KB

WITHDRAWN

ACTION, ORGANISM, AND PHILOSOPHY IN WORDSWORTH AND WHITEHEAD

By The Same Author

About Wordsworth and Whitehead: A Prelude to Philosophy (Philosophical Library, 1982).

Aspects of Wordsworth and Whitehead: Philosophy and Certain Continuing Life Problems (Philosophical Library, 1983).

ACTION, ORGANISM, AND PHILOSOPHY IN WORDSWORTH AND WHITEHEAD

Alexander P. Cappon

Philosophical Library
New York

Library of Congress Cataloging in Publication Data

Cappon, Alexander Patterson, 1900—
  Action, organism, and philosophy in Wordsworth
and Whitehead.

  Includes bibliographical references.
  1. Wordsworth, William, 1770-1850.   Prelude.
2. Wordsworth, William, 1770-1850—Philosophy.
3. Whitehead, Alfred North, 1861-1947.   4. Philosophy
in literature.   I. Title.
PR5864.C36   1985   821'.7   84-14897
ISBN 0-8022-2468-7

To
Dorothy Churchill Cappon
and
Frances Cappon Geer
in great gratitude

Contents

vii

Acknowledgments:

Two of my previously published books—*About Wordsworth and Whitehead: A Prelude to Philosophy* and *Aspects of Wordsworth and Whitehead: Philosophy and Certain Continuing Life Problems*—list acknowledgments that have a bearing on the current book, and need not be completely repeated here. Publishers always need special appreciative mention.

The Macmillan Company and Cambridge University Press have been especially valuable with respect to the writings of Whitehead, and Oxford University Press has been especially valuable with respect to the works of Wordsworth. We have also valued greatly publications of Simon and Schuster; Doubleday and Co.; G.P. Putnam's Sons; Thomas Y. Crowell; Charles Scribner's Sons; Yale University Press; Harvard University Press; W.W. Norton; George Allen and Unwin; University of Chicago Press; D. Van Nostrand; Brunner-Mazel Inc.; Farrar, Strauss and Giroux Inc.; Beacon Press; Barnes and Noble; Open Court; Delacorte Press; New American Library; Tudor Press; Little, Brown and Co.; Duke University Press; Holt, Rinehart and Winston; Harper and Row; Princeton University Press; Hodder and Stoughton; University of Michigan Press; University of

North Carolina Press; Athenaeum; John Knox Press; Harper and Brothers; Greenwood Press; Columbia University Press; Free Press; Houghton Mifflin Co.; Longmans, Green and Co.; and Arlington House—other publishers have been of real value, though less specifically, in connection with our work and thought on Wordsworth and Whitehead, and are definitely appreciated. Philosophical Library Publishing Co. has brought out very many books which have been of great value in regard to insight and reflection, among them perhaps the finest of Whitehead: *Essays in Science and Philosophy*. We want to express our thanks to Rose Morse, the Director of the company.

Our thanks also to the University of Missouri-Kansas City, and to librarians of the world.

The dedication to this book represents a very special gratitude.

Alexander P. Cappon
University of Missouri-Kansas City

Introduction

Action is characteristic of Americans. So it is often said. And the dynamic is prominent, moreover, in modern industrialism. In this sense an energy (or energics) is a feature not only of our own country but of Great Britain, Germany, Italy, France, and every other country that has been centrally affected by the Industrial Revolution. Our world-outlook or philosophy in America is often characterized by energetics, which is perhaps a better term than energics for our present purposes, although energics is a perfectly good word in that it is suggestive of science and technology, as these things are at times in the background of philosophy and of democratic industrial life particularly in the late twentieth century. But in what way can our technological life be called democratic? Does it today lack democratic features? These are philosophical questions.

We are all interested in democracy—at the very minimum if for no better reason than that we would wish to see a perpetuation of our way of life. Doubtless there is a more satisfactory basis than this, since we would like to expand, to grow—not merely perpetuate ourselves: we desire in many ways to modify our thought and the kind of lives we live. Modification of thought implies a critical treatment of it. This is a characteristic procedure in human beings. Modification of ourselves, and our lives, involves a gradual change in our outlook. Here we have philosophy; we are philosophical when we reflect on something and then allow our broad thought to take new forms.

Thinking of Bertrand Russell, who was a close friend of Alfred North Whitehead for many years, we may be brought to a consideration of what philosophy mutually meant to both of them. Two points of view can often provide valuable correctives, the one to the other. This is true of Russell and Whitehead. But their attitudes on many things are so far from simple that comment on them necessarily has an emergent rather than a neat and immediate quality. Russell, writing in 1945, called philosophy a combination of "inherited religious and ethical conceptions"[1] plus such scientific points of view as we are able to combine in our general outlook. Presenting his ideas in another book (in 1959), he suggested that philosophy has its start "when someone asks a general question,"[2] and this he says is true also of science. He then proceeds to a consideration of very early philosophers.

Often it is held that an understanding of the first development of Greek culture is one of the best ways to secure insight into the term philosophy. We would agree. Russell pays great respect to the early Greek philosophers by saying that their "outburst of intellectual activity is one of the most spectacular events in history." This development began near the end of the seventh century B.C. But it is not our purpose now to define philosophy on the basis of the Greeks. An idea in regard to the matter will be brought forward increasingly in the chapters of the present volume; the conception will grow gradually, and in this sense it could be almost considered what Whitehead calls an organism. An idea can be an organism. Matters cannot be understood well unless they are seen in the process of growing like living beings. So at least William Wordsworth implicitly believes, and so Whitehead definitely declares in his late works.

Whitehead's statement itself always has to be understood as a growing conception. In an earlier book, *About Wordsworth and Whitehead*, we have dealt with the thought of the two men as that thought can be seen in its relation to the first six books of Wordsworth's 1805 *Prelude*. We chose this early form of the poem as a basis to work with because it is expressive of the poet's very definite attainment of maturity and vitality. In a second volume, *Aspects of Wordsworth and Whitehead: Philosophy and Certain Continuing Life-Problems*, we centered attention again on this, the poet's major work, devoting the discussion especially to the core of the poem (the seventh through the eleventh books) in relation to the thought of the philosopher and certain vital problems in the modern world. In the present volume we shall cover rapidly, with new perspectives, parts of the ground of our first two books, and then concentrate on the final divisions of *The Prelude* in connection with philosophy. Any one of the three books, however, may be read first without knowledge of the others. Each volume is integral to itself.

Bertrand Russell admires the early Greek thinkers, as we have seen. This admiration (and also his interest in philosophy) he might well have obtained from Whitehead. When Russell came to Cambridge University his interest was in mathematics. He was a very shy young person, and felt drawn greatly to Whitehead because the philosopher seemed to show a recognition of promise in a youthful student. At any rate both men refer frequently to the contributions of the early Greeks to human culture. Russell's words concerning the "outburst of intellectual activity" in Greece (which we have quoted) led in his volume to this further remark: "Nothing like it has ever occurred before or since."[3] This is a strong statement with which Whitehead would heartily agree. There are many evidences of the extreme admiration which he too felt for early Greek philosophy.

A preliminary sense of the first Greek attitudes toward a world-view can be very helpful, we have said, to an understanding of what is implied in the term philosophy itself. From time to time in the present volume we shall, for this reason, make reference to the Greek philosophers prior to Plato. The main problem one has in pursuing philosophical thought is to try to see things without prejudice. Whitehead, thinking of philosophy, declares that "the curiosity of the human spirit permeated with criticism, and divorced from hereditary superstitions" gave rise to science; this science, as he holds, "had its birth with the Greeks." Whitehead explains that "among the Greeks Thales was the earliest exponent known to us."[4] Thales is associated with the thinkers of the coastal town of Miletus in Ionia (on the eastern shore of the Aegean Sea), about one hundred fifty miles from the Greek mainland, a region which is now a part of Turkey. It was Thales (the first syllable pronounced as bay in Green Bay), born about 624 B.C., who, so far as the Western World was concerned, virtually invented philosophy. And here we may quote Whitehead's statement that "Greece was the mother of Europe; and it is to Greece that we must look in order to find the origin of our modern ideas."[5]

Certain things in the philosophy of Thales seem strange to us at first, for example the thought that all things come from water and, moreover, that "all things are full of Gods."[6] These conceptions are often held to be the most basic features that can be brought out with reference to him. But an incident in his life which is more immediately revealing might be cited. Thales was once snobbishly "reproached for his poverty" and this was deemed to be an evidence that his discipline was without "use."[7] According to legend he was able to make predictions—for example, with regard to harvests and other matters. In answer to the reproaches (so the story goes) Thales cornered the olive presses "at a low price because no one bid against him." Finally, he was able to rent or sell the presses according to his pleasure "and made a quantity of money." He was able, through this, to show "that philosophers can easily be rich"; however, "their ambition is of another sort."

Merely to sit back in thought with a concern about manipulations in regard to costs and prices is not enough even for philosophy as it touches economics. Underneath all, human factors are important as well. We cannot rest satisfied in simplicity with a much-quoted aphorism such as *Let the buyer beware*. Ethics must be entwined with politics or economics, if Thales is to be satisfied philosophically. And a profound ethics also needs to be a factor in social custom. Social control is a problem here.

Thus we can see that at an early stage philosophy—in Thales as in his followers—showed an awareness of the question of social status resting on utilitarian self-serving in contrast to disinterested reflection. Thales had evidently to deal with the problems of snobbery and downgrading, which relate to the philosophy of an elite in contrast to incipient democracy and a world-view directed toward equality of rights and the values of life which may be enjoyed. Philosophy aims at disinterestedness. The question of justice and what it entails appears very early among the Greeks. Of this more will be considered in a moment—especially concerning tyranny and the basic human response to it.

Thales held that what is "most ancient is God, for he is uncreated."[8] And to Thales that which is "most beautiful is the universe, for it is God's workmanship." He was much given to concentrated or epigrammatic utterance of this kind. In his view evil deeds cannot be hidden from the gods, nor can "an evil thought." He was also deeply aware of the need of self-knowledge. The larger problem of "the divine," in addition, preoccupied him. This he held to be identified with what "has no beginning nor end." One might well wonder what in his view could be regarded as the strangest thing that could ever be seen. He was asked this question. The observations of Thales led him to give his own terse personal answer in these words: "An aged tyrant." Such a thing would be a real rarity. In his conception tyranny cannot last long because people will not endure it.

This problem of tyranny and its overthrow arose in Wordsworth's thinking and had connection with his sympathy for the French Revolution. The necessity of direct action is implied here. And yet Wordsworth, like Thales, was exceedingly humane. We can with effort "lead the best and most righteous life," Thales believes. Such a life can exist through following the basic principle of "refraining from doing what we blame in others." Whitehead's point of view can be thought of as comparable in some respects to that of certain leaders of early Greek thought. In the present book we shall refer to this early aspect of human culture at times because it can be highly illuminating to an understanding of philosophy and of both Wordsworth and Whitehead. Dominantly, however, there will be reference to matters most important to us in the modern world.

Wordsworth is basically modern, and Whitehead rather remarkably parallels him in many respects. The one figure is revelatory of the other. We can valuably look back from the philosopher to Wordsworth, or glance from the poet's period forward toward Whitehead's time and toward our own. The effects of such looking or glancing are reciprocal in their relation one to the other. And the philosopher Whitehead favors such backward-and-forward reciprocal processes in thought.

Notes

[1]Russell, *A History of Western Philosophy* (New York: Simon and Schuster, 1945), p. xiii.

[2]Russell, *Wisdom of the West* (New York: Doubleday and Company, 1959), p. 10.

[3]*Ibid.*, p. 10.

[4]Whitehead, *Adventures of Ideas* (New York: Macmillan, 1933), p. 180.

[5]*Science and the Modern World* (New York: Macmillan, 1937), p. 10.

[6]Russell, *A History of Western Philosophy*, p. 26. Russell in a footnote mentions that John Burnet questions the last point as applied to Thales.

[7]*Ibid.*, p. 26. The quoted words are from Aristotle's comments on Thales in his *Politics*.

[8]Quoted in Drew A. Hyland, *The Origins of Philosophy: Its Rise in Myth and the Pre-Socratics* (New York: Capricorn Books, G.P. Putnam's Sons, 1973), p. 114.

A Word to the Reader

Our purpose in the present volume on Wordsworth and Whitehead is not only to deal with philosophy and with the relationships of the one figure to the other, but to do so in such a way as to provide for careful verification by anyone who questions a given matter. Frequently we shall use single words in quotation marks not only to stress the importance of the concept represented by the single term in Wordsworth or Whitehead, but also to help a reader trace the thought in the original context where it appears. At times it may seem fussy when we quote a few of Whitehead's words that end with a period; but this is done because the source may be spotted more easily if a reader watches for the period with which a sentence in the original book ends.

In comparing our quotations from Whitehead (or any other writer) with the original source, one should note that all quotations after the first one will be found in the page originally cited unless otherwise indicated; this is true even of quotations in subsequent paragraphs. Short quotations are used in the main. The use of short quotations we have found helpful in order to focus on very precise aspects of thought. It is this very special kind of centering of thought which can be of value in dealing with problems of philosophy. We have tried to avoid the use of petty detail or technicality in this volume, but we would now emphasize the point that Wordsworth's 1805 *Prelude* (which we have used) is different from the poet's 1850 version, which is most commonly read. The latter, despite signal merits, in certain ways reflects his point of view in his declining years. The line numbering of the late version is often extremely different from that of the earlier work; moreover, the earlier poem consists of thirteen books, whereas the 1850 version has fourteen.

Still, we would emphasize the fact that the 1805 *Prelude* (which we use) is freighted with special thought, particularly in its last parts. For this reason the final four chapters of our present book deal with the concluding part (the last book) of the 1805 *Prelude*. But all this will be sufficiently clear in the end.

Many readers have found Whitehead's work fascinating, but have been dismayed at running upon passages that are somewhat esoteric (which Whitehead sometimes even indicates may be skipped and returned to later if need be); this same procedure, of judicious skipping, may be followed in the present volume. But our main purpose all along has been to indicate something of the story (the inner story) of Wordsworth and also to bring about, little by little, an understanding of Whitehead. The full reaches of his philosophy contain clairvoyance and represent in the end a profound world-view.

We shall refer at times to Wordsworth as "the poet" and to Whitehead as "the philosopher," but without any intention of doing so honorifically. The purpose of such references to the men will be to avoid an awkward repetition of their names. The spirit we have tried to follow all along is that of an impartial inquiry; the person who reads must be the one who decides for himself in all cases whether respect or honor may be due.

Chapter One

Childhood and School-Time: Wordsworth's Retrospect as Connected with Whitehead

We are concerned in the present volume with the relation of the philosophy of Wordsworth to that of Whitehead, and this brings us to the things which they valued. The personality, the self which we possess, is valued, at least by ourselves. And we value the self, or personality, in others—particularly in those who mean a great deal to us. We consider value from the point of view of something which is sustained in its realization. For Whitehead personality is important: it may be cited as "the extreme example of the sustained realization of a type of value."[1] Most of us would probably tend to agree with what the philosopher is stating here.

Wordsworth, in the 1805 *Prelude*, recognizes again and again the importance of personality: his own, and that of his friend Coleridge, and that of any person who might cross his path. The poet seeks in many ways to examine personality, or what we would now call

1

identity. In our introduction we spoke of early Greek thought about philosophy, and here we can mention that among these Greek thinkers there was some concern about the problem of identity; for example, Thales of Miletus has such an interest in stressing that one "know oneself."[2] This, he holds, is the most difficult of all things. Again, he is reported by Hyland to have urged that the individual should not be too much an individual but should "remember friends" and without presumption "study to be beautiful in character." Here again Thales is interested in the problem of personality, although he has a deeper feeling about what he regards as the divine.

In our introduction we explained that we would have further things to say, going beyond Thales, about certain of the earliest Western philosophers and their relation to the development of ideas. Can we think now of the essential principle within the world as something comparable to material substance—water or air (as the more primitive Greeks at times thought), or could we reflect on material substance as something which we could liken to a *breeze* of air in its vital quality or in its dynamic motion and infinite changefulness? This seems on the face of it a little absurd, but it is with such thoughts concerning a principle within the universe that reflection about philosophy often begins. We might have emphasized strongly the concept of water as it was central to the earliest Greek thought, for we often think how essential moisture is to the violet or to the human being and, indeed, to all other living forms. As Whitehead thinks of the people in ancient Ionian Greece he says that their "genius was philosophical"[3] and that they tried to clarify their world in a structural way. They were "primarily asking philosophical questions."

An example of this would be: "What is the substratum of nature?" We quote Whitehead here. In answer, the early Greeks thought of the possibility of water, of the divine, of air, of fire, of ordinary physical matter (earth) as being central, and they recognized other foundational possibilities or "combinations," Whitehead says, as providing answers. It is surprising to see the number of cases in which Wordsworth echoes insights that appeared thus early in Western philosophy. At any rate in our present book we shall make some further references to this aspect of developmental philosophy, for thought about it is one of the very best ways of understanding the term philosophy. This is true also of the ideas of other thinkers of Miletus whom we shall mention.

There was the possibility, appearing, subsequently to Thales, in Anaximander (born close to 610 B.C.), that the intangible, as thought of in relation to the unending, might be the underlying principle of the universe. There is some controversy about this in that Anaximander may not have centered his thought on the intangible, or even considered this aspect, but he was nevertheless concerned about the endless, the eternal, and the divine. From his point of view the divine— although not limited in space or time—might have been a substance in the tangible sense; that is, the parts of the divine could be extremely fine and yet comparable to air, breath, earth, water. The divine is, however, unlimited, in his view; it is, evidently, the greatest thing and it is without any generation. He is reaching toward the spiritual.

Anaximander also advanced the "conception of justice—of not overstepping eternally fixed bounds"—in the words of Russell, "one of the most profound of Greek beliefs."⁴ According to Russell, "gods were subject to justice" quite as much "as men were," but he says justice must not be regarded in the Greek sense as the "supreme God." Justice is balance. For Russell, writing in another volume, there is the important fact that Anaximander was aware that "some sort of evolutionary process does go on."⁵ This early philosopher also believed that the human being was derived "from the fish of the sea," which "he backed up by observations on fossil remains" and in other ways. From our point of view, however, what is most important in Anaximander is his concern about the unlimited as the source of all things that exist, in addition to his thought about evolutionary process. He was preoccupied with time and eternity. He was trying especially to understand, insofar as a human being can understand it, the greatest thing that exists, or the divine. This was his fundamental objective.

Not long after the time of Thales and Anaximander the view was advanced or promulgated, also in the town of Miletus, that the fundamental principle in all things is breath. This idea is associated with Anaximines (the accent here is on the third syllable); Anaximines, who held that breath, or air, is the substratum of all things, seemed to be "guided by the observation that the more closely anything is compressed, the harder and more solid it becomes."⁶ In the third paragraph of this chapter we quoted Whitehead with reference to the Greeks and the subject of nature. The philosopher, in this context, when speaking of nature and its substratum, does not mention Anaximines and the theory concerning air as the universal substratum of things, but this idea of certain ancient Greeks was very well known to him and others. As Robert S. Brumbaugh says, "At that time it conveyed the idea of 'breath,' the 'soul' that 'animated' men and animals."[7] And Brumbaugh stresses the fact that this involved "a connection between life and matter."

In Wordsworth's 1805 *Prelude*, Book One, the poet is writing about development—childhood and early school days—but his mind moves backward and forward in time, and it touches on many things. He is at least semi-philosophical here, and he is thinking about the principle of the universe when he refers to a force which blows its creative breath from without upon the individual. This force, this breath, is connected with the "creative breeze" blowing within the self. Near the beginning of our chapter we referred to a *breeze* of air in its vital quality, and the term "vital" is used by Wordsworth in his present context. In the passage he speaks of

> A vital breeze which travell'd gently on
> O'er things which it had made ... (44—)

The very air becomes for Wordsworth a symbol or a principle which is within human beings; this air, or breeze, is capable of becoming for him, for anyone, a thing which is tempestuous, or at times "redundant," and it can be deleterious in its effect upon "its own creation." We have been drawing material from Book One of the 1805 *Prelude*, a part which Whitehead especially admired. But here we would also emphasize the thought of the poet concerned with democracy, an emphasis which is important in the work of Whitehead. Thus we find Wordsworth thinking of the spirit of freedom

> which fifteen hundred years
> Surviv'd, and, when the European came
> With skill and power that could not be withstood,
> Did, like a pestilence, maintain its hold,
> And wasted down by glorious death that Race
> Of natural Heroes ... (196—)

The word "pestilence" seems scarcely suitable here; but, when we think of the Greeks, the figure of pestilence may be comparable to the symbol of fire (for destructive force) that we mentioned in our third paragraph. Whitehead himself speaks of "fire,"[8] a kind of pestilence, or destruction, which, at an early stage, was at times thought to be fundamental in the universe. The destructiveness of fire was at times considered an inescapable or fundamental principle. And in Wordsworth a kind of destructiveness "wasted down by glorious death" the "Heroes" who were attempting to establish a better world than had been in existence before the day of their efforts. The problem of evil appears at this point. Not only in his early *Prelude* did the poet use this extreme figure for a destructiveness which is a factor within the universe. In the 1850 edition of the work he left his expression for it unchanged. His use of the term "pestilence" was probably carefully considered. For Whitehead as for Wordsworth the question of destructiveness is an important one. For the philosopher even God suffers in the face of it. God feels emotion.

In Whitehead, parallel to the "Heroes" whom Wordsworth mentioned, are "the Titans who storm heaven, armed with a passionate sincerity."[9] Destructiveness is part of "the multifariousness of the world"; there is a seeming permanence and there is destruction. We have used Whitehead's words here though in his passage he is not speaking of Wordsworth. Still, the context is fitting to the part of *The Prelude* we have quoted. Whitehead goes on to suggest that, despite the multifariousness, "Life refuses to be embalmed alive."[10]

Wordsworth's statement about the "Heroes" concerns destructiveness, but also permanence. Whitehead desires "a God available for religious purposes."[11] But near the end of the chapter from which this is drawn, the philosopher thinks of God as "the supreme ground for limitation"; thus the cosmos for Whitehead, as he elaborates it, includes destruction as well as a creativeness which is forever potential. Religion exhibits a "character of gradual development"[12]; this, for Whitehead, exemplifies the way we have to deal with it. He refers to theology, but he is thinking foremost of religion, and points out in the very next page that the fact of development in our understanding of religion is "a commonplace to theologians, but it is often obscured in the stress of controversy." Some destructiveness, or seeming destructiveness, is inevitable. Whitehead says in his last paragraph of the volume *Adventures of Ideas*: "We have always the dream of youth and the harvest of tragedy." But these can be reconciled.

Near the outset of this chapter we spoke of the Greeks and their very early concern for a principle within life or nature, whether water, the approach to infinity, or air; we could have stressed the mathematical as well as the Orphic element of music, expressed in generality. Pythagoras (born about 582 B.C.) exemplifies this latter tendency. He seems to have developed his thought partly under the influence of Anaximander. In search of a principle within a universal life the young Bertrand Russell found an inspiration in Pythagoras, partly because the mathematical appeared in Greek philosophy very early and doubtless also because of the element of art or the aesthetic (the Orphic) and the kind of order that this implied.

Speaking of Greece and the mystical and Orphean factor Russell says, "In the East, the mystical element reigned supreme."[13] This Orphean element of course needs balance. A corrective on the side of carefully examined truth is required. As Russell puts it, "What is needed is a passionate search for truth and beauty. It seems that the Orphic influence provided just that conception." Truth is an important factor. And some pages later he connects Pythagoras definitely with the Orphic as a "pioneer of this new spirit"[14]; he regards it as Apollonian. Whitehead also admired Pythagoras. In Wordsworth, at any rate, there is an ideal aspiration

> towards some philosophic Song
> Of Truth that cherishes our daily life;
> With meditations passionate from deep
> Recesses in man's heart, immortal verse
> Thoughtfully fitted to the Orphean lyre . . . (230—)

Whitehead, we have said, found a stimulus in the early Greeks and there are many ways in which his philosophy can be connected with such preliminary thought. About forty years later than the time of Pythagoras, somewhat evolutionary or unfolding ideas began primitively to develop as to organisms—for example, in the derivation of various aspects of the universe through seeds or in other somewhat similar ways. From this thought, as we shall see later, and from that of certain other Greeks, there developed the idea that the soul has in its early stages a kind of seed-time. We can think analogously of certain conceptions that are to be found in Wordsworth and, somewhat more highly developed, in Whitehead, who pays notable respect to early Greek thought. Related to this we may recall the "seed-time" of the spirit in Wordsworth and how he

> grew up
> Foster'd alike by beauty and by fear . . . (305—)

But it is not our intention to cover with fullness the ground of Book One in Wordsworth's *Prelude* as related to Whitehead. All we have aimed to accomplish here is to mention suggestively a few points not treated in our earlier examination of the Wordsworth-Whitehead problem. Still, we should surely recall the reference which is made to Newton near the end of Chapter I of our volume *About Wordsworth and Whitehead: A Prelude to Philosophy*; there, and near the end of Chapter II, we spoke of the preoccupation with Newton that Wordsworth showed at a very young age, and we indicated that the poet, like Whitehead, later moved philosophically far beyond the influence of Newton.

Notes

[1] *Essays in Science and Philosophy* (New York: Philosophical Library, 1948), p. 66.

[2] Words of Thales, quoted in Drew A. Hyland, *The Origins of Philosophy*, p. 114.

[3] *Science and the Modern World*, p. 10.

[4] Russell, *History of Western Philosophy*, p. 27.

[5] *Wisdom of the West*, p. 18. Inference by Russell is involved on this point.

[6] Edward Hussey, *The Presocratics* (New York: Charles Scribner's Sons, 1972), Hussey goes on to say: "This suggests that we may explain solid, liquid, and gaseous things by the varying degrees of compression of one basic material."

[7] Robert S. Brumbaugh, *The Philosophers of Greece* (New York: Thomas Y. Crowell, 1964), p. 28.

[8] *Science and the Modern World*, p. 10.

[9] *Process and Reality* (New York: Macmillan, 1929, 1960), p. 513.

[10] *Ibid.*, p. 515; note on p. 532.

[11] *Science and the Modern World*, p. 249.

[12] *Ibid.*, p. 261.

[13] *Wisdom of the West*, p. 13.

[14] *Ibid.*, p. 20.

Chapter Two

Later School Days
as Connected with
Wordsworth and Whitehead

The habits of mind, or the elements of conscious life, are disseminated—"first sown, even as a seed" in Wordsworth's phrase—but they also can be thought of as analogous to water, or to a river; we can think of a "portion of the river" (which represents mind) as coming from some particular source. But there is danger in assuming that we can designate the precise origin of things within consciousness. The poet himself does not make psychological attributions of influence casually. Here, now, in Book Two of the 1805 *Prelude*, he speaks of his friend Coleridge as being one who is "deeply read" in what is essentially the psychology of the self:

to thee
Science appears but, what in truth she is ... (216—)

9

Science is very important, Wordsworth believes, but is not to be regarded as "our glory and our absolute boast"; the danger of absolutism is felt here. An idea has to be regarded as a "prop," for its value lies (and this is scientifically notable) in the fact that it leads to other things. For Wordsworth, as for Whitehead, science needs careful study, but it is not a be-all and an end-all for philosophy. The poet in Book Two of his *Prelude* is carrying forward the topic that he used at the beginning of the work; that is, he is extending his treatment of childhood and its development into various stages of school time. Thus he thinks of the child "in his Mother's arms" where it attains kinship in the deepest sense with another person—"manifest kindred with an earthly soul"; and again, as in earlier cases he resorts to the image of a "breeze" which can be connected with our inward psychology, and the awakening of forces that operate within it. The child combines factors, making "one appearance" of what might be thought of as fragments of isolated factors. Hence it is that the child's

> organs and recipient faculties
> Are quicken'd, are more vigorous, his mind spreads,
> Tenacious of the forms which it receives.   (252—)

Psychology and human development are important in the philosophy of Wordsworth as they are in Whitehead's thought. For the poet the factors connected with personal evolving, or growth, are very significant. The unconscious mind operates in such a way that what we feel is unremembered, though we have an "obscure sense" of various things—for example, a sense of "sublimity" which we entertain as only an as-if, or a *possibility*. Still, a possibility works upon us in many cases as a functioning force, and thus we are able to

> aspire,
> With faculties still growing, feeling still
> That whatsoever point they gain, they still
> Have something to pursue.   (338—)

Wordsworth had a feeling for the complexity of inorganic things which can be related to that of Whitehead. Beneath the surface of physical objects there are forces at work, but he is well aware that these things exert themselves upon us psychologically in that certain effects at first seem absolutely polarized, or disparate; they nevertheless are often being *silently* brought together. He realizes how knowledge is gained in part by "the great social principle" which works upon us. For the poet, too, there are special moments, so that he tells us how insights or powers were brought to him in a sort of "revelation" whereby he believed that he

convers'd
With things that really are . . . (412—)

The poet, while still in preparatory school, received an education which stressed science (as was indicated near the close of Chapter II of our volume *About Wordsworth and Whitehead*); this early training, though it rested primarily upon the classical humanities, included importantly a recognition of what had been contributed to mankind by Newton and Francis Bacon. The training he received was given under the influence of William Taylor, a former Cambridge University fellow. Wordsworth at that time wrote a poem in which he mentioned Francis Bacon.

Whitehead suggests certain dangers in the seventeenth century Baconian influence, at least as Bacon has been very widely understood. According to the philosopher, if you concentrate on the "efficient causes," neglecting a long-range grasp of matters, you will have a limited view of science; from this narrow view, or from a merely effectual perspective, the tendency is to "interpret large features of the growth of structure in terms of 'strife.'"[1] Destruction is a factor here. But there is the possibility of a more profound interpretation of Bacon, and this Whitehead brings out in *Science and the Modern World*, where he indicates that the Bacon of a later stage (in his *Natural History*) "discriminates between *perception*, or *taking account of*, on the one hand, and *sense*, or *cognitive* experience, on the other hand."[2] Here "Bacon is outside the physical line of thought which finally dominated the century." Whitehead, in referring thus to the seventeenth century, feels that in a very subtle sense Bacon was expressing "more fundamental truth than do the materialistic concepts that were being shaped as adequate for physics."

Did Wordsworth in his early stage recognize the more profound aspect of Bacon, revealed in Bacon's later publication? Probably not. But the poet did ultimately come to a position which brings him into close kinship with Whitehead. In Bacon as he is usually conceived there is the advantage of the effort toward precision. Historically considered, ideas need to be examined from the point of view of their vibrant creativeness, for in history we have, as Whitehead explains, "a tragic mixture of vibrant disclosure and of deadening closure."[3]

Pythagoras (born about 582 B.C.) could be cited as an early Greek example of disclosure in Whitehead's sense. Many very important figures may be seen as illustrating closure: Plato would be one example. "The sense of penetration," Whitehead says, can vanish; it can be "lost in the certainty of completed knowledge." We are at times too easily certain. So Plato is often hastily conceived, with a loss of his truest value. Whitehead stresses the importance of trying to understand potentiality. The most profoundly usable aspects of the past lie in our will to employ them: in their movement into a new future. Our view should be backward and forward. We need to give character to the future through what Whitehead calls "the sense of the form having dual activity in the present."[4]

What he objects to is an absence of a sense of value; we must go beyond the view "that we ought to describe detailed matter of fact, and elicit the laws with a generality strictly limited to the systematization of these described details."[5] For this is the unduly restricted view. It denies the beyond. "Whenever we attempt to express the matter of immediate experience, we find that its understanding leads us beyond itself, to its contemporaries, to its past, to its future, and to the universals in terms of which its definiteness is exhibited." But these universals are relative universals. They are relative to each other. Wordsworth's thought, like Whitehead's, leads us, in its quest for understanding, to the present, to the past, and to the future in all variableness. Understanding comes about in the process.

Notes

[1] *Adventures of Ideas*, p. 39. Section IV, Part I.

[2] *Science and the Modern World*, p. 61.

[3] Whitehead, *Modes of Thought*, Capricorn Books (New York: G.P. Putnam's Sons, 1938, 1958), p. 81.

[4] *Ibid.*, p. 138.

[5] *Process and Reality*, p. 21.

Chapter Three

Residence in Cambridge as Connected with Wordsworth and Whitehead

Complexities of feeling have an important place in the philosophy of Wordsworth, as we see in Book Three of *The Prelude*. Feeling also plays a part in the structures upon which Whitehead reflects. Wordsworth's experience as indicated in this part of his poem, Book Three, includes his activities in the university, but it takes him also to the regions around the outskirts of Cambridge. There he responded to "every natural form," including the rocks, and fruits, as well as "the loose stones" on the highway; he "saw them feel" or associated them with "some feeling," and altogether they were part of a "quickening soul," being filled with "inward meaning." They were in fact not simply *filled* but seemed to breathe forth their deeper presence and inner significance. So it is that he says:

> Thus much for the one Presence, and the Life
> Of the great whole; suffice it here to add
> That whatsoe'er of Terror or of Love,
> Or Beauty, Nature's daily face put on
> From transitory passion, unto this
> I was as wakeful, even, as waters are ... (130—)

To these things he was as "obedient as a lute" that responds to the breezes of the wind. He goes on to tell the tale of himself in a variety of ways, purposing to include, so far as possible, its inward meaning. Whitehead speaks of feeling as being present not only in animals at every level but in the world of organisms below that of animals; in this area of what he considers the organic, he holds that there is "a vague feeling of causal relationships with the external world, of some intensity, vaguely defined as to quality, and with some vague definition as to locality."[1] But this does not mean that Whitehead accepts pantheism. His conception of God is "of an actual entity immanent in the actual world, but transcending any finite cosmic epoch—a being at once actual, eternal, immanent, and transcendent."[2] His objection to the pantheistic doctrine appears by implication in many places, and explicitly in *Adventures of Ideas*, where he refers to the "pantheistic" idea of God "as essentially immanent and in no way transcendent."[3]

Whitehead, as we have emphasized before, had a great regard for the early Greeks. In *Science and the Modern World* he looks upon Greece as "the mother of Europe" and as a source of certain "modern ideas."[4] He refers at once to the fact that "on the eastern shores of the Mediterranean there was a flourishing school of Ionian philosophers"; Whitehead regards these figures with considerable respect. They help us understand philosophy. Among those who were thus associated with the eastern regions of greater Greece were Thales, Anaximander, and Anaximines, to whom we have referred. The first of these men received much discussion in our Introduction and the two others were given comment in the latter part of our initial chapter.

These early Greek philosophers were interested in nature, as Whitehead says, and this implies science, but their "school of thought had not attained to the complete scientific mentality." They were in quest of science. In certain respects, however, what these thinkers had attained "was better." They were interested in "philosophical ques-tions." And it is philosophy in its further reaches which is White-head's main theme in *Science and the Modern World*. The problem of changefulness or flux among the Greeks comes up here. But White-head quickly passes over the point about flux. He goes on to stress the fact that "Mathematics interested them mightily. They invented its generality" and made "discoveries of theorems by a rigid adherence to deductive reasoning." Whitehead, however, realizes the dangers that may arise in this kind of deductive intellectuality. He admits that mathematics tends to have notable limitations.

Some points beyond those already stated about Pythagoras might fittingly be mentioned here. Pythagoras himself, though he spent his flourishing years in the western part of the Greek commonwealth, was at an early stage close to the influences of Ionia. Russell, perhaps under the influence of Whitehead, was attracted to Pythagoras. The tradition of Pythagoras emphasizes, as Russell puts it, the "detached contemplation of the world."[5] But detachment in Pythagoras finds its connection with the Orphic; Russell specifically stresses this "influ-ence embodied in the Pythagorean attitude to life." The point deserves repeated stress. Russell seems quite enamored of Pythagoras and later rather extensively adds various related ideas (p. 38) with regard to mathematics, particularly about the theory of number.

John Burnet, thinking of Pythagoras, speaks of the value of music "fully recognized in the psychotherapy of these days."[6] Burnet refers here to ancient "priests, who treated nervous and hysterical patients by wild pipe music," and he explains that this practice "was followed in turn by a healthy sleep from which the patient awoke cured." He adds that "there is much to be said for the view that the originality of Pythagoras consisted" in the fact that he held "scientific, and espe-cially mathematical" reflection as of value to the spirit. In Plato also this view is found, as Burnet declares, "and it frequently recurs in the history of Greek philosophy."[7] Burnet feels that Pythagoras probably was the first to use the word *philosophy*, and that "we need not hesitate to ascribe to him the saying," recorded by Plato, "that philosophy is the 'highest music' "; the Orphean tendency, then, included music as a factor in philosophy.

A basic feature of the thought of Pythagoras, as Whitehea(

declares, is a harmony which passes on through various thinkers; the conception, actually, becomes prominent in Whitehead himself. Ultimate things, Whitehead says in *Science and the Modern World*, are "together in a harmony which excludes mere arbitrariness."[8] In saying this he has in mind going beyond science to a "deeper faith." A moment later he explains, "To experience this faith is to know that in being ourselves we are more than ourselves: to know that our experience, dim and fragmentary as it is, yet sounds the utmost depths of reality"; and he adds a reference to the fact that "this system includes the harmony of logical rationality"—following this reference immediately with three further references to the word *harmony*. It is thus that he closes emphatically his first, very important chapter in *Science and the Modern World*. He is making a very conscious effort to keep the factor of harmony before us.

But aside from this harmony, and perhaps more important, Whitehead at a later stage in his volume refers to "the nature of mathematics." And he proceeds thus: "The idea, ascribed to Pythagoras, has been amplified, and put forward as the first chapter in metaphysics."[9] It will be helpful now to turn back to our earlier indications of Whitehead's respect for the Greeks. Close to the midpoint of our first chapter we spoke of early Greek philosophical thought, and we touched upon mathematics. We might well have referred there to the proposition of Pythagoras, and made reference to the generality represented by the Pythagorean theorem about the relation between the square (which may be very large) on the hypotenuse of a right triangle and the sum of the squares on the two legs. Here the matter of infinity and the infinitesimal as limits could be given attention. Pythagoras is famous for his thought about this problem and also about mathematical matters connected with the number ten.

Whitehead, having referred to Pythagoras, might well have commented on a figure born some twelve years after the birth of Pythagoras, Xenophanes (the first part of the name pronounced like Zen); Xenophanes, an Ionian, was born about 570 B.C., inland in Colophon about fifty miles north of Miletus. Thus the school of thought in Miletus (including such figures as Thales, Anaximander, and Anaximines) could well have had an influence upon him. He traveled away from the eastern Mediterranean region, however, to Sicily, and shortly thereafter his career was associated with certain thinkers on the western coast of Italy in Elea.

Xenophanes was concerned with what exists in a larger sense than that involving material substance (though the conception of substance had not been very much clarified in those early days); still, he was in advance of the ideas that were usual: the multiplicity of all things, he said, must be regarded as one. He is extremely satirical in referring to the tendency of having anthropomorphic conceptions of God: if animals had art "horses would draw the gods shaped like horses and lions like lions"; they would make "the bodies of the gods resemble their own forms."[10] He strongly attacked adultery, and the tendency to portray gods as liars and thieves. Xenophanes expresses, as William Guthrie says, "a surprisingly high level of religious thought for the sixth century B.C. in Greece."[11] He has a marked emphasis, moreover, on unity, quality, and being in the sense of reality.

Whitehead was interested in philosophy in its further reaches, and like Xenophanes he has a decided concern for religion; this appears in the volume *Science and the Modern World*, from which we have quoted. He speaks of the medieval heritage which has come down to us, and which is related to the idea of "the rationality of God, conceived as with the personal energy of Jehova and with the rationality of a Greek philosopher."[12] These Judaic and Greek factors needed to be combined, Whitehead believes.

Certainly we must remember that the main Ionian philosophers to whom Whitehead had referred lived as we have said on the coast of Asia Minor at Miletus, and were by no means far from Hebraic cultural influence; a combination could thus have occurred. Jerusalem, indeed, was less than five hundred miles distant from the Grecian colonies of Asia Minor. The influence of Asia on the early Greek philosophers was doubtless very important. Whitehead's reference to the idea of "the personal energy of Jehova"[13] is illustrative of this. Whitehead is concerned, in this context, with the development of thought even through medieval times and through "the impress on the European mind arising from the unquestioned faith of centuries." Here, as he says, he does not refer to "a mere creed of words."

We would emphasize Whitehead's opposition to "a mere creed of words." The philosopher in this context indicates that he is opposed to a view of God as "arbitrary" and "impersonal"; such conceptions, as he believes could not have "much effect on instinctive habits of mind."[14] The philosopher is explaining his point of view in regard to what he feels is important in the development of ideas through the ages. He is opposing the conception of occurrences in the world as "due to the fiat of an irrational despot" or as being the result of "some impersonal, inscrutable origin of things." The tendency he opposes does not give "the same confidence" that we feel "in the intelligible rationality of a personal being." The last six words here might well have been underlined. European thought was moving toward an effective conception of rationality. A *possibility* or an as-if was being developed. What Whitehead believes is that "modern scientific theory" is an outgrowth of this sense of a possibility; and in science itself "an unconscious derivative" drawn from a developing religion was having its effect. Religion was in process of change, and in its change it was also producing a modification in science.

Wordsworth's developing philosophy during his Cambridge years parallels the kind of evolution that Whitehead has presented in *Science and the Modern World*. The poet does not conceive a universe which is under the rule of an "irrational despot," to use Whitehead's phrase, or which is the result of "some impersonal, inscrutable origin of things." For the purpose of emphasis we are repeating the philosopher's words which could be related to some expressions of Xenophanes. The poet, as we have seen, responded to his world sensitively. He was establishing connections between himself and what he regarded as the world's inward meaning. He had his moments of triviality, among his fellow students; but he did at times spend serious hours in which he tried, perhaps somewhat pedantically, to study. Often, however, "indecisive judgments" ruled him.

All told, his university experience, in this first year, represented "a goodly prospect," in spite of a tendency he had toward unconstructive solitude. In the end he revealed to others the fact that his "heart" was strongly "social" and that like most youths he was drawn to the leisurely waste of hours and the thoughtless pursuit of idle "joy." Thus it was that he, with others,

> talk'd
> Unprofitable talk at morning hours,
> Drifted about along the streets and walks,
> Read lazily in lazy books, went forth
> To gallop through the country in blind zeal
> Of senseless horsemanship, or on the breast
> Of Cam sail'd boisterously; and let the stars
> Come out, perhaps without one quiet thought.   (251-)

Wordsworth was a youth, then not unlike many another in certain respects. His imagination often was asleep, but "yet not utterly." After all, as he says, "Newton's own etherial Self" had walked these grounds, and though the great scientist was actually "humbled" in Wordworth's eyes by the commonality of the experience at Cambridge, he was nevertheless through his very closeness to the poet much more to be loved as a great memory. It is important here that, for Wordsworth, Newton is not associated with materialism, but with something decidedly beyond our material world: the ethereality of his inward being or identity.

Notes

[1] *Process and Reality* (New York: Macmillan, 129, 160), p. 268.

[2] *Ibid.*, p. 143.

[3] *Adventures of Ideas*, p. 154.

[4] *Science and the Modern World*, p. 10.

[5] *Wisdom of the West*, p. 21.

[6] John Burnet, *Greek Philosophy from Thales to Plato*, Part One (New York: Macmillan, 1924), p. 41.

[7] *Ibid.*, p. 42.

[8] *Science and the Modern World*, p. 27.

[9]*Ibid.*, p. 248.

[10]Quoted by W.K.C. Guthrie, *A History of Greek Philosophy*, I, p. 371.

[11]*Ibid.*, p. 373.

[12]*Science and the Modern World*, p. 18.

[13]*Ibid.*

[14]*Ibid.*, p. 19.

Chapter Four

Wordsworth's Summer Vacation: Its Connection with Philosophy

Is it true that in our lives there can be moments of very special significance? Something like this belief seemed to occur to Wordsworth when, after returning home from college to the cottage where he had lived, he stepped out in the evening to roam the surrounding fields. Are such special moments possible for us to attain provided that we have not previously been quiescent and inert? According to the poet a human being can reach, under certain circumstances, a stage of spiritual nakedness as in the presence of the divine. So it was, in his feeling, on the occasion of this walk. He felt that the force of living reality can have the capacity of pervading the mind of a person in such a fashion that a special "power," a sense of being, could thaw the "sleep" that too often takes a long-standing possession of us. Through such a force he believed that a person can spread

abroad
His being with a strength that cannot fail. (160—)

There is a reality, a power, within the self that need not fail in higher purpose. The poet uses the expression "cannot fail." But these two words are preceded by an if-clause; that is, the individual needs also to be, and can be, operative. This is often forgotten by those who consider the poet and do a kind of block-thinking, centering all emphasis on such words as "cannot fail." Wordsworth is not an easy optimist, nor is Whitehead. In Book Four of *The Prelude* a stock-taking of the self is prominent; this occurs at a stage, after his first university year, when he is well aware of what he has lacked in many ways. He thinks warmly and sympathetically of the ordinary, unprivileged people of the world. He surveys widely and consciously his own surrounding world of actuality, his eyes carrying his thought to "White Sirius, glittering o'er the southern crags," and other surrounding heavenly bodies, including "Orion with his belt, and those fair Seven" which had meant much to him even as a child.

He considers, furthermore, the "shadings of mortality" which had rested upon "these objects heretofore"; in his thought, earlier, the fact that the material universe would not last forever had seemed more than a probability, but finally he had been able to overcome this sense of gloom and to see that life can be meaningful and readily open "to delight and joy." Now, for a moment, he thinks of himself "down-bending," looking over the edge of a boat and seeing in the "still water" the countless "discoveries" which

his eye can make,
Beneath him, in the bottom of the deeps,
Sees many beauteous sights, weeds, fishes, flowers,
Grots, pebbles, roots of trees, and fancies more;
Yet often is perplex'd, and cannot part
The shadow from the substance . . . (250—)

Here, before Wordsworth's eyes, we see an illustration of the human feeling about the mystery of appearance and reality. It is a mystery to which Whitehead also refers in various works. But there is in addition the problem of the poet's own appearance and reality, which, as we have said, needs stock-taking. But change is also a factor. He must try to know better how he himself appears and, so far as possible, whatever the reality of that self may be. Know yourself. In what sense is the self permanent? In what respect does it have existence; is it an existent entity? What do we mean by saying that it is an *existent* entity? How is it existential? Does it retrogress? Here we may think of the early Greek philosopher Heraclitus (the third syllable is pronounced like light), who was concerned about that which is or is not lasting and pondered the light in a fire with its evanescent quality. Our discussion will include more about Heraclitus in the last part of this chapter.

The mystery of self is a problem in early Greek thought as it is in Wordsworth and Whitehead. The poet returns to personal stock-taking repeatedly, considering, for example, his tendency toward "an inner falling-off." He was ruled often by "a swarm" of idle things: "gawds" and "dance" and "public revelry" and "sports and games," rather than by a somewhat better form of what he calls "eager zeal"; he had let himself be led astray, he says,

> in societies,
> That were, or seem'd, as simple as myself.   (284—)

What does the poet mean when he refers to people who "were, or seem'd," as simple as himself? Does he imply that he only *seemed* simple, but was not: that *they* were the ones who were really simple? Or is it his thought that the other people *seemed* simple but that some of them, possibly, were not so? All of the tendencies that Wordsworth has repeatedly shown would indicate the latter. He has charity. Again and again he exhibits a tendency not to judge people too hastily; that is, he is not judgmental.

If we consider the matter in greater generality we will find that Wordsworth has the habit of weighing things carefully before leaping to a conclusion. We notice frequently that he is concerned with matters that *seem* and yet perhaps *are* not. As he was walking, on a certain occasion, he "mounted up a steep ascent" where the road, glittering under the moonlight, "seem'd" before his eyes to be a "stream" flowing back toward the valley behind him. The as-if often has a place in his thought as it has in many of Kant's statements. On this particular evening, in "exhausted mind," he stole along (the image is Wordsworth's), his

> body from the stillness drinking in
> A restoration like the calm of sleep . . . (386—)

This part of *The Prelude* comes some forty lines after his famous self-dedication passage, where he made no particular personal vows but where vows were nevertheless, he felt, made for him. Book Four of *The Prelude* ends, very shortly after this, with an exemplification of his feeling concerning the importance of simple acts of humanity. In this case, the incident concerns a veteran of the tropic wars who needed help. Wordsworth stood a long time before making the decision to be of assistance. He finally overcame his "specious cowardise" and did the act of assistance.

We have said that the poet is not unduly hasty in making decisions; he is not prone to judge others. He is, if anything—like Whitehead— overly judgmental of himself, a valuable trait if it is not carried too far. Is it, at times, best to be overly judgmental of oneself? Can such a tendency contain true value? Again the problem of the as-if arises. One can think of oneself as if one is at fault; this can be a valuable corrective to thinking that might be especially weighted on the other side. To think perfectly is impossible. Even to insist on trying to think perfectly can cause one to err. Thought itself needs to be put into action, as a process involving discord as set against structure. Some things must be destroyed. Destruction and creativeness function together to effectual purpose.

We have referred to the early Greeks from time to time as a deliberate procedure in the present book, and we may think here of Heraclitus (born about 535 B.C.), who, in his emphasis on destruction and fire, stands opposite to Xenophanes among the pre-Socratic thinkers who can help us exemplify the meaning of philosophy itself. Heraclitus was born in the eastern Mediterranean region (in Ephesus); Whitehead probably was somewhat influenced by the early Greek doctrine of the passing, or passage, of all as it is seen in Heraclitus. In a crucial passage of *Process and Reality* Whitehead, indeed, alludes to Heraclitus and flux, or eternal change, implying that there appears in the Greek writer an "immortal" expression rendering the idea of change with extraordinary "completeness"[1]; it is the flowing quality that Heraclitus is presenting in relation to Permanence. We are considering here what Whitehead, on the same page, calls "the metaphysics of 'flux.'"

Inspiration plays a part in the theory of Heraclitus when he speaks (almost like Pär Lagerkvist) of "the Sybil" who "reaches over a thousand years with her voice, thanks to the god in her."[2] There is always, as here in Heraclitus, something largely hidden from us; indeed, according to his theory, much learning may drive us mad, if it is merely mechanically accumulated. And yet he stresses learning. He is paradoxical. The whole cosmos, or world, continually shows to us a spectacle of "an ever-living Fire, with measures kindling, and measures going out."[3] In the words of Heraclitus: "All things are an exchange for Fire, and Fire for all things, even as wares for gold and gold for wares."

Bertrand Russell also quotes and emphasizes these words written by Heraclitus, probably from the same source, Burnet, that we have used. Ephesus, where Heraclitus lived, was a city of commerce and the idea of "exchange" in relation to "wares" was very natural to him. But the language he uses is symbolic. If he is thinking of economics he is thinking of economics as process. It is the intangible relationships, rather than money, that he has in mind. There is a melody, an *attunement*, he believes, that we need to understand. In this respect Heraclitus echoes earlier Greek thought in Pythagoras concerning the relationship between philosophy and music. When he speaks also of war as necessary (as a form of fire) it is not militarism that he would endorse. He has in mind that something akin to oxidation (our modern term) is occurring the world over, and these changes appear not merely in ways of physicality. There is a kind of logical quality and an activity, also, that Russell like Burnet sees in Heraclitus. In a sense we have a self (in our actual existence), and in a sense we are nonexistent. We change in our flow just as a river changes. "We are and we are not," Russell avers, "is a somewhat cryptic way of saying that the unity of our existence consists in perpetual change, or to express it in the language later forged by Plato, our being is a perpetual becoming."[4]

We have quoted from John Burnet's *Early Greek Philosophy* at certain points: for example, the statement by Heraclitus about "measures kindling and measures going out." This involves motion, change. But the idea of measure is important here metaphysically, as it also is in the ethics of Heraclitus. In his philosophy "the measures are not absolutely rigid, provided they do not exceed the bounds."[5] So Russell puts it, explaining Heraclitus, and he adds: "They may in fact oscillate within certain ranges," the oscillations or periodicities being potentially very complex. In Russell's view we might "connect the notion of oscillating measures with the Pythagorean construction of irrational numbers by continued fractions, where successive approximations alternately exceed and fall short of exact value." Russell admits that we cannot be sure that "the early Pythagoreans did evolve this method," but he explains that "by Plato's time it was certainly well known"; hence it is possible that it was grasped by Heraclitus, though we cannot be absolutely certain of this. The important point is measure and its variation.

Basically, the feature that Heraclitus moves toward is harmony in the midst of complexity and the terror we feel in the face of seeming destruction. It is the universal, as he would deem it, that he emphasizes most prominently. But change is for us—in this life—eternal. "We step and do not step into the same rivers; we are and we are not."[6] We have identity, but that is a quality that is not so absolute as we suppose. Words themselves are flowing—they are clairvoyant—and the human being also flows and is clairvoyant. It is evident that Heraclitus recognizes that one of our greatest problems is self-knowledge. But how can we attain self-understanding in view of our changefulness? "Man is called a baby by God," just as a child is often called a baby "by a man."[7]

It would seem that anyone who views Heraclitus as a materialist, because of the apparent emphasis on flux in his work, is far from being accurate. It is not a loose relativity or an ethics of convenience that he would endorse. We can learn many things from him. But it is possible to understand him wrongly. Whitehead says ironically, "Mathematical physics translates the saying of Heraclitus, 'All things flow,' into its own language. It then becomes, All things are vectors."[8] But we need more than this if we are to have insight into Heraclitus, and we need to advance carefully through Heraclitus toward Whitehead. A philosophy of organism brings us onward toward more adequate insights into Whitehead's world in contrast to that of Heraclitus.

In Heraclitus the spirit of the ideal human being is a kind of flame that moves upward. It seems to die down, but actually this is not the case. It fluctuates and yet it can attain to great things. This is human. But in comparison with God, or the divine, we should not think of the greatness in the self. Still, greatness should not be neglected; we need to be awake to it, although Heraclitus, like Thoreau, feels that people are, in general, pretty much asleep.

Is Heraclitus aristocratic in his philosophy? He is concerned with the *best* as it may be represented in human beings. He is no aristocrat as measured in terms of money or material values. Ought we to estimate Heraclitus on the basis of what his thought has contributed to mankind, or ought we to approach him strenuously, trying to ascertain what in exactitude he actually was? Are we to seek that which has an as-if value and be concerned most profoundly with the usable past? What has Heraclitus which could be thought of as a value in an understanding of the developing Wordsworth or the ever-changing growth characterizing Whitehead: this should be the focal center of our present thought.

Did Heraclitus think of fire, the fundamental thing, as a form of physicality or of materialism? So he is sometimes viewed. But it is not materiality of this kind that thinkers like Wordsworth and White-head have inherited from the early Greeks, and it is not necessary to ponder this aspect of ancient thought in our present context. It has been asserted by Burnet that Heraclitus in referring to God "meant Fire."[9] It is no simple thing to which this ancient Greek is pointing in his key expression. We can scarcely doubt that what he has in mind leads us toward the point that "the opposition and relativity which are universal in the world disappear." For the ethics of Heraclitus "the greatest fault is to act like men asleep"[10]; this interpretation drawn from Burnet requires a balanced understanding of total philosophy, insofar as one can attain such a wide view. Necessarily we have implied here something which is a far cry from perfection.

Notes

[1] *Process and Reality*, p. 318.

[2] Burnet, *Early Greek Philosophy*, p. 147.

[3] *Ibid.*, p. 148. These words quoted from Heraclitus are crucial.

[4] *Wisdom of the West*, p. 25.

[5] *Ibid.*, p. 26.

[6] Burnet, *Early Greek Philosophy*, p. 153.

[7] *Ibid.*, p. 154.

[8] *Process and Reality*, p. 471.

[9] *Early Greek Philosophy*, p. 188.

[10] *Ibid.*, p. 191. Some people talk as if they are asleep. See Frag. 73.

Chapter Five

Stored Learning in Books:
Wordsworth and Whitehead

Is there ultimate evil in the world, and, if so, would this evil cancel out whatever good there is to be found in the universe? We have spoken here of *the world*. This is an initial aspect of the problem. But are we aware that we can get beyond the reaches of the world we immediately know to further reaches? Does such an awareness exist? There is the complex world inside ourselves which may be thought of in combination with the intricate world of all other consciousnesses, past and present. Often the human being does not think very much further than the surface of his own earth with its small layer of atmosphere. But beyond our atmosphere human beings have been able to travel to other physical regions—indeed, to the moon itself, where men have created a spontaneous primitive art that they have enjoyed: in the dance. This is exemplified in the excitement of the

astronauts as it was revealed on television. The men danced, as
Compton danced at the climax of a discovery concerning cosmic
rays. In our volume *About Wordsworth and Whitehead* we made
certain points as to the world—in time and space considerations.
These space-time considerations are a factor exemplified in travel.
Time was a subject also referred to in several of the chapters of our
other book, *Aspects of Wordsworth and Whitehead*, where we spoke
of the matter in connection with Ludwig Wittgenstein. But now we
must stress the fact that Whitehead, thinking of time, declares that
"by reason of the body, with its miracle of order," as he puts it, "the
treasures of the past environment are poured into the living
occasion."[1]

Whitehead speaks of the *percipient* "route of occasions" as the
experience advances, and he tells us that this percipient factor ends,
wandering "in 'empty' space amid the interstices of the brain." A
moment after the reference to space and the brain he explains that
"this culmination of bodily life transmits itself as an element of
novelty throughout the avenues of the body." It seems evident that he
is thinking here largely of the action of the unconscious mind. But he
is leading up to an aspect of his philosophy of time. In the "higher
actualities" of the world (which are largely within the human person)
there is, finally, a haunting "terror at the loss of the past, with its
familiarities and its loved ones." Yet there is the need of action, and
there is advance into the physical and mental future. We can die, but
before we die there is the need to "attain" something. This is the
foundation of ambition. The human being has forever a sense of
incompleteness.

The important values in what human beings have experienced
before our own present time—"the treasures of the past"—are constantly in Whitehead's mind, it would seem, in view of his references
to them. We have cited in the Introduction and in Chapter I the
example of his interest in the early Greek philosophers and our debt
to them; in Chapter III this point was briefly developed further. But
now we would recall the problem of permanence and change. From
his point of view "it is not 'substance' which is permanent, but 'form.'"[2]
This is characteristic of his philosophy of organism. We can think of
the particularity of forms, thought of in the plural or in multitud-
inousness. "Forms suffer changing relations; actual entities 'perpetu-

ally perish' subjectively, but are immortal objectively." This statement brings to mind the ancient Greeks and their effort, their quest
for a substratum beneath that which is constantly passing. We have
referred to these Greeks in relation to philosophy and its meaning.

The Prelude in Book Five is concerned with reading, and the poet
tells of a dream which a friend had about an "Arabian Waste" where
the friend imagined himself "in the wide wilderness" seated "upon the
sands." This was a dream which the poet himself had, and it concerns
the ephemeral. In the dream a man approached, who "seem'd an
Arab," carrying under his arm a "Stone" and in one hand a "Shell" of
special brightness. The two objects are symbolic books. The dreamer
questioned the "Newcomer" and found that the stone represented
"Euclid's Elements"; the shell is referred to as a "Book" which sent a
message

which foretold
Destruction to the Children of the Earth . . . (97—)

The "Newcomer" explains that he plans to "bury those two
Books," representing, on the one hand, mathematics which can unite
humanity by "purest" union, "undisturbed by space or time," and
indicating, on the other hand, inspired poetry connected with "a
God" or with the divine. These things need to be preserved in the
event of the destruction, in large part, of our physical world. Here is a
problem that Heraclitus thought of and that we think of today. What
can be destroyed in a holocaust? Whitehead's theme in *Process and
Reality* to which we last referred focused on the ephemeral, and
Wordsworth in Book Five of his poem has this same problem in
mind, with a strong stress upon the human need for a sense of
permanence. Here, as we think of mathematics in its purity "undisturbed by space or time" (in the poet's words), we may return to the
thought of the early Greeks and the development of their ideas.

Behind Plato and Aristotle, as Whitehead says, there were "three
or four generations of thinkers."[3] reaching back ultimately to Thales,
Anaximander, Anaximines, as well as Pythagoras, Xenophanes, and
Heraclitus, on all of whom we have commented; but we can profitably look backward still further "beyond them." Whitehead had been
thinking of the early Greeks, although he does not specifically refer to

all of the ancient philosophers we have mentioned. For the moment he goes on to "the Academy of Plato," which provided a "group of thinkers, to whom the modern world owes its speculation, its criticism, its deductive and inductive sciences, and the civilization of its religious concepts." He is looking forward. But in understanding this heritage we need to look back, he says, to "the confused traditions of Egypt, Mesopotamia, Syria, and of the sea-borne Greek civilization." In this way Whitehead looks backward and forward, as he often does, into the story of human culture.

A key figure among the early Greek thinkers, as we have seen, was the mathematician and philosopher Pythagoras, and here we would mention him further as part of our deliberate procedure. In speaking of mathematics, Bertrand Russell declares that he regards it as "the chief source of the belief in eternal and exact truth, as well as in a super-sensible intelligible world."[4] It is in connection with his presentation of Pythagoras that Russell makes this statement. Russell is interested in the possibility "that thought is nobler than sense, and the objects of thought more real than those of sense-perception." He reiterates the point that "mathematical objects" may be regarded as "eternal and not in time." He emphasizes the fact that "eternal objects can be conceived as God's thoughts." Of course, Russell is speaking of very early Greeks, but his comments recall to one's mind the *eternal objects* of Whitehead as discussed in *Science and the Modern World* and in *Process and Reality*.

We will re-emphasize here that Wordsworth's subject of discussion— like that of Whitehead to which we have referred—concerns the ephemeral. The poet's whole purpose in *The Prelude* is to recapture the ephemeral, the passing, and to try to sound out its significance. But his center of attention now is on books and on value. The ideas from Whitehead that we have dealt with in the present chapter could never have been attained by him without attention to books. But, whatever we may chance to feel about Whitehead, Wordsworth is not heavy-handed as he deals with books. Still, he would prefer not to present mere passing incidents with regard to his reading; such a treatment of the casual, or the anecdotal, he would prefer to leave

in its endless home
Among the depths of time.   (197—)

Wordsworth's reference here to the "endless" is of interest in its bearing upon experience and the universe. As he speaks generally with regard to reading, or, as he says, "in memory of all books" that are helpful to people, we must not forget "the low," even the very small, "wren-like" literature—if we can agree with him to call it that—associated with "Cottagers and Spinners at the wheel" or casual travelers we might meet who would make a seemingly trivial allusion to something they had read, or, indeed, might allude to "ballad tunes" or to things which, with their "hungry ears," small children attend to carefully; he would "assert the rights," the "honours" these elemental authors deserve—

> speak of them as Powers
> For ever to be hallowed; only less,   .
> For what we may become, and what we need,
> Than Nature's self . . . (219—)

The poet, here, like Whitehead, is dealing with "what we may become," or with the problem of incompleteness; more broadly, like the philosopher he is interested in the essence of becoming in and of itself. What we have here quoted from Wordsworth about time is only one example of many. He was fortunate in experience; he might indeed, except for happy chance, have been "dried" up, he says, in childhood, "body and soul." Luckily, however, he and Coleridge (Wordsworth thinks also of his friend here) had not been "shut out" from *becoming* or from the "touch of growing grass." Literature had its values and was very much open to their eyes. The factor, the phenomenon, of *growth*—of change in its relation to time—is emphasized here as it is stressed in many places in *The Prelude*. It is also a prominent feature in the philosophy of Whitehead, and it brings our thought back, once again, to the early Greek Heraclitus, who was so deeply concerned about the passage and change in the world that he was sometimes rather ironically called the weeping philosopher.

But Heraclitus, as otherwise understood, had small reason to weep. Martin Heidegger sees in Heraclitus' presentations the importance of togetherness in a very profound sense: "*that which is permanently together*, collectedness."[5] Even death, and seeming destruction of all things, can be surmounted; we need not be pessimistic. The very essence of life with all its wonder can be gladly perceived to be a slow process including "death."[6] We need not despair. This may be profoundly true: "Everything that enters into life also begins to die, to go toward its death, and death is at the same time life." So Heidegger says, and believes, inspired by Heraclitus. He is no Sartre; he does not view life with nausea. In this view Greek thought had, for Heidegger, "reached the very gates"[7] of the divine. Thus it appears that Heraclitus was a forerunner of religious developments.

The basic feature of this early thought is, according to Heidegger, a very profound unity standing in opposition to the common: "what is commonly believed and said, in hearsay, in *doxa*, appearance."[8] The problem of appearance and reality is dominant in Heraclitus, and it brings us to conflict: a conflict within our own minds. We struggle with opposites. If we may see Heraclitus, as quoted by Heidegger, we will note: "Opposites move back and forth, the one to the other; from out of themselves they gather themselves."[9] How close this is to Whitehead's backward and forward movement we can see in a further statement concerning Heraclitus which is Heidegger's interpretation: "Conflict of opposites is a gathering, rooted in togetherness." In another sentence, he adds the point that Heraclitus brings forward "the supreme radiance" which is "the greatest beauty, that which is most permanent in itself." The war of opposites can be a profound thing that is no war.

As opposed to the Heraclitus of flux, as usually viewed—in contrast with the wholeness of things—stands Parmenides (the name is accented on the second syllable); this philosopher, born about 515 B.C., lived for the greater part of his life in the western region of the extended Greek commonwealth in Italy. He traveled to Athens on one occasion in his old age and was reverenced there. He was constructive, very far from a weeping philosopher. His great concern was centered in that which is existent, and he followed Xenophanes, also of Elea, in his metaphysical emphasis upon the grandeur, rather than the triviality, of the world. Both thinkers were decidedly independent. And they are related, in their development, to Heraclitus. They are far from the orthodoxy of their own time or of any time.

Parmenides is concerned with logic and time. But he is also very imaginative. He presents a goddess who speaks wisdom to the youth who is central to his story. From one point of view Parmenides may be regarded primarily as a symbolic poet (he wrote poetry in hexameters), bringing us, as Sartre has done, a story of a quest or an inquiry, emphasizing the value, the extreme essentiality, of persuasion. Viewed otherwise, he is basically analytical, centering his attention upon the necessity of logic in its narrower sense. Actually, he has both tendencies: the inspiring semi-mystical concern for a way that can lead us to profound insights, and the unbending logical emphasis upon the greatest thing in the world that exists or is existent. This greatest thing rules out any conception that emphasizes transciency and that which is passing. It may seem difficult to see how this approach can possess elements that are highly logical. But the logic in Parmenides is often the main feature that is remembered about him.

The goddess (in a spirit of fair-mindedness) is concerned that the youth should take the path, or the route, which is right and that will lead to what in an ultimate sense *is*: that which, in other words, possesses true being. But she nevertheless indicates that he should know the wrong—the other side of the problem; he needs to reflect upon the the ephemeral, mainly to perceive its nonexistence or to understand the majority of his fellow human beings, who are unenlightened. Mourelatos points out that the youth's "encounter with the divine," in various figures in the story, "lacks any hint of worship."[10] Mourelatos at once adds that Parmenides even "avoids the word 'divine' with reference to 'what-is' " and "seems to withhold from it any of the epithets which had been traditionally bestowed upon the gods." The point of importance, however, we would say, is that Parmenides wishes to depart as far as possible from the dogmatic: from any traditional notion of the gods of his time. His purpose is very far-reaching.

The place of the conception of eros, notable in Plato and Whitehead, appears in Parmenides in the form of symbolism indicative of a deeper factor within the poem; as Drew Hyland wisely emphasizes, it is "intimately bound up with the theme of the quest"; and it is bound up with "incompleteness and the impetus toward the overcoming of that incompleteness."[11] Our human incompleteness may be connected with the divine (as in the thought of Karl Jaspers),[12] or it can be seen primarily in connection with the psychology of the person. The feminine element in the poem of Parmenides is therefore worthy of special remark. Lately the notion of the feminist has been indicated as having reference to anyone (regardless of sex) who is strongly concerned about women's rights and the rights of all persons in the world. The feminine characters (the goddesses) in Parmenides are notable, and there is a larger element of the feminine in the poem than these characters alone represent. The theme is itself part of the universalizing tendency in his philosophy.

The goddess beyond the doors of Night and Day stresses the problem of change with the aim of indicating that it is illusory. This fact has seemed to most readers to set Parmenides in strong opposition to Heraclitus. But Martin Heidegger attempts to bring the two thinkers together and Drew Hyland, with some qualifications, defends "the view set forth by Heidegger"[13]; it is the eternal *one* that Hyland has in mind. For Heidegger, even a few words of Parmenides in a specific case stand "like Greek statues"[14]; evidently they have a permanence that can be associated with art. The few remains of the writings of Parmenides "might perfectly well replace whole libraries of supposedly indispensable philosophical literature." Heidegger follows this remark with even higher praise.

A connection between mathematics and the thought of Parmenides is brought out by Robert S. Brumbaugh in the suggestion that Parmenides may have known "the Pythagorean proof that the diagonal of a unit square is incommensurable with the side"; this proof surely could have been extended "into pure logic."[15] We can see that Parmenides, if he is doing this, does so through extending such a "proof from relations of quantity to philosophy." Other factors to be found in Pythagoras undoubtedly could have led Parmenides toward thought about the infinite as a limit in its relation to one's pondering about ideas connected with the divine. Space presented a problem in his thought, and he used notably the figure of a globe as symbolical of being. That-which-exists extends in globular fashion in all directions (here we have an approach to infinity as a limit) from a center; time is inevitably a factor here, and being (reality) therefore stretches endlessly in time, as it extends in all directions.

Parmenides is opposed to dwelling upon the particular, except as it is an integral feature in universal being. This leads to or implies what Brumbaugh refers to as some measure of the clairvoyant or the mystical, and he explains "a mystical experience" as "a vivid intuition of the oneness of all reality."[16] Brumbaugh re-emphasizes the point by saying that "it is possible to have an intuition of the unity of all things, and a sense of the transparent unreality about the particular items that appear." This would be an approach that might seem contrary to that of Wordsworth and Whitehead, but it is one which they could both understand. Michael C. Stokes shows perception when he conceives of Parmenides as "endeavoring to obliterate variation in both time and space"; Stokes points out that this effort "inevitably came into conflict on these two fronts with customary human belief."[17] Speaking of Parmenides, he adds that it is easy to conceive how Parmenides could reject both facets of common sense because they at once led to the being of what is not and thus not only distinguished Being from not-Being but also confused the two. Our reference to the early Greeks is part of a planned procedure.

We, as thinkers, though we are incomplete, can achieve thought which moves toward, and theoretically could unite to a degree with, the basic reality of the universe. Thus thought is—or in the end can be or can lead toward—that which is the ultimate: being. Plato later shows respectful consideration for Parmenides, but develops more complex views of being and not-being, as does Whitehead. Has Wordsworth, like Parmenides, a marked sense of the phenomenal world—that of the appearances that surround us—as well as a realization of the need to try to move beyond appearances in the direction of the divine? We shall find that it will indeed be increasingly evident that he has such a view.

Notes

[1] *Process and Reality*, p. 516.

[2] *Ibid.*, p. 44.

[3] *Adventures of Ideas*, p. 182. Anaximander, Anaximines, Xenophanes, and Heraclitus are not specified.

[4] Russell, *A History of Western Philosophy*, p. 37.

[5] Heidegger, *Introduction to Metaphysics* (Garden City: Doubleday Torchbooks, 1961), p. 109. Italics in Heidegger.

[6] *Ibid.*, p. 111.

[7] *Ibid.*, p. 107. Heidegger mentions Christ here as the logos.

[8] *Ibid.*, p. 109.

[9] *Ibid.*, p. 111.

[10] Alexander P.D. Mourelatos, *The Route of Parmenides* (New Haven: Yale University Press, 1970), p. 44.

[11] Drew A. Hyland, *The Origins of Philosophy*, Capricorn Books (New York: G.P. Putnam's Sons, 1973), p. 181.

[12] Human beings, in thinking of the divine, cannot "encompass this reality"; that is, we cannot *completely* encompass it, for "merely to think it leaves us empty." See Jaspers, *Way to Wisdom* (New Haven: Yale University Press, 1954, 1959), p. 47. He refers here to thinking of a proposition.

[13] *The Origins of Philosophy*, p. 180.

[14] Heidegger, *Introduction to Metaphysics*, p. 82.

[15] Brumbaugh, *The Philosophers of Greece*, pp. 52-53.

[16] *Ibid.*, p. 55.

[17] Michael C. Stokes, *One and Many in Presocratic Philosophy*, Center for Hellenic Studies, Washington, D.C. (Cambridge: Harvard University Press, 1971), p. 126.

Chapter Six

Cambridge and the Alps: Philosophical Retrospect

We find Wordsworth still thinking about reflection and reading near the close of the first thirty lines in Book Six of *The Prelude*: he is now looking backward to the time of his early twenties, when he was a student. He recalls how, having returned to Cambridge following what we would call his sophomore year, and having completed his vacation, he was reading more and *reflecting* more. He seemed, that is, at this stage in his twenties, to be moving in the direction of something that was at least "promising." Still, even if we add a space of greater time, coming down close to the end of his junior year at the University, he was continuing without any "settled plan." He was somewhat "detached," as he says, given to following the thought (as we may guess) which merely happened by chance to cross his mind. Nevertheless, he did gain special value from mathematics, though he speaks with due humility about this. It is significant that he was drawn to a consideration of mathematics in relation to the frame of "Nature"; that is, he was preoccupied with structure and the "Laws" that can be discerned in the physical world, generally conceived.

But the poetic and the symbolic also find a place in this part of *The Prelude*. Still, as he thinks of science, it is a sense of permanence for which he feels a need (somewhat as the early pre-Socratic Greeks, notably Parmenides, felt a need); Zeno of Elea, born about 490 B.C. and a pupil of Parmenides, had a similar urge. Zeno battled charmingly but somewhat confusedly against pluralism, but he was strongly concerned about permanence and the one. Plato shows the personable Zeno at the age of forty speaking to Socrates. Zeno says that his writing was "meant to protect the arguments of Parmenides against those who ridicule him"; he would protect Parmenides against those who "urge the many ridiculous and contradictory results which were supposed to follow from the assertion of the one."[1] Zeno uses ridicule against ridicule.

It was a sense of permanence for which, as we have said, Wordsworth felt a need. He reflects upon this as it may have a relation to the divine. Something like a feeling of peace and the transcendental seemed to come to him, and this was a "comfort," he says, to his "youth." Wordsworth had a need for philosophy, then, even in his relatively youthful college days. He thinks of a person stranded on an island who has but a single volume—as it happens, a work on geometry. Did Wordsworth himself feel stranded at some point during his university study? Did he feel at times "beyond common wretchedness depress'd," and did he, like the character to whom he refers, draw "diagrams" within his mind? At any rate he speaks of comfort that can come from

> those abstractions to a mind beset
> With images, and haunted by itself . . . (179—)

Here, thinking of a mind beset or loaded with images—indeed, a mind "haunted by itself"—we may recall Bertrand Russell's experience in his Cambridge University days. The poet Wordsworth, as he thinks of mathematics, is struck by the effect of "clear Synthesis" which it can provide, and he thinks of it as if "aloft" in its pure gracefulness, even though one might be also reflecting on it somewhat as one thinks of "a plaything, or a toy" which can manifest itself before one visibly, though indeed

it is
In verity, an independent world ... (185—)

As we reflect on Wordsworth's employment of the words "plaything" and "toy" as related to thinking, it is of value to recall Erik Erikson and his book *Toys and Reasons*, with its fly-leaf quotation from Blake about the "toys" of youth and the adult's "reasons" which may be thought of as but "the Fruits of the Two Seasons."[2] That is, there is a kind of toy or play aspect involved in a certain sort of inventive or creative thinking, and this can, in effect, be connected with Plato's references to leaping or jumping, and play, as Erikson explains at the outset of his volume. Make-believe has value if it creates a structure. Erikson refers to play in the Introduction. It is interesting that, in Wordsworth's context, the poet is deeply involved with the value of the fanciful in relation to structures of thought which the human being can build.

Where Wordsworth refers (seriously) to the "plaything" and the "toy" which is given a sense-form, Erikson also thinks of the serious aspects of our creativeness which, though "they are *playful*," may go further and become part of the philosophical and even of a religious perspective; moreover, they help us to bring about or to "renew the *surprise* of recognition."[3] Back of this, as Erikson develops his idea on the next page, we see there is a sense of the clairvoyant or the divine. Here we have the problem of appearance and a deeper reality; behind the appearance there is in Erikson's view "a pervasive element which is best called the *numinous*." This thought of Erikson concerning the numinous or spiritual has a very close relation to that of Wordsworth, but is even more nearly affiliated with Whitehead's reflections.

As Erikson sees things, he recognizes also a danger in the "deceptive and self-deceptive trends which are the shadow of all make-believe"[4]; but for him even ritualization may be of distinct value, although it can also bring about distortions which are hurtful to thinking. When it has this distortional effect, it leads to blindness reflected in *isms*; Erikson in contrast to healthy ritualization speaks of what he calls "more simply, *ritualism*." His dislike of such pseudo-forms is evident, though in itself he has no objection to a ritual. He is friendly to ritualization when it is undistorted, but *ritualism* appears in "mere compulsive compliance with daily rules" or in "the obsessive-repetitive expression of fanatic and delusional visions." We must beware of any ritualism of this shadow kind "which distorts the reverence for the truly numinous." There is in such cases a loss of the extremely valuable "playful" aspect of thinking. What Erikson desires is the generative, the creative, the playful in thought. He uses the term "generational" for this, and he stresses the fact that it leads to integration.

The early Greek Zeno had this impulse most markedly. Whitehead likewise in this sense desires the generative in thinking which can bring about surprising new examples of unification. As we think of the integrative (which is connected with creative thinking) it is of value to recall Wordsworth's use of the term "Synthesis" (1. 182)—a "Synthesis" which may appear to some eyes, the poet says, as "a plaything or a toy," rather than as a factor connected with profound thinking. Wordsworth, Whitehead, and Erikson are close together in their insight as to this matter of synthesis and the play of the mind.

Erikson's use of the conception *play* (and Wordsworth's use of it) may be set beside Whitehead's remark that "all our knowledge is the play of our own mind."[5] He objects even to the use, the "silly trick" he calls it, of the plural in the word "our," for he centers and emphasizes creative thought within the experience of the single self. But, as he points out on the page following, that very individual thing, the self or the consciousness (although we have it), possesses also the "nature" which we ourselves apprehend; the "apprehended nature" is a part within the self. For "our consciousness exhibits its significance" concerning the "factors of fact beyond itself." Here he holds that space and time are understandable as interacting forces.

We need to remember Whitehead's reference to "play" in the expression about "the play of our own mind." There are many examples of such play in the poetry of Wordsworth. He comes to a point in Book Six where he gives an account of a fourteen-week walking trip which he and a friend, Robert Jones, took in 1790; in it they traveled through regions of France, the Alps, and Switzerland.

The poet tells how, at a certain stage, the river Rhone served as "the wings on which" they "cut" through the "lofty" mountains. In the description there are references to such things as the "single Cottages" and "lurking Towns" and "deep and stately Vales." The vast grandeur of the valley regions impresses Wordsworth. Many examples are also given of the psychological effect of the French Revolution, which was taking place. We get a sense of the people and their state of mind as they, along with the poet and his friend, share meals with "flowing cups elate" and with "happy thoughts"; having greatly enjoyed their sociality they finally

> rose at signal giv'n, and formed a ring
> And, hand in hand, danced round and round the Board . . . (406—)

Near the middle of the present chapter we made reference to Erik Erikson and the value he found in play: in thought that jumps or leaps; this idea traces back, as we have said, to Plato's *Laws*. The poet's thought leaps when he sees "the naked huts, wood built and sown like tents" near lawns and close to the "river-side." Appearance and reality are constantly in his mind. When he and his friend first saw Mont Blanc it seemed far different from the picture they had carried in their minds, for it was now merely a material or "soulless image on the eye"—a usurpation. But together, at the sight of the rivers "broad and vast" of "Chamouny," they became "reconcil'd," in spite of all, to the wonders of the "realities" around them. In this region they felt that winter "walks" down from the peaks and glaciers in friendly spirit

> make sport
> Among the cottages by beds of flowers.   (467—)

Realities and appearances were in Wordsworth's mind, then, as he reflected on things and people and events, the latter notably when he was thinking of reaching the topmost height of the path up and over the Alps. In a famous passage concerning this he tells how, without knowing the exact point, he nevertheless *had crossed the Alps.* He italicizes these words in the poem. The event becomes symbolical. Our awareness of the physical actuality of crossing the mountainous divide—that is, covering a certain entity which is spatial in our own particular experience and occurring seemingly at one exact instant of time—this is not the important thing. It is the event itself which he feels can overwhelm us; for us, "Tumult and peace" and "darkness and the light" can coalesce and become

> like the workings of one mind, the features
> Of the same face, blossoms upon one tree,
> Characters of the great Apocalypse,
> The types and symbols of Eternity . . . (568—)

Wordsworth had used the concept *leaps*, a concept which might have made Plato glad, as we saw some paragraphs back, and Coleridge made a comment on this portion of the poem. For the later version Wordsworth made a change in which he referred to how a stranger might "look with bounding heart" at the scene which he and Robert Jones beheld. Coleridge had not objected to the fact that Wordsworth's "heart leap'd up," but he was troubled by the words "leap'd up" and the expression "look down" (toward the "deep haunts")—terms which are in close juxtaposition in the 1805 version; still there was more life and play in the writing of 1805 than in the later revision, and more of the quality that Plato was concerned about when he wrote his *Laws*. The play of the fanciful is important here, as it was in Wordsworth's writing of his short poem "My Heart Leaps Up," about the rainbow, near the time in which he was working on *The Prelude*.

Space and time (in regions) play an important part in Wordsworth's poem, as we have seen; a rainbow, observed in childhood, and also in adult periods, is actually a staggering example of multiple curves and also of the problems of curved space and time. An igloo put together with blocks of ice in a multitude of curved spatial arcs is another example. The Eskimo was not playing (and yet in some sense he *was* doing so with the play of the mind) when he primitively created, or evolved, this astounding form. Whitehead, in the essay from which we have quoted near the middle of this chapter, is concerned with combined unity and diversity, as well as with the problem of consciousness related to space and time. Does our consciousness literally *possess* the significance of factors which are beyond consciousness itself? The significance of factors which are beyond consciousness itself is a matter of importance to the idealists.

But Whitehead does not accept the position of the idealists at this point "so far as they consider such an external significance" as if it were "peculiar to consciousness" and from this "deduce that the things signified have a peculiar dependence on consciousness."[6] He is against subjectivism. Whitehead places a very great importance upon realism—upon realities outside ourselves. He would be at one with Wordsworth in feeling the *real* existence, the actuality, of "chestnut woods" as well as "garden plots" and "lofty steeps, and pathways roof'd with vines," of

> cloistral avenues
> Where silence is, if music be not there . . . (597—)

The poet is sensitive to spaces and times and regions exemplifying differing features under various actual conditions; he looks back to the period after his junior university year, when the occurrences of his trip flowed over him like a stream, affecting him not in "instantaneous" moments but rather by something like a process which is "circuitous." The sociology of his experience, however, was also important, especially when he notes, concerning the Revolution, the "triumphant looks" (1. 682) which served as "the common language of all eyes." The glance of an eye can be not only a language but a gesture, as he well knew even if he did not use this word to describe its *action*. The people of Switzerland he found, like the people of France, were "exulting"; he was youthful then but he was undergoing creative advance and was not insensitive to "the cause of Liberty." He does not pretend that he, the "Stripling," knew, as yet, much about the problems, as he says, of "social life," but he was nevertheless definitely "touch'd" by them; he compares himself in his stage of development to the lower creatures, "a bird" or "a fish," but he had the "spirit of pure youth," responsive directly to all of the things which were "spread" everywhere about the path that he had taken in going abroad. In our next chapter, and later, we shall make further references to the pre-Socratic Greeks, as part of our continuing, planned procedure—with the intention of adding illumination to the meaning of the word philosophy and the thought of Wordsworth and Whitehead.

Notes

[1] Hyland, *The Origins of Philosophy*, p. 225. Hyland also deals with points not presented here which are important.

[2] See Erikson, *Toys and Reasons* (New York: W.W. Norton, 1977), fly-leaf, p. 3.

[3] *Ibid.*, p. 88. See also p. 89.

[4] *Ibid.*, p. 90.

[5] Whitehead, "Uniformity and Contingency," *Essays in Science and Philosophy* (New York: Philosophical Library, 1948), p.106.

[6] *Essays in Science and Philosophy*, p. 107.

Chapter Seven

London:
Wordsworth as Related to Whitehead

Very important to Wordsworth was his experience in London, but the effect of it, as we shall see, was in some ways almost overwhelming. The events that occur to us in our human life are in part made up of anticipation, first response (or appearance), and, last, the actuality. What aspect of an event is the actuality? An event is capable of reaching into things to come. Thus we might think of the social aspects of knowledge and creative advance to which we referred in the last paragraph of the previous chapter. Wordsworth himself does so in anticipating the fact that such social aspects at a given *time* will become enriched by a later insight—for example, insight into a revolution actually taking place in time, in a given nation. For some people the experience, the event, of being in London (or in Hamburg or in Chicago) may itself be a revolution.

For Whitehead an event is "the grasping into unity of a pattern of aspects. "[1] Such an event has a power to produce effects, and this "effectiveness" reaching into the beyond "arises from the aspects of itself which go to form the prehended unities of other events." Whitehead's concept of the prehended unities is difficult, but Wordsworth exhibits the power of prehension in more ways than one. According to the philosopher "it would hardly be possible to express more clearly a feeling for nature, as exhibiting entwined prehensive unities,"[2] than Wordsworth does in certain parts of *The Prelude*.

The poet's powers of prehension are exhibited in many ways. But here we would like to emphasize the tendency whereby he shows in Book Seven the capacity of reflecting upon appearance (as related to anticipation, false or otherwise) and actuality. In addition there is the power reaching into things to come whereby they are made more and more meaningful. Thus he had thought of London while he was still very young, and his anticipated notions of the city far surpassed what he had conceived earlier with regard to "Gardens" from the creations of the "Genii of Romance"; many such fantastic notions "fell short" by far from what he "in simplicity believed" about London.

His early fantastic conception, his *belief* at that early time, is thus contrasted, in *The Prelude*, with what he finally came actually to know. Perhaps he was somewhat susceptible to unthinking belief (he considers this possibility), but he says that a neighbor boy, after a trip to London, *seemed* surprisingly lacking of transformation on his return home from the city. Wordsworth had a conception, an expectation, of "beams of glory" that might well, through city experience, be conferred upon the boy in "that new region." The youthful Wordsworth questioned his friend a great deal, but the responses of the boy

> Fell flatter than a cagèd Parrot's note,
> That answers unexpectedly awry,
> And mocks the Prompter's listening.   (107—)

The expressions of language may be thought of as naked words or they may, for the poet, be a representation of "wond'rous power"; words can change things when for example we think of "pageant fireworks" or of the Thames in London "proudly bridged" as well as of the "Whispering Gallery of St. Paul's," not to speak of

> Statues, with flowery gardens in vast Squares,
> The Monument, and Armoury of the Tower. (134—)

In Wordsworth's mind we see again and again the problem of the attempt to represent, anticipatorily or otherwise, the reality of things. If, he declares, matters seemed in reality not to be so great as he had supposed, perhaps he was the one who was wrong; what he failed to see in actuality perhaps had a "prescriptive right" and should be recognized as what "ought to be." Thus when a male chauvinist, in our own day, pulls rank upon us, we may often be tempted to yield to this rank and to say that he may be an *authority* concerning what he says. This may be a problem for example with regard to university faculty members or other officers in their capacity as representers of truth, as Wordsworth earlier had come to know. Cambridge was a good illustration of this. What the poet is to tell of London seems now to be in part a "work of fancy"; we have here, again, the question of seeming and being.

Near the beginning of our first chapter and later as a planned procedure, we spoke of the early Greek interest in philosophy, and we might have gone beyond the search for a universal principle in water, air, or other physical substance, or in what we also included in regard to mathematics. If we had gone beyond the reference to the approach to infinity as connected with mathematics we could have touched upon the problem of appearance and reality—that is, the problem of seeming and being; as an example of this Xenophanes could once again be cited in that he had begun to reflect more actively about the qualitative and probably about spirit, rather than about matter as a source of universal being. Mind or soul was central for him. The development of the concern about spirit in early Greek times is a much-disputed matter, but Wordsworth, like Whitehead, is an inheritor of the increased spiritualization of thought in the ancient world. In the succession of thinkers in early Greece there is an increasing sense of unity and also of the *power* of the written or spiritual word, or logos, along with a concern about organism in contrast to seemingly dead material substance.

Whitehead stresses organism in contrast to material things, but his conception of the philosophy of organism reaches far into a totally interactive universe. Near the close of the last chapter we alluded to the philosopher's realism and to the way he rejects idealism and its magnifying of consciousness or of subjectivism. In his essay "Uniformity and Contingency," he speaks of ascribing "external significance to every factor of fact," such as the "colour green" or a "bath-chair."[3] He believes in this external reality. Correlatively he believes not only in the *actuality* of the "colour green" (and the actuality of bath-chairs) but in a less tangible actuality connected with consciousness. To explain this he has his own special way of using the word *patience*. This use of the word is for some readers rather troublesome. Nature is active. Whitehead thinks of the patient enduring of consciousness by nature; that is, nature *actively* endures consciousness. In the same context the philosopher deals with interactionism; he speaks not only of the *enduring* of consciousness by nature, but of the exhibiting by nature of the *fact* that nature itself is "apprehensible by consciousness." This again is troublesome. But often, if we bear enduringly with Whitehead, our endurance brings reward.

One additional comment at this point may deserve patience. It will be brief. Continuing the discussion of "nature as apprehensible" by the conscious mind Whitehead explains that this is an exhibition, an endurance (or "patience") revealed by nature in connection with the active ingression of sense objects to our consciousness; nature in this respect, then, is itself interactive and real, apart from our consciousness of her. Nature provides a "stratification into layers of simultaneity" (in our experience)—an essential character of the ingression that occurs; but this stratification "is at the same time an adaptation of nature" and it is also "an adaptation of consciousness for the apprehension of nature." Here, then, is the play of thought as well as interactionism. And it involves complex space and time. Interaction occurs between that which is within us and that which is outside us.

But enough for the present of the problem of Whitehead and the activity of nature in her patient assimilation, as well as her action while enduring recipiently. We through our consciousness provide part of the adaptation which, in nature, enables experience in complex space and time to occur. The stratification "is both a fact of nature, and is also the way in which we apprehend nature." Now Wordsworth, as we see in *The Prelude*, is experiencing the complex reality of London (which is a part of the total span of nature, broadly viewed), and he is also noticing the surface: things that seem. He sees "allegoric shapes" and, in reproduction, "the physiognomies of real men"—for example, "Admirals of the Sea" or the countenance of

> Newton, or the attractive head
> Of some Scotch doctor, famous in his day.   (182—)

The phantasmagoric play aspect of London takes on many shapes: "a company of dancing Dogs," the "Dromedary" carrying "Monkies on his back," puppet-masters, or the "English Ballad-singer."We hear vendors'"London cries" which "entangle us awhile"; the poet appeals to all of our senses and possibilities of association. But this is enough for the present, except for his reference to hanging sheets of paper on which "ballads" are inscribed and to giant advertisements which "press" upon him "in all colours" as well as his remembrance of

> .   a Face turn'd upward . . . strong
> In lineaments, and red with over-toil . . . (216—)

We can continue our references to this book of Wordsworth's *Prelude* by emphasizing his concern for the working-class people (his sense of the need for a developing of democracy) and his feeling about life's mystery to the vast majority of human beings. The mystery of change and destruction is indirectly present in many passages of Wordsworth's *Prelude*: for example, in Book Five the reference (1. 98) about "Destruction to the Children of the Earth" and, at the end of Book Seven, the theme of London as a "blank confusion" to almost every person, a world in which things are "undistinguishable" for all practical purposes; this is the case as one encounters the city

> Living amid the same perpetual flow
> Of trivial objects, melted and reduced
> To one identity, by differences
> That have no law, no meaning, and no end . . . (701—)

For Wordsworth, London represents a Heraclitian perishing or destruction which was moment by moment in process: a process of events moving into the past. But it is also a present thing undergoing a growth involving possibilities of transformation. Using Whitehead's terms we can say that even Wordsworth's London with its perishing past "transforms itself into a new creation." There is also, however, the point that one may feel caught or to some extent trapped within the city: the fact referred to by the poet at the very end of Book Seven that London should be conceived, from his point of view, as a "vast receptacle." Plato has a concept related to this.

The problem of the receptacle is given some treatment in our book *Aspects of Wordsworth and Whitehead*. The receptacle is not merely a trap. In Chapter VII of the volume *Aspects of Wordsworth and Whitehead* we have indicated that the poet's concept of democracy has an important relation to the receptacle-concept in the philosopher. Cambridge was a receptacle and Paris was a receptacle. Whitehead speaks of the idea of the receptacle as it first underwent Platonic development; he refers to it as "a difficult notion,"[4] and he is somewhat undecided about an adequate sense of its meaning.

Part of the problem concerns life and motion. In the next page Whitehead does not present his own philosophy as involving a "static world." His philosophy is active. And he refers to "life and motion" as "essentials in Plato's later thought"; it is "operation" that Whitehead wishes to emphasize. He presents a modern adaptation or development of Plato's "notions" and does so through starting with "actuality as in its essence a process." It involves the physical "perishing of the past as it transforms itself into a new creation."

Ideas and action are prevalent, wildly prevalent, in London; they are so now, and were so when Wordsworth was in the great city. For the poet it became evident that (to use Whitehead's language again) London "passes into the future." The city is dynamic and, with all its evil and, at times, triviality, it possesses a potential growth. This sense of dynamic process which is a factor of growth is more evident in *The Prelude* later, when Wordsworth tells of his experiences in Paris. For the poet the city, anywhere, presents a possibility of profound adventure: a general philosophical and moral adventure. Book Seven ends with a few lines of definite hope about a "Soul of Beauty and enduring life" which he experienced in the city as "diffused" even though in "meagre lines and colours" and as appearing surrounded by "self-destroying, transitory things"; the final paradoxical note for the poet is a resolution of seemingly unresolvable difficulties. The difficulties in establishing a philosophy can, for Wordsworth and Whitehead, be in considerable degree creatively resolved.

Again we may say that in the chapter that follows and in later pages we shall find value in further references to Zeno of Elea and other pre-Socratic thinkers in Greece, with the purpose of expanding upon the idea of philosophy itself, as well as in adding illumination to the thought of the poet and Whitehead.

Notes

[1] *Science and the Modern World*, p. 174.

[2] *Ibid.*, p. 122.

[3] *Essays in Science and Philosophy*, p. 107.

[4] *Adventures of Ideas*, p. 354.

Chapter Eight

Nature and Human Kind:
Wordsworth, Whitehead, and the One

Having reflected upon cities and their confusion, Wordsworth proceeds in Book Eight of *The Prelude* by coming back to his experience in the countryside in his home region. We will notice here the *proceeding by coming back*, which reminds one of the backward-and-forward movement characteristic of Whitehead's philosophy. The poet tells how he often thought of open nature even when he was in the city, and he reflects also upon love of one's fellow human beings, though this may require growth and may at times be difficult to attain. What he has in mind, he tells us, is general "kindliness" which can be felt toward the stranger who crosses one's path, a person who can be thought of as "a Brother of this world"; toward such a person he was gradually moved in kindliness through the influence of nature. So he believes. He recalls in Book Eight a kind of peak experience of his which had occurred: he had beheld "while yet a very child" a mountain scene of "mists and steam-like fogs" moving and recoiling, within

> loop-holes of the hills, wherever seen,
> Hidden by quiet process, and as soon
> Unfolded, to be huddled up again . . . (89—)

As the mists moved, this processive scene included a shepherd with a dog, circled in the mists; the figures seemed to belong to "an aerial Island" which floated on as if by "the soft wind breath'd forward." Were these things real or did they merely seem? They have an aspect of seeming. In some respects they are homely, but they seemed nevertheless to speak to him from an invisible world. This may serve as an example of the interactionism occurring in the poet's experience. Yet it is a symbol. He was moving to an increased sense of kindliness toward shepherds and his fellow members of humanity everywhere. He believed that the change in himself had occurred under the influence of *nature*. What does this mean? In considering nature, is it the universal world of which he is thinking? Is his view of natural phenomena a wide one carrying him beyond mere woods, and fields, and flowers?

Clearly, nature in the narrow sense could not in itself lead him to love of humanity. But a philosophy of active organism holds that feeling occurs not only in plants and animals but throughout the world, and this philosophy could do so. Whitehead's thought follows these lines. In a context bringing out this aspect of the philosophy of organism, he says "that 'feeling' survives as a known element constitutive of the 'formal' existence of such actual entities as we can best observe."[1] The poet Wordsworth is concerned about the feeling and thinking of human beings in their homely labor, and he uses the term "a fragrance breathing of humanity"; here he is thinking of the joy to the person in being free, carrying on

> his wants,
> His comforts, native occupations, cares,
> Conducted on to individual ends
> Or social . . . (153—)

Does Wordsworth, when he is speaking of "individual ends," have in mind only a self-focused individualism? Does he sharply divide the two tendencies, individual and social? Certain things in our experience may be profoundly personal, and the ends or aims may be individual without being actually self-directed. It is such an end or purpose that is being referred to in this part of *The Prelude*. Whitehead speaks of "personal freedom" and a heightening of the individual into "absoluteness."[2] Is such heightening desirable? He is thinking of "Imperial Rome" as well as "of England in the eighteenth and nineteenth centuries." Elsewhere he says, writing in 1933, that industrialism can move into a situation in which "it is a grim joke to speak of freedom. All that remains is the phantasm of freedom, devoid of opportunity."[3] Individualism is baneful if it is unsocial. Freedom with democratic opportunity concerns both Whitehead and Wordsworth; all other freedom is mere bondage, whether we self-concernedly glory in it or are miserable in consequence of its evils.

The social also plays a part importantly in the development of the idea of philosophy itself. We have been steadily occupied with the term philosophy, though often indirectly, and this interest, as we have explained before, has accounted for our calling attention to early Greek thought. This was notably so in the references near the outset of Chapter VI in which we mentioned Parmenides and Zeno of Elea and stressed what Zeno referred to as "the assertion of the one."[4] It is in the creative work of Plato that this remark by Zeno is reported.

We can well believe that Plato actually met Zeno. At any rate oneness is of importance in early Greek thought. But Zeno, for most people, presents great difficulties. These difficulties arise because, although his theme is oneness, he deals largely with flux and also indirectly criticizes the conception of the unit. In an essay on Zeno in Drew Hyland's *The Origins of Philosophy*, Howard De Long quotes a passage from Plato suggesting that Zeno "makes the same thing appear to his hearers like and unlike"[5]; although we do not here give all that Plato said with reference to Zeno, the few words given suggest that a thing may *appear* from one point of view in one light and from a different point of approach be seen in quite another light. This tendency to see around a subject (or an object) can be of immense value. The matter of play is here, as well as an important part of philosophy's essence. It touches the social and politics.

The idea of the unit, for Zeno, tends to give fragmentation. This he would like to avoid. Fragmentation would cause the larger oneness to be lost. Most people, however, accept *both* the idea of the separate unit and the conception of oneness. Therefore, to such people Zeno's thought seems unfortunately paradoxical. But we must not shy away from paradoxes if we are to gain knowledge of Zeno. His philosophical contribution is full of seeming paradoxes. To understand an aspect of Zeno initially we can imagine a tall tower based on a square foundation, with the square top of the tower having sides a little longer than one hundred forty-six and six-tenths feet. We mention a number of this sort deliberately. Actually numbers themselves, in their approximations and in their quantitative flow, present important factors related to wider thought. The six-tenths decimal we have mentioned repeats itself indefinitely. This repeating decimal gives rise in itself to a philosophic question concerning fragmentation and the one and the many. It is suggestive of reaching toward infinity as a limit.

We may think now, however, of a guided missile of the same length as the side of the tower. Let us suppose that this missile is directed in flight from the north so that it passes the east side of the tower, near the tower-top. We are speaking definitely in order to aid visualization. The missile passes the tower, we may imagine, in an instant, (or, for the sake of concreteness, let us suggest in a second); at the same moment another missile of the same size coming at the same speed (say about one hundred miles an hour) from an opposite direction also passes the square side of the tower on the tower's west side. The missile coming from the north also passes the tower side in a second. We could add multiplicity in that we could have two missiles coming from the south, immediately following each other, and two missiles similarly coming from the north. And we could have two towers almost exactly next to each other. But what we want especially to consider is the swiftness with which the one missile passes the other as first indicated.

Since both missiles are in rapid motion in opposite directions it takes half the time for them to pass each other as it would take for the missile (either missile) merely to pass the tower. The speed with which they pass each other would then be half a second, or some might say half an instant. Zeno was deeply interested in various aspects of this seemingly paradoxical problem concerning speed, the unit, and the instant. In one sense it might seem that the missile passing the tower could, for an exceedingly short split-second, be regarded as stationary. Our example is mechanistically modern, but the ancient Greeks under the influence of Zeno, thought of such things as applied to chariots and racing. Zeno wonders whether the universe, in the light of such matters, is characterized by *change* or by wholeness— whether it is, or is not, basically a thing of flux. Mathematics, in the thought of Pythagoras, who preceded Parmenides and Zeno, is a related subject for consideration here. Can a moment, or an instant, or a unit be isolated? Wordsworth was interested in oneness and he was also concerned about mathematics. The same was true of Whitehead.

We have tried to see a problem of Zeno displayed in a modern picture. Bertrand Russell suggests that we might imagine three drill-sergeants who are standing still while "two files of soldiers march past them, in opposite directions."[6] Russell's analysis of this picture as related to Zeno is of interest, but his conclusion about Zeno is what we would stress now. We *can* finally escape the difficulties that are before us here, as we think of Zeno, Russell says, "by denying the reality of space and time altogether."[7] This Russell concludes is probably what Zeno did, and Russell adds that a "large number of philosophers have followed him."[8]

We have stressed the fact that Zeno was interested in the one. From Bertrand Russell's point of view modern education needs to emphasize this sense of the one much more than it has generally emphasized it in the past. Wordsworth would agree. The problem of doing this is not so difficult as is often supposed. In mathematics we may gain something of this sense of the true one, Russell says, by considering certain "general truths, truths which are not asserted to hold only of this or that particular thing"; we need to think of an assertion as holding for "any one of a whole group of things."[9] We need "the power of understanding and discovering such truths" because in them "the mastery of the intellect over the whole world of things actual and possible resides"; it is the "ability to deal with the general as such" which "is one of the gifts that a mathematical education should bestow."

But this gift unfortunately is bestowed far more rarely than need be, as Russell strongly emphasizes. He is thinking anticipatorily, of group theory. Zeno, we have seen, had a very great tendency to be preoccupied with the one, or unity, and also with the problem of flux, or change. Permanence and change probably arrest the attention of everyone at one time or another. Russell speaks of the problem of the infinitesimal and the infinite, and he also brings in references in these respects to Zeno. In the past there were great difficulties for the individual attempting to advance toward an understanding of higher mathematics; these areas of difficulty existed because students had often been required "to give assent to arguments which, on first acquaintance, were rightly judged to be confused and erroneous."[10] It is hard to give assent to what is confused.

Whitehead parallels Russell in his concern for a richer democratic education (and a sense of the one), through training in mathematics and thoughtful enlightenment in other subjects; indeed, Whitehead precedes Russell in developing and promoting such ideas concerning the one. But we need to return again for a moment to the early Greeks. The world (as Russell says in another essay) opposed Zeno's main thought "from that day to our own,"[11] but at last Zeno's position finally received new consideration by a group of thinkers most of whom probably knew little of humanity's debt to Zeno. Among these thinkers was Karl Weierstrass (1815-1897); he, by "banishing from mathematics the use of infinitesimals," at last revealed "that we live in an unchanging world" and in this sense we live in a world characterized by the one.

Zeno had attacked the view that human life, as well as the world, is most basically characterized by change. His "only error," Russell says, "lay in inferring (if he did infer) that, because there is no such thing as a state of change, therefore the world is in the same state at any one time as at any other." Russell is suggesting that Zeno may *not* have inferred this. Change is necessary for social advancement. Zeno was interested in politics. The attitude presented by Russell toward Zeno is not simple, especially when we are faced with "the problems of the infinitesimal, the infinite, and continuity."[12] But the statement and clarification of "the difficulties involved" brought insight of value to an accomplishment of "perhaps the hardest part of the philosopher's task." Russell adds, "This was done by Zeno."

Although Zeno has seemed to many people a propounder of confusing paradoxes, he was, according to Russell, actually a clarifier of difficulties. At present we shall not attempt anything like an extensive approach to the matter of infinity, the infinitesimal, and continuity. For more than two thousand years, Russell says, "the finest intellects of each generation in turn attacked the problems, but achieved, broadly speaking, nothing." This is his considered view.

In our own modern time the three problems (the very small, the ultimately large, and continuity) have been actively attacked by Weierstrass and also by two other figures (Russell should probably have added himself as a fourth), and the results of their work were most beneficial. The two other figures are Richard Dedekind (1831-1916) and George Cantor, the Russo-German mathematician (1845-1918); Russell regards the achievement of these two men, along with that of Weierstrass, as "probably the greatest of which our age has to boast," and he adds that he knows "of no age (except perhaps the golden age of Greece) which has a more convincing proof to offer of the transcendent genius of its great men."

Russell's admiration for the ancient Greeks speaks eloquently here. Some twelve years after writing the two essays from which we have quoted, he again, in another work, refers respectfully to Zeno, indicating that Zeno's thought "afforded grounds for almost all the theories of space and time and infinity which have been constructed from his day to our own."[13] This statement appears in the revised edition of *Our Knowledge of the External World*. In 1945 Russell used the thought of Zeno to try to refute a certain view of change: a view "which is," he says, "not unlike Bergson's."[14] Bergson presents and attempts to refute certain aspects of the thought of Zeno, one aspect of which concerns the flight of an arrow—to which we could liken the flight of a speeding motorcycle or missile.

The speeding vehicle (or arrow) is conceived of as passing a comparable thing which is at rest. Another similar thing coming from the opposite direction likewise passes the object (which could be conceived of as a stationary motorcycle); this illustration is basically the same as that which was earlier given concerning the guided missiles and the square tower—but there is value in seeing the matter through a slightly different picture. The problem concerns the relativity of the speeds of the moving objects in relation to the stationary object. Bergson was interested in Zeno's ideas.

Russell explains that Bergson's effort at a reply to Zeno's view concerning the arrow, "or a closely similar one concerning Achilles and the Tortoise," appears in "three books."[15] Bergson's replies are, in Russell's view, quite without merit. All of the technicalities of Zeno's thought, and those which Russell presents concerning the ideas of Bergson, need not be covered here, but it is worth noting that Russell's interest is such that he returns thoughtfully to the ideas of Zeno. Indeed he does so also in a still-later book of 1959 in which he says that Zeno's arguments "are in the main an attack on the Pythagorean concept of the unit."[16] Zeno, as Russell declares later, is concerned with things and their relation to the "infinite in size."[17] There are some weaknesses in Zeno's thought at various points, but Russell believes that Zeno does present "a perfectly sound criticism of the theory of units."[18] Most important is the fact that Zeno, through demolishing "the Pythagorean theory of discrete quantity," or instants, accomplished the purpose of laying "the foundations for a theory of continuity."[19] This involves the one.

Russell's continuing interest in Zeno is evident in that the various remarks we have quoted come from publications over a span of fifty-eight years. Zeno is famous for his creative paradoxes concerning change in contrast to permanence. He is interested in permanence. In a part of Russell's material a tribute is paid to Zeno in a statement indicating "how little modern orthodox metaphysics has added to the achievements of the Greeks"; Zeno's paradoxes were not devised for idle amusement but for the sake of the one and for the sake of Zeno's "master Parmenides, in whose interest the paradoxes were invented."[20]

The book from which we are here quoting contains also a full expression of Russell's indebtedness to Whitehead about "the problem of the relation between the crude data of sense and the space, time, and matter of mathematical physics."[21] Russell says, "I have been made aware of the importance of this problem by my friend and collaborator"; to Whitehead (Russell says) also "are due almost all the differences between the views advocated" in the volume *Our Knowledge of the External World* and those "suggested," a year earlier, "in *The Problems of Philosophy.*" Russell proceeds to enumerate specifically a number of the factors that he had drawn from his friend. Speaking of Whitehead, Russell says the material developed on these topics in *Our Knowledge of the External World* "is, in fact, a rough preliminary account of the more precise results" worked out for *Principia Mathematica*; that is, in future writing, Whitehead planned to contribute them to a "fourth volume" which would have served as the conclusion of the total work. In a footnote concerning what Russell had gained from Whitehead, Russell indicates that his own indebtedness includes the material in the first, second, and third volumes of *Principia Mathematica*.

The fourth volume of this immense work was never finally written, but most of the substance for it was probably included in other volumes and essays later published by Whitehead. The early indebtedness of Russell to Whitehead over more than a decade should never be forgotten, whatever later differences there were between the thought of the two men. That Whitehead, like Russell, reflected carefully on Zeno's thought is evident in one of the passages of *Science and the Modern World* in which Whitehead refers to "the objection which Zeno might make to the joint validity of two passages from Kant's *Critique of Pure Reason*" and says this objection could be constructively dealt with "by abandoning the earlier of the two passages."[22]

Observe that Whitehead considers respectfully the *objection* which Zeno might make. Zeno lived more than two thousand years before Kant. Why worry about what Zeno might think about a man of Kant's stature? Whitehead speaks of Kant's "*Extensive Quantity*" in the *Critique of Pure Reason* and the "subsection on *Intensive Quantity*." The italics are Whitehead's. He goes on to quote somewhat further from Kant. The subject being dealt with has a bearing on the problem of changefulness and, on the other hand, it includes the one, or an approach to permanence and unity. A part of the material from Kant which Whitehead uses favorably runs as follows: "*Points and moments are only limits*, mere places of limitation, and as places *presupposing always* those intuitions which they are meant to limit or to determine."[23]

Kant's words here (and "intuitions" should be especially noted) are very important to Whitehead. A notable passage written by Kant is quoted further: "Mere places or parts that might be given before space or time could never be compounded into space or time." What is needed is a continuum. Whitehead declares that he is "in complete agreement" about this material "if 'time and space' is the extensive continuum"[24]; he at the same time indicates his disagreement with the earlier passage from Kant, which he had quoted but which we do not need to use here. The passage from Kant that we are not using is opposed by Whitehead because "Zeno would object that a vicious infinite regress is involved." That is, in such a view, "Every part of time involves," as Whitehead explains, "some smaller part of itself, and so on. Also this series regresses backwards ultimately to nothing"; and Whitehead notes that "the initial moment is without duration and merely marks the relation of contiguity to an earlier time." Because of this, "time is impossible," according to Whitehead, in the complete context of Kant.

Whitehead is concerned about what he calls *realization* and its bearing on a conception of space and time. But his view does not dangle from Kant's philosophy; it "does not depend on any peculiar Kantian doctrine."[25] Actually, Whitehead is close to Plato. What Whitehead has said "assumes that Zeno understated his argument." Whitehead presents what he views as an epochal theory, a very large theory which involves a field-pattern including the realization, in the actual, of events which are contained in a process. He is aiming toward a realization involving his total organic philosophy.

It would be tempting to speak further here of the relation of Whitehead's thought to that of Zeno and other early Greek philosophers. But enough has been said to suggest that early Western philosophy can be helpful in moving searchingly into problems concerning time, experience, permanence, change, and reality having a bearing upon the modern world. Zeno should be important to us. Such would be Whitehead's view. There is an element of wonder we may note in Zeno. A person may perhaps grudge this effect of wonder, even of the uncanny, that is felt. But it is possible, as Howard De Long says, to feel a reaction also against an *absence* of wonder, "against the so-called common reality."[26]

De Long points out that it is thus that the great Argentine writer Jules Luis Borges reacts to Zeno. This reaction of Borges to Zeno, De Long refers to as "haunting"; the haunting quality appears in this statement by Borges: "Art—always—requires visible unrealities." And Borges goes on, "Let it suffice for me to mention one: the metaphorical," and he sees the unrealities he seeks in the skillfully written dialogue in great drama. "Let us admit," he says, "what all idealists admit: the hallucinatory nature of the world."[27] And he adds, "Let us do what no idealist has done: seek unrealities which confirm that nature. We shall find them, I believe, in the antinomies of Kant and in the dialectic of Zeno."

These words from Borges have a value in relation to our understanding of Wordsworth. But let us add a few words from Howard De Long. "In Zeno, we not only have a person committed to following an argument wheresoever it leads, we have a philosopher who disturbs our firm belief in 'common reality,' and who thereby helps create that sense of wonder which both Plato and Aristotle saw as the true origin of philosophy." We may be grateful to Howard De Long and to Drew Hyland for their contribution to an understanding of the nature of philosophy. And we can be grateful to the early Greek thinkers for the efforts they made to move out of primitive confusion into a world including an extended grasp of a more profound way of life.

Notes

[1] *Process and Reality*, p. 268.

[2] *Adventures of Ideas*, p. 56.

[3] "The Study of the Past," *Essays in Science and Philosophy*, p. 117.

[4] Hyland, *The Origins of Philosophy*, p. 225.

[5] *Ibid.*, p. 205. From Plato's *Phaedrus*, 261 D.

[6] *Our Knowledge of the External World*, revised (London: George Allen and Unwin, 1926, reset 1952), p. 182.

[7] *Ibid.*, p. 183.

[8] *Ibid.*, p. 184. Russell's own personal position is not indicated here.

[9] Russell, "The Study of Mathematics," *Mysticism and Logic* (Garden City: Doubleday and Co., 1957), p. 60. The earliest edition was published in 1917 by Barnes and Noble, Inc.

[10]*Ibid.*, p. 61.

[11]*Ibid.*, p. 76, in the essay "Mathematics and the Metaphysicians." Russell speaks of Zeno as being "immeasurably subtle and profound" and is eloquent in admiration of this ancient thinker.

[12]*Ibid.*, p. 77.

[13]Russell, *Our Knowledge of the External World*, p. 183.

[14]Russell, *A History of Western Philosophy*, p. 805. Zeno's view does not, however, "touch the mathematical account of change," Russell says.

[15]*Ibid.*, p. 806. The tortoise is given a head start and, according to Zeno's paradoxical account, the swift runner, Achilles, is never able to overtake the creature, if we make certain assumptions.

[16]Russell, *Wisdom of the West*, p. 40.

[17]*Ibid.*, p. 42.

[18]*Ibid.*, p. 43.

[19]*Ibid.*, p. 43.

[20]*Our Knowledge of the External World*, p. 170.

[21]*Ibid.*, pp. 7-8.

[22]*Science and the Modern World*, p. 183.

[23]*Ibid.*, p. 184. The italics appear in Whitehead's volume.

[24]*Ibid.*, pp. 184-185.

[25]*Ibid.*, p. 186.

[26]Hyland, *The Origins of Philosophy*, p. 223.

[27]*Ibid.*, pp. 223-224. The words of Borges are quoted by De Long from *Labyrinths* (New York: New Directions, 1964), pp. 207-208.

Chapter Nine

Revolution

In Book Nine of *The Prelude* Wordsworth refers to permanence, change, and revolution as they appear in society, but he also has references to the revolution which during the period was occurring within himself. He is strikingly aware of the inner and the outer occurrences that are correlated in human life. These have a backward and forward movement. This is exemplified in his feeling about a "devouring" sea that lies ahead if he is now to tell about himself and certain things that happened; he thinks of himself at the moment as a kind of river—he has again and again measured

> back his course, far back,
> Towards the very regions which he cross'd
> In his first outset . . . (5—)

67

Actually the poet is referring directly to a river here, but he is likening it to the river of his life. He dips back for the moment to his more recent experiences in London which were like those of "a colt," but now he proceeds almost immediately to Paris, where he soon finds social turmoil of Revolution surrounding him. At first he is a dispassionate spectator, and he decides after a while to move on to a more quiet part of France. He did not know much about political science (to use a term of our day)—he lacked "the main Organs of the public Power," which if understood could give "form and body" to his thought. For the moment, things where he now lived seemed "quiet." After a period of time he left the retired, or out-of-the-way circles where he had interested himself more or less as a spectator; he

> gradually withdrew
> Into a noisier world; and thus did soon
> Become a Patriot . . . (122—)

Wordsworth, that is, was drawn to the democratic side representative of the "People," for, as he says, his "love was theirs." Thus he changed personally in many respects, especially through knowing Michel Beaupuy, who became a great influence upon him. The poet applies the word "Patriot" to himself but also to Beaupuy, using the term mainly as synonymous with a sympathizer of the Revolution. This involved being "bound" in devotion to the cause of democratic "service" through an "invisible" tie such as one might follow in "a religious Order." As to Beaupuy, there was

> a kind of radiant joy
> That cover'd him about when he was bent
> On works of love or freedom . . . (320—)

The character of Beaupuy, who died in the cause of his devotion, serves as an example of the ideals to which Wordsworth was drawn while in France. The poet finally closes Book Nine of *The Prelude* with an account of two lovers who, shortly before the French Revolution, were separated by social injustice. The leading character of the story, Vaudracour, in the end sank into a state bordering on agoraphobia,

> Nor could the voice of Freedom, which through France
> Soon afterwards resounded, public hope,
> Or personal memory of his own deep wrongs,
> Rouse him . . . (929—)

This story, which tells of Vaudracour, Julia, and their daughter, serves as a somewhat vague symbol representing Wordsworth's own experience, for it was at this time that he left Annette Vallon, who was soon to give birth to their daughter.

In our last chapter, as part of our planned procedure, we referred to the early Greeks, and, among them, to Zeno, for the purpose of an understanding of philosophy and some of its perplexities. Zeno was concerned with paradoxes, with motion, and with relative speeds of motion and of change. He was also concerned with politics. How are these related to the one, or reality? We think of objects, and also of happenings in society, realizing in our thought, so it seems, that they do change—for example, in position. Objects may undergo change of position. Happenings concerning people may occur in position prominently in Paris or Athens or on the western coast of Greece; we think of these things believing that they are not only in a certain physical position but in particular moments in time. Uprisings occur and changes are in the air in society, in city or nation.

But does society greatly change or do things change prominently; is change deep down an illusion? Is there something that we call the one, which is stable? Life is paradoxical; so at least Zeno believes. It is paradoxical to Wordsworth and it presents contradictions or antinomies to Whitehead, as it did also to Kant. What can we find which will help us hold things together? Do the activists have a point in thinking that life can be made better by turmoil? It seems absurd to seek peace by war, and perhaps it *is* basically nonsensical. Time is a problem here." Consider, for example," as Whitehead says, "an act of becoming during one second. The act is divisible into two acts, one during the earlier half of the second, and the other during the later half of the second."[1]

In the context Whitehead had been speaking of Zeno and he refers back to his own book *Science and the Modern World*, where he had spoken earlier of Zeno and where time receives treatment. The focus there was upon time and its relation to a large or "epochal theory" in which things are seen in relation to "a complete organism."[2] This view of time involves the organic in that the organism holds "in its essence its spatio-temporal relationships (both within itself, and beyond itself) throughout the spatio-temporal continuum."

Having referred back to this earlier volume, *Science and the Modern World*, Whitehead proceeds with his argument about the charming Zeno, who, long ago, had an anticipation of a complex problem concerning time. Basic to this problem, if we consider Zeno's thought about the arrow in flight earlier referred to, is the fact, as Whitehead says in *Process and Reality*, that "the true difficulty is to understand how the arrow survives the lapse of time."[3] In proceeding, Whitehead refers to the race of the speedy runner who is trying to overtake a tortoise that is some distance ahead. The race, described by Zeno, includes "details which have endeared the paradox to the literature of all ages"[4]; these details involve the problem of series. But if we think of such serial details we must remember that we are considering change and something that becomes. Here we need to recall a principle that Zeno, as Whitehead says, seems to have overlooked: "the principle that every act of becoming must have an immediate successor, if we admit that something becomes."

Whitehead is thinking here of a matter involving the spatial isolation of parts in an experience, and he concludes that, while time has extension, "the act itself is not extensive, in the sense that it is divisible into earlier and later acts of becoming which correspond to the extensive divisibility of what has become." Whitehead's thought, as he goes on concerning Zeno and the philosophy of organism, touches upon "the notion of continuous transmission which reigns in physical science."[5] Whitehead proceeds to explain "physical transmission." Without covering his technical treatment of this (which is readily available in *Process and Reality* in the context to which we have referred), we will go on to his reference to occasions of experience and "*physical* prehensions."[6] These prehensions concern physical events. But there is also to be considered the "*conceptual* prehension." This can be understood in terms of "the transmission of mental feeling." Whitehead would not "assimilate the conditions" for the conceptual prehension "to those for pure physical prehensions." To do so would be to take us into the doctrines of the materialist. Whitehead is finally concerned here about "the instinctive apprehension of tone or feeling in ordinary social intercourse."

To move from the abstraction of our present discussion we may say that tone of feeling in ordinary social relations can well be imagined in Zeno and in the case of Wordsworth's discussions with Michel Beaupuy. This tone was very much the opposite of one that would be associated with a materialistic outlook upon life. Yet atomistic materialism was a factor in the Revolution. Wordsworth had been interested, earlier, in scientific advances in the modern world, as he understood them, and Whitehead was enthusiastic about similar interests—or he would never have gone to the labor of writing *Science and the Modern World*. But science, for Whitehead as for Wordsworth, had an important relation to human social interaction and, finally, to the effort to attain social harmony. Conflict and change present a problem with respect to this. Revolution in the offing or in actuality confronts the person who thinks of the matter.

It would be tempting at this present point to turn to the rise of science in early Greece and its importance to a later understanding of science, mind, and the changing human condition. Anaxagoras (born in Ionia in Asia Minor about 496 B.C.) contributed to the rise of science, as did Empedocles of Sicily (who was born about 492 B.C.), and also Leucippus the atomist, who came about a decade later and whose career has been associated with Ionia in the East but also with distant Italy in the West, perhaps because it has been thought that Zeno of Elea influenced him. Zeno's interests touch upon science.

The problems of change and flux were undoubtedly in the mind of Leucippus as he developed his atomistic philosophy. This atomistic philosophy has ever since his time been associated with the rise of science. What is known of Leucippus would suggest that the psychological and ethical considerations were of interest to him, along with atomism and science. At any rate a statement from his work *On Mind* involves the problem of determinism, in that he says, "Nothing comes to be at random, but all things for a reason and of necessity."[7] The atoms were thought of in this period as solid individual bits of matter. Thus in pouring water from a pan we are pouring an enormous number of quite invisible ball-bearing-like particles that roll or flow seemingly in a mass.

Centrally important in a profound atomism is the question of change in relation to freedom or the absence of freedom. Can this matter have held importance for Wordsworth during the time of his concern about social change as it was taking place in America and also in France? Did the problem of such freedom (or the absence of it) have importance in the philosophy of Whitehead? The two foregoing questions scarcely need to be put here. They were decidedly important to both men. As we think of the early Greeks, mention must surely be made of the teaching of Leucippus and its importance to the development of materialism in the young Democritus (born about 462 B.C.). who was reputably the pupil of Leucippus. He grew up on the coast of the northern part of the Aegean Sea (in Abdera), where it is sometimes said that Leucippus also for a time lived.

Democritus (the accent is on the second syllable) traveled to Egypt, Persia, and other places in the East, apparently with the intention of seeking knowledge most broadly. His problem was basically to understand variety and change. What he desired was happiness and equanimity, and the ability to get along with others. The atomism of the young Democritus is most often mentioned, but he also devoted attention to mathematics and to human relations and, perhaps rather simply, to ethics. He had a somewhat self-directed moderation as his watchword, and he showed a tendency to gravitate toward uninspired conventionalism. There is a danger, however, in that he may be underestimated. Thus he says, "It is noble to prevent the criminal; but if one cannot, one should not join him in crime."[8] This statement can be interpreted as clearly ethical, in that nobility is a consideration; it may seem, however, to invite unworthiness, or it may be recognized as stressing the fact that we need always to use crude common sense.

The statements of Democritus are often cryptic, and some of them, like certain remarks of Zeno, may contain unrecognized humor. Thus, in Fragment 227 Democritus urges one not to have children, unless one *takes* them, carefully chosen, from "friends."[9] In so doing one will have "one child out of many" to his "liking" rather than be forced to "accept" a child "as he is." This has often been cited as an example of the selfish, mechanistic thinking of Democritus, comparable to that of William Godwin or Jeremy Bentham, prominent in the eighteenth century, when Wordsworth was in his early developmental stage. But Democritus believed that in individual behavior we should act, even if no one could be aware of our act, in such a way that we could gladly thereafter face ourselves.

Democritus thinks mechanically about light, and even about the soul of a human person, as consisting of *atoms* which are almost infinitesimal in size. Light may also be related to reflections on atoms of various kinds. For him there are gods that exist (made also of atoms) but we can know little about them or their interests. They are superior beings who are unconcerned with our level of life. Whitehead in *Science and the Modern World* speaks of the tendencies of the "seventies" of the nineteenth century in which "some main physical sciences were established on a basis which presupposed the idea of *continuity*."[10] In contrast to the continuous he speaks of "the idea of *atomicity*" used to complete the work in "the foundation of chemistry." There he refers to Wordsworth's contemporary, John Dalton (1766-1844). "Ordinary matter was conceived as atomic"; however, one *could* think of other effects which "were conceived as arising from a continuous field." These effects were electromagnetic. In the atomistic, and in field theory, Whitehead declared that basically there "was no contradiction." As he indicates, these notions "are not logically contradictory." However, at that time "there were but faint signs of coalescence between the two." He is referring to Dalton's time.

In this connection Whitehead recalls the early contributions of Democritus as well as others. Science, in its power to produce effects, made use of the efficient ideas of atomism. But were the ideas *sufficient*? Whitehead had in mind very particularly the eighteenth century, a time in which well-educated people almost universally "entertained ideas about atoms." But later developments moved beyond mechanism and simple atomicity. In subsequent developments and in Whitehead's own philosophy "the notion of material loses it fundamental position."[11] He is thinking here of materialism. In the process "the atom is transforming itself into an organism" and science moves to "the analysis of the conditions for the formation and survival of various types of organisms."

At another point in his book he considers "a theory of science which discards materialism" and deals with other entities than matter: "primary entities."[12] In seeking to find an answer based on this quest he suggests: "We must start with the event as the ultimate unit" in nature. "An event has to do with all that there is, and in particular with all other events." To understand this philosophy we need to remember that every part of the configuration or, better, the "interfusion," includes "sounds, scents, geometrical characters, which are required for nature and are not emergent from it."

In a later book, after referring to Wordsworth, Whitehead comments on the subject of atomism and points out how "Hume discovered that an actual entity is at once a process, and is atomic," and Whitehead stresses the point that "in no sense is it the sum of its parts."[13] It is more. Hume's basic thought at times seems subjective, but he "retained an obstinate belief in an external world which his principles forbade him to confess in his philosophical constructions." This belief affected "his historical and sociological writings" and "his *Dialogues concerning Religion*." He describes process. He is social. Whitehead finds merit in Hume's thought, in that "the process described is within 'the soul.'" In Whitehead's philosophy such a term as soul, or the term *mind* used by Locke, is usually "replaced" by "actual entity," which may also be thought of as an "actual occasion" that in its actuality brings an emotional tone.

In Whitehead's view, "We prehend other actual entities more primitively by direct mediation of emotional tone, and only secondarily and waveringly by direct mediation of sense."[14] Perception is affected here. His view is a departure from the sensation doctrine of materialism. He comes back later to the thought of the early Greeks when he mentions that "mathematical physics also accepts the atomistic doctrine of Democritus."[15] But Whitehead relates this atomistic view to quantum theory. His opposition is directed against a physical materialism; "what has vanished from the field of ultimate scientific conceptions is the notion of vacuous material existence with passive endurance, with primary individual attributes, and with accidental adventures." Such conceptions he rejects.

It is often thought that what gave rise to the French Revolution was atomistic materialism, but is this altogether true? For George Herbert Mead the Revolution had as its basis *rights*, and this basis is in its nature ethical. Kant for Mead was the father of the Revolution. Consider simple questions concerning which everyone is seeking an answer: for example, livelihood, including shelter. This applies to all. If we move toward the universalization of the matter, we have to consider the many—the multitude of people. This is paramount if we are to be reasonable persons. We must endeavor to find what the community most *deeply* wants. Here we have the problem of what we would all *will*. Mead is close to Whitehead.

Can we bring the sum total of all our human volitions in some way together? Not absolutely surely, but we can proceed in that general direction. We can work with an *as if*. Broadly speaking, we know various things concerning the sum of such things as nine and three. "We believe these things," Mead says, "and, if other people did not, we should still continue to believe them"[16]; we tend to feel, and Kant felt, that they cannot but be true. They are "necessarily true." In Mead's chapter heading there is reference to Kant as the "Philosopher of the Revolution." For Kant there are certain laws concerning things that are necessarily true, and they are based on forms transcendental in nature within our sensibilities and also on similar "forms of the mind."

Kant further asserted that "judgment" within the mind "has certain other forms, which he called the 'categories.' "[17] In Mead and in Kant also there is a tendency toward reflection on the problem of our movement *toward* the universal. The human being—man as man—through his nature "can give laws to society," if those laws express human "rights."[18] Weighing and considering probabilities will enter into all this. But if, following Mead, we think of Kant in his ideas as the philosopher of the Revolution (though certain aspects of these ideas were anticipated before Kant wrote), we can see how the rights of human beings were regarded as having a wide basis. And this basis was something other than atomicity. Such a conclusion would conform to the reflections of Wordsworth in *The Prelude* and also to the thought of Whitehead in our own later period of modern times.

Wordsworth, we have said early in the present chapter, left Annette Vallon, who was soon to give birth to their daughter, but he did not return directly home; rather, he stopped in Paris for a period of time, observing further stages of the Revolution going on. Why did he do this? Was he still in process of watching his own development? Was he realizing himself from the point of view of his obligations, or was he *not* doing so? Was he, again, trying to understand the world in relation to himself—that is, trying to grasp the meaning of a total world in turmoil? Was he thinking of the one? Was he thinking, or trying to think, of a duty: the duty to realize himself from the point of view of world obligations—the very obligations which the world has to its own development? This sounds rather fantastic, but it is a part of the problems of the Revolution, as we may see further in Mead's view of the philosophy of the Revolution in its relation to the thought of Kant. In any event, Wordsworth himself, as we shall see in the following chapter, attempted to philosophize about the problems of individual and social change as well as about their relation to the universal, if such a universal could be found.

Notes

[1] *Process and Reality*, p. 106.

[2] *Science and the Modern World*, p. 186.

[3] *Process and Reality*, p. 106.

[4] *Ibid.*, p. 107.

[5] *Ibid.*, p. 468.

[6] *Ibid.*, p. 469. We have discussed prehensions earlier.

[7] W.K.C. Guthrie, *A History of Greek Philosophy*, II (Cambridge University Press, 1965), p. 386.

[8] Fragment 38, Hyland, *The Origins of Philosophy, A Collection of Early Writings*, p. 299.

[9] *Ibid.*, p. 309, and also p. 293, as well as Russell, *History of Western Philosophy*, p. 72.

[10] *Science and the Modern World*, p. 145.

[11] *Ibid.*, p. 149.

[12] *Ibid.*, p. 151.

[13] *Process and Reality*, p. 213.

[14] *Ibid.*, p. 214.

[15] *Ibid.*, p. 471.

[16]George H. Mead, *Movements of Thought in the Nineteenth Century*, ed. Merritt H. Moore (Chicago: University of Chicago Press, 1936, 1950), p. 39.

[17]*Ibid.*, p. 40.

[18]*Ibid.*, p. 41.

Chapter Ten

France and Further Problems

Wordsworth did not return from Annette Vallon directly to England. Further experiences in France, bearing among other things upon the guillotining of people in Paris, presented a psychological problem for him in connection with his own complicity in evil in that he was decidedly a sympathizer with the French revolutionary events that had occurred. Again and again it is evident that he is interested in the question of *judging* as it is applied to a variety of circumstances. He is concerned about the existential—about things that actually exist whether in the world of outer events or in the psychology of the person. The guillotining of a woman, man, or boy is not a mere ephemeral or atomistic thing to him; when he tries to think of the good that can be brought about by a revolution he has to weigh the destructiveness or evil that occurs. It presented a problem that he was still revolving in his mind in the period (ten years later) when he was writing *The Prelude*. There is a matter for reflection when he decides that some people make a "senseless sword" into "a judge"; yet people seem during revolution to bow down all too readily to the material entity in its efficacity: the guillotine.

Masses of people can become a machine; this is a social fact. The person, in his imagined or self-styled humanism, may be worshipping himself through a destructive material entity like a sword. The problem of destruction (in its manifold forms) becomes a factor to be considered in philosophy, for Wordsworth and for Whitehead as well. Wordsworth venerates the conception of "a Republic" (which had at last for the French become a fact) although

> lamentable crimes
> 'Tis true had gone before this hour, the work
> Of massacre, in which the senseless sword
> Was pray'd to as a judge . . . (31—)

This was the situation in Paris, figuratively presented by the poet, where, "enflam'd with hope," he had "returned." He "rang'd" the "wide City" with even greater eagerness than he had shown when he was there some months before. It was indeed a receptacle in the sense in which London was a receptacle. Now the king ("with his Children and his Wife") was in bondage, and the "Palace" had most recently been attacked by "a numerous host." How could a person judge these things? The final two words in the quotation from Wordsworth at the end of the previous paragraph concern "a judge"; and that judge is not human. For Wordsworth the problem of judgment was a matter of importance as, we have said, it had been for Kant, and as it was likewise for Whitehead.

Judging, Whitehead says, "requires an Inspection to provide the material from which decision arises."[1] Here we have to consider "those fundamental modes dominating experience. Such modes are modes of division, each division involving differences with essential contrasts." Wordsworth, before he does any judging, follows the principle of *inspection* in countless instances; *The Prelude* is full of examples of this. He also follows "modes of division" (as Whitehead expresses the point) in trying to arrive finally at a judgment, and he is strongly aware of *essential contrasts*. The words we have quoted are from Whitehead, but the prior *ideas* are in Wordsworth.

Whitehead—continuing his thought concerning judgment by presenting ways (or modes) of division—lists as important "Clarity and Vagueness, Order and Disorder, The Good and the Bad." We cannot here go into his full theory about these three ways of division while a person is making a "Judgment" (Whitehead capitalizes the term, thus calling attention to his sense of its importance), but we may note that he closes the chapter in which he discusses this matter by re-emphasizing "the three primary grounds of division"[2] we have listed. For Whitehead, judgment involves a creative functioning of the mind and it is important to "the immediacy of the present."

Wordsworth is confronted with the immediacy of the present in relation to the French Revolution; he has the problem of judging the events that have occurred as best he can. Judgment, for him, takes time. It requires the long view. As to this, the poet alludes to Shakespeare and oddly, it might seem, to the first speech in *As You Like It* having to do with horses being "taught their manage"; but the reference to Shakespeare concerns the irony of the *neglect* of human beings, and the great need of an education which might produce better results than have been attained heretofore. The "wind" of time, according to the quotation Wordsworth uses, moves slowly in these things:

> Year follows year, the tide returns again,
> Day follows day, all things have second birth;
> The earthquake is not satisfied at once.   (72—)

These lines concerning time represent the young Wordsworth's thoughts as he attempts to justify the carnage and brutality of the Revolution. But for him Paris was then "a place of fear" much like "a wood where tigers roam." He finally returned to England because of "absolute want" of money, he says, leaving Annette Vallon and his daughter whom he had not seen; he was unable to see his child, Carolyn, for a full decade. What does an extensive revolution do to a person who is in the midst of it? Psychologically, is it often unbalancing to the person? Here the underlying conceptual formulations that have been developing in society are a factor.

After the midpoint of the last chapter, as a part of our planned procedure, we referred to the early Greeks and the stage in their development in which atomism became rather specially prominent under the influence of Democritus of Abdera. We cited the example of pouring water from a large pan and the fact that to the Greek atomist this would be conceived as pouring an enormous number of quite invisible ball-bearing-like particles that roll or flow seemingly in a mass. The particles themselves contain nothing except their own hard mass. Viewing life atomistically may give rise to a kind of uninspired social conventionalism or it may lead to a tendency for one to be far-out in a disorganized way, or, finally, it may involve a fluctuation backward and forward between the two extreme poles. In rare cases it may lead to a balanced, humane, and even somewhat creative adjustment to one's world. Its effect is unpredictable.

Following the time of Democritus by about two decades, Protagoras (also of Abdera in Thrace, on the northern shore of the Aegean) became greatly interested in the fact that it may seem almost impossible for anyone to have a sense of values. A kind of new Grecian world was opening up in which economic class barriers were being crossed, and it seemed to many people that truth should be viewed sophistically merely as something which could provide a self-oriented advantage. Protagoras, a Sophist who was born about 482 B.C., came to believe that the human being must be thought of as the center of the universe; man, that is, knows those "things that are not," and has the task of summarily rejecting such things. Likewise the human being has the problem of taking the *measure* of those "things that are" and keeping focused steadily upon such realities. Man has this capacity. He can be a measure. Here we need not go into the problem of the variability of the Sophists: there were many of them, and in some cases they were of fortunate or of unfortunate influence.

Protagoras has come to be regarded as probably the greatest Sophist of all. Plato reacted to Protagoras to the extent that he touches upon the Protagorean point of view in two dialogues. Part of the difficulty in dealing with the thought of Protagoras lies in the fact that it often appears ambiguous and seems quite paradoxical. He may be understood—or often is understood—as believing that a thousand different points of view are each to be regarded as acceptable; one may justify all kinds of insurrections and uprisings, or one may justify a rigidity of social life which is maintained by violence. One may accept any kind rigidity. Protagoras does not say that he favors a violent interpretation of life. But he does seem to stress our great ignorance and our need for an emphatic self-importance.

As to education Protagoras urges the necessity of repeated practice, and he seems somewhat mechanical in regard to his interpretation of the social in life. Plato brings out the point that if Protagoras's philosophy is to be regarded seriously there is no reason for feeling that the Protagorean view itself should be accepted; evidently one could without thought take one's choice of any of the philosophies that have existed. One could thus turn definitely to a belief in the thinking of Parmenides or of Socrates, or of any other figure. Protagoras's philosophy is not the necessary or sufficient answer. Perhaps Protagoras would say to this: "Yes, there should be many points of view, working together in a vast mixture. This would be best."

In the French Revolution as Wordsworth encountered it there was a vast mixture of thought. Perhaps most important in this array of material, we might mention a number of ideas centered in Kant, the "Philosopher of the Revolution," and having to do with rights that, as Mead says, are so "generalized" that the human being can be thought of "as giving laws to nature as well as to society."[3] We are not thinking of the human being as giving laws by fiat; but there are "necessary objects in experience" and "there is universality in it." Mead follows Kant here. The problem of the transcendental arises here, and it is related to the question of judgment. For Kant the human being is capable of forming, "in advance of an experience, a judgment as to what that experience could be." Such a judgment was to be thought of as "transcendent in the sense that it transcended the experience itself." Here we have to think of certain forms related to human thought. And that brings us precisely to judgment. We may judge that a given object in the landscape is a house. Later we judge that it is a certain house which we have seen years ago.

Mead gives the psychological example of seeing something in a dark box in which a spark is suddenly introduced. We see something but do not know what we see. Again a spark is introduced and we see part of a structure. When certain later sparks are given we gradually form the sense of a picture, possibly that "of a cathedral, or of a castle."[4] Mead explains, shortly, that "our perception is just such a process as that." The whole problem is connected with the unity and our forming of it; it is a process which is "essentially that of judgment." What we arrive at "is more than the mere sum of the parts."

All of this, for our purposes, has a connection with one's perception of the French Revolution and with social change, as we shall see in the following chapter. Mead's view of Kant's place with reference to the Revolution, brings insight into the Revolution, and it is for this reason that we pursue his thought. Mead is in many ways close to Whitehead, and philosophy of the social is illuminating to the social problems which Wordsworth faced.

Notes

[1] *Modes of Thought*, Capricorn Books (New York: G.P. Putnam's Sons, 1958), p. 103.

[2] *Ibid.*, p. 116.

[3] Mead, *Movements of Thought in the Nineteenth Century*, p. 41.

[4] *Ibid.*, p. 44.

Chapter Eleven

The Restoration of Imagination: Wordsworth and Whitehead

In France Wordsworth had been in a receptacle, in the sense implied in his remark about London. We have seen Whitehead's use of the term when he speaks of "the essential unity of the Universe conceived as an actuality, and yet in abstraction from the 'life and motion' in which all actualities must partake."[1] It is the abstract understanding of the total universe in which we live, in all its complexity, that Whitehead emphasizes here while endeavoring to clarify his conception of the Receptacle. Yet this total unity, as an actuality, *partakes* in " 'life and motion' " insofar as it can have being. The concept is difficult, Whitehead himself says, in the previous page. Yet he feels that his adaptation of it is important to his philosophy. What he has especially in mind is our complex experience and its transformative power. And this transformative power, this power of transformations, must not be forgotten when we think of such receptacles as London, Cambridge, Paris, or even a local village or community near which we may live.

Imagination is essential to an appreciation of transformative power. In Book Eleven of *The Prelude* Wordsworth refers to the importance of hope and things to hope for in connection with the problem of his recovery from a state of profound depression following the days of his experiences abroad—especially when England attacked France. Consider Whitehead here. In our volume *Aspects of Wordsworth and Whitehead* we refer to this fact and to the place of hope in the philosopher's thought, as well as to his view of the togetherness in a time-and-space perception of the things in the universe. He uses italics to emphasize the separative and cohesive factors in such complex perception: "the *separative* and the *prehensive* characters of space-time."[2] This second character—the prehensive— has relation to continuity and to the *event* in a space-time sequence. Something of the transcendent has an ingression into the event.

Wordsworth is an example of a poet who helps us appreciate joyfully "the apprehension of the things which lie around us."[3] And this apprehension, though it could have simplicity, is not necessarily a simple thing. Elsewhere in the same volume Whitehead stresses the importance of considering "what Wordsworth found in nature that failed to receive expression in science."[4] An example of this is that the poet does not separate the inorganic aspects of the world from the organic and keep them forever in absolute isolation, the one from the other. Wordsworth, as Whitehead emphasizes, "dwells on that mysterious presence in surrounding things, which imposes itself on any separate element that we set up as an individual for its own sake." And in the same page the philosopher goes on to speak of a major part of *The Prelude* as constituting the greatest poem "by far" that Wordsworth ever wrote.

Near the beginning of Chapter VII of the present book we spoke of Whitehead's appreciation of the prehensive quality of Wordsworth's poetry. The philosopher refers to this in *Science and the Modern World*. In his view Wordsworth has a depth of concreteness which science, as usually practiced, fails to appreciate. Whitehead's comments here deserve careful reading in full; such an examination will provide an enrichment to what we have been able to say within our more narrow limits. Elsewhere in speaking of receptiveness and prehension he refers to the fact that broadly speaking "the animal body is composed of entities, which are mutually expressing and feeling."[5] In Chapter XI of *Aspects of Wordsworth and Whitehead* we spoke of the philosopher's interest in "the aesthetic intuitions of mankind"; there has been a discord between this aspect of human beings and the mechanistic side of "science."[6]

For Whitehead, "Wordsworth is the poet of nature"—nature viewed as being "the field of enduring permanences carrying within themselves a message of tremendous significance." But Wordsworth does not, according to Whitehead, neglect the "eternal objects"; this being so, the relation between the poet and the philosopher, on a fundamental issue, is very evident. Notice the relation between the two figures: we cannot emphasize too strongly the fact that according to Whitehead "nature cannot be divorced from its aesthetic values"; and "these values arise from the cumulation, in some sense, of the brooding presence of the whole on to its various parts." The philosopher has used a variety of expressions very similar to those presented by him in this context, where he is stressing the importance of Wordsworth in connection with the complexities of organism. For Whitehead there are exceedingly important values in a philosophy which includes "change, value, eternal objects, endurance, organism, interfusion." And all six of these we have tried to exemplify in the present volume. But we should stress a seventh point, and that is the spirit of humanity which may be shown every day toward the people you meet. This seventh point, we have emphasized strongly in the present book.

Wordsworth had gone down into the depths of depression, and in Book Eleven of *The Prelude* he attempts to tell how he emerged from this state. In Book Ten he had mentioned how in desperation he turned to mathematics (1. 904) to find either an escape or a relief from his situation. What he needed, however, in order to attain relief, was a combination of reason in the highest sense, as connected with the creative, along with direct and profound perception; both of these factors become a part of his philosophy, as they are also a part of Whitehead's outlook upon the world. An illustration of the combination of these matters can be seen in Wordsworth's "spots of time," brought out near the end of Book Eleven (for example, a criminal hanged in chains), which can be related to Maslow's peak experiences.[7] For Wordsworth these spots of time almost always have a connection with a fellow human being met in the common walks of life.

We have spoken of George Herbert Mead near the end of Chapter X, mentioning his interpretation of Kant as the "Philosopher of the Revolution." Mead was particularly interested in Whitehead and in Kant's doctrine of unity in relation to experience; in Kant's view our "experience consists in judging."[8] If it is truly experience, "it is an experience of things having a unity"; it may be noted "in perception and thought." It comes from something which is in part given "in advance of the actual experience." Herein lies its transcendental character. Do we ever really know "what things we are going to see"? Do we know, moreover, that if we have an intelligible experience it will necessarily "have a certain unity" and is this a character which is in advance of the actual happening? Our experience of unity is important. Can we say in the case of a moral act that it has a certain unity? This is a point that Kant as the "Philosopher of the Revolution" puts before us.

We cannot well comprehend the French Revolution in its most important aspects, Mead would say, unless we go back to Kant. Notice Mead's words. Our problem is a matter of perception; it does not include "simply the association of one sensation or image with another but the organization of them—of the appearance of a face into that of an acquaintance," and an acquaintance is not *merely* a face. Often, going beyond sensation, we speak of perception, but we may stop at the bare mention of perception before thinking carefully of the problem before us. This is a mistake. Kant, and George Mead also—like Whitehead—would have us go beyond a hasty view which would overlook the significance of our perceptual experience of organization and unity.

We must look beyond the usual view, Mead says, so that we will see "more than perception in the sense of having sensations." For Kant this looking beyond is summed up as "apperception." It might be thought of as increased or more profoundly structural perception, or more fully conscious and *feeling* perception. Feeling tone is a significant factor here. In the philosophy of Kant, as in the philosophy of Mead, perception reaches into the beyond in a significant way. Judgment, for them, involves this quality of reaching into the beyond, and it has this very quality in the thought of Wordsworth with regard to infinity as a limit as it does also in the process thinking of Whitehead. Stressing the importance of structure in Kant, George Mead shows how Kant returns to "the fact of judgment, to an 'I judge.' " Here a reference to the self that judges has a quality that is transcendental; it has "something given in advance of perception." In this context Mead is referring to Kant's earlier conception with regard to judgment. Kant undergoes further growth.

In a later chapter, Mead stresses the importance of judgment as a concept by bringing in a reference to Kant's *Critique of Practical Reason* and, indeed, by going further than this work to a reconstruction of "the world from the observation of certain ends and purposes—those involved in the very processes of living, on the one hand, and those involved in art, on the other hand."⁹ It is the *Critique of Judgment*, a later work by Kant, which Mead refers to here. That work "sets up a sort of end or purpose as determining the life-process of living things," an end or purpose "which determines the structure of that which delights our aesthetic tastes." Wordsworth is deeply concerned with the very same processes of *living* to which Mead refers and also with those involved in art. Some of Mead's lines might almost have been written by Wordsworth. And Whitehead is close to Kant.

In Mead's later chapter, which we have mentioned, he gives still further exposition with regard to the *Critique of Judgment*. There Mead relates "the *Critique of Practical Reason* and the *Critique of Judgment*."¹⁰ He connects these two works to "the period of the revolution." They go back to thought with reference to the French Revolution and the philosophy of rights to the effect "that one could claim for himself only that which he recognized equally for others." We can share values. And this leads to freedom: not only that given to the other person but that which receives (and deserves) honor as given to oneself. We must feel able to face ourselves. This is responsibility. This we can have. The cosmos indicates, in effect, that we must have this freedom-in-responsibility. And if we must have it, we *can* be possessed of it. So Kant, Mead, and Whitehead believe.

But the philosophy of judgment does not call for responsibility only in the sense that we are ready to take the *consequences* of our action, painful though the end-results might be. This pseudo-responsibility is a point of view often held by people who nevertheless persist in wrong action. The doctrine of judgment we are here seeking goes deeper. Freedom needs to be centered, not in self-serving behavior, but in thought about the freedom-needs of other people. Those others are you. In any profound understanding this needs to be realized. Basically, in seeking a cause we need to get beyond a focal center "in a mechanical world."[11] Mead explains this by drawing on Kant and indicating that "our whole understanding of that which is living and our whole understanding of that which is beautiful, which is art, implies ends."

It is a larger purpose that Mead has in mind here. For "there is something in our comprehension of the world which transcends the order of the world as science presents it to us." This is a key thought of Kant in Mead's chapter "Kant and the Background of Philosophic Romanticism." We know that this point of view of transcendence is in Kant. We may still ask: Was something of it personally in Mead also? Is it to be found in Wordsworth and likewise in Whitehead? Part of the answer to this may be evident in what we have already disclosed.

Wordsworth had suffered injury during the French Revolution even reaching into the very depths of his imagination. His ethics was involved. That injury is an important factor—the most important factor in Book Eleven of *The Prelude*—and it is a key factor to be remembered in the underlying purpose of our present eleventh chapter, as well as in the eleventh chapter of the volume *Aspects of Wordsworth and Whitehead*. The central factor concerns this question of personal responsibility. But a deeper insight into freedom and responsibility, as well as transcendence and an approach to the infinite, needs to be disclosed in the sections of the present book which are to follow.

Notes

[1] *Adventures of Ideas*, p. 355.

[2] *Science and the Modern World*, p. 94.

[3] *Ibid.*, p. 23.

[4] *Ibid.*, p. 121.

[5] *Modes of Thought*, p. 32.

[6] *Science and the Modern World*, p. 127. Whitehead refers to Shelley also in this context.

[7] See Abraham Maslow, *Toward a Psychology of Being*, second edition (New York: D. Van Nostrand, 1968), p. 71.

[8] Mead, *Movements of Thought in the Nineteenth Century*, p. 45.

[9] *Ibid.*, p. 68.

[10] *Ibid.*, p. 76.

[11] *Ibid.*, p. 77.

Chapter Twelve

Imaginative Restoration Concluded: Its Relation to Wordsworth and Whitehead

In the last chapter the main theme concerned what had occurred to Wordsworth's imagination in the way of psychological injury as an aftermath not only of the French Revolution but also of the subsequent nationalistic factors connected with his own homeland. England had directed an attack against the internationalistically-minded country of France. So at least Wordsworth at this point conceived the situation. World happenings were, of course, more complicated than his view of them. Still, it is his personal circumstances that are important here. During a war a state of inward peace is difficult to attain. Imagination as a faculty—which Wordsworth regarded as one of man's most profound possessions—had, he felt, virtually left him, and in any event was very seriously impaired for a matter of a few years. Book Twelve of *The Prelude* presents a continuation of his concern about this problem. What he needed was a more complete sense of peace.

91

Whatever it was that militated against the workings of the imagination had presented a very grave problem. It was a source of continued pain and depression of spirits. What had happened to him toward the end of his experience in France and upon his return to his homeland had occurred, he says, to other young men of his age at that time; examples of this could be cited, but in the poet's case the discovery of the source of his trouble involved, as we have suggested, a new philosophy and a better sense of what justice to other human beings meant. With this awakening of inward and outward concern there also came a new and more profound sense of the self. For the self, on any close and adequate analysis, is social. It is not an isolated entity, and it can of course be social for good as well as for evil. In any case a restoration and a redevelopment of it, and of the attendant imagination, may occur after circumstances of strain and trial. Although he is thinking that it is his goal to become a philosophical poet, he anticipates such an accomplishment with modesty. At times he realizes that this purpose could well have grandeur of scope. He is ambivalent in his feeling about himself. He feels dull. In his despair he is not like Dante in exile, for the Italian poet in his troubles probably had sudden and perfectly magnificent spurts of imaginative creativeness.

If Wordsworth at his period of trial lacked a strongly creative movement of the spirit, power nevertheless was reflected in the fact of memorable experience itself—in the remembrance of "spots of time" and their ingress of imaginativeness. Such, we saw, was the moment when, as a small boy, he came upon the scene where a criminal had been hanged "in iron chains." This we have referred to in Chapter Eleven. Of the many things connected with Wordsworth's conception of peace and imagination, ethics is one and a state of balance or harmony is another. The imagination as such is not extensively described in *The Prelude*, but the dangers of presumption or of pride have a relation to its impairment.

The poet has been slow in his recovery of a dynamic imagination, but the cause for this slowness of recovery is not entirely to be found in the world outside himself. The human being should be aware of his own faults and take responsibility for them. This Wordsworth tries to do. What he has to struggle with chiefly is not the whole cosmos but the personal complicity in evil, as people often say. The cosmos, along with the efforts of man, can aid in overcoming the evil that has been wrought. What Wordsworth had needed, he realized, was a revolution as it were in himself which would be contributory to the workings for good coming from outside himself. Such a metamorphosis can be aided through the imagination, a power which is not merely a faculty in man but is in part a force in the universe. So Wordsworth believes. This is what Whitehead, too, has in mind with regard to the creativity within the world. The "spots of time," we said in the last chapter, could be thought of as related to the experience of something close to absolute being—as applied to psychology by Maslow in our own day.

At the opening of Book Twelve of *The Prelude* Wordsworth refers to twin factors—strong emotion and calmness—which, coming together as a gift to man, serve as "bounties," horns of plenty, or sources contributing to the growth of the self. They are part of nature's "glory," if we think of nature for the moment as that which surrounds us. This enveloping world includes other persons and, from one possible perspective, our own inward constitution as well. In Wordsworth the twin factors of emotion and calm had been illustrated earlier, in Book Eleven, in connection with the event when he, as a youth, had waited near Christmas time for the arrival of the two horses on which he and his brothers were to return home, the poet himself riding probably in tandem fashion with a partner. From the lonely aspect of the experience, before the horses arrived, he had strangely gained comfort. In thinking of the experience later, indeed, he drank of it as at a fountain. The figure is characteristically Wordsworthian. In similar fashion he found solace in the related subsequent experience concerning his vision of the hill surmounted by a "Beacon on the summit" and of the girl he met who "seem'd with difficult steps to force her way," as she was undergoing the resistance of "the blowing wind."

Both of these experiences involved emotion and a subsequent tranquillity as he was recollecting them, not only after they occurred but at later stages and doubtless even as they were being used for *The Prelude*. The circumstance is reverberant of one of the phases concerning the affective and the tranquil, famous in his theory of poetry. They have a place, then, in his philosophy, on the side of aesthetics: they are examples of the generative and creative principle, or what he calls "Genius," and they involve as he says the alternative use of "peace and excitation"—always as a natural phenomenon. Excitation, one would suppose, should come first, and "peace" should follow it. Why, then, did Wordsworth reverse this order? Perhaps he did so for the sake of emphasis: that is, to bring out the extreme importance of peace in relation to aesthetics or poetic composition.

In any event, the thought concerning "peace" was probably foremost in his mind in other connections. When a person deliberately, or through an inward source, energizes himself, the creative, whether in art or in other ways, is manifested, though of course it also shows itself when objects are intuited. This would seem to fit in with Wordsworth's conception of how we interact with nature. It occurs to poets and also to other persons. The creative impulse, he says, undergoes a kind of rousing, or is awakened, and it "aspires, grasps, struggles, wishes," or, in other words—as indicated in these expressions—is extremely active.

In view of this activity-principle, one may ask wherein does the creative person find the "peace" which the poet also includes in his aesthetics? What Wordsworth says can be understood only through a reconciliation of opposites. Such a reconciliation theory may be found in the aesthetics of Coleridge and of many later literary figures and critics even far down beyond the middle of the twentieth century. It is found in Wordsworth. The creative impulse also demands something more which is related to being or reality and which may be associated with the "spots of time" conception: a "stillness of the mind," a receptiveness, which enables the mind to obtain the gift of the imagination which sometimes comes without any seeking on our part. Indeed, it is a "benefit" which

> souls of humblest frame
> Partake of, each in their degree . . . (15—)

In referring here to the humblest people, Wordsworth may seem patronizing. But he is finding a place of importance for all people in his philosophy—a place of importance connected, indeed, with what he regards as the highest principle of change in humanity: the generative principle. In the passage we have quoted there is a key to the democracy of his acceptance of his fellow human beings. We find a parallel in Whitehead in a context that stresses the danger in our

educational procedure which, being never perfect, continually needs
to be strengthened anew to the end not of mechanical and routine
thinking but of creativity. The potentialities in virtually all men are
far greater than our society permits them to realize. Our modern
psychology will bear this out. In this conception Whitehead goes
quite as far as does Wordsworth. The philosopher, in his hope for
humanity, remarks that "some measure of genius is the rightful
inheritance of every man."[1] In the belief of Wordsworth and Whitehead we all in our basic nature share a great deal with our fellow men;
neither would glorify a class as *class*, whether an intellectual elite or a
group holding pretensions to aristocratic status. What we can share
implies a deep, a profound similarity between persons. This is
fundamental.

We see in Wordsworth, then, imagination in process, and we see
something of the poet's theory of beauty, but we should also keep in
mind that in large part the theme of *The Prelude* here concerns a
social or democratic philosophy. He feels that, in view of his observations of individuals, it is his right, as well as his duty, to speak of what
he himself has "known and felt" about people, a task that he considers
especially congenial in that he has been led to it not only by "gratitude" but by "confidence" in its "truth." Gradually he had gone
through the process of overcoming his state of illness (it was no less
than that) and had begun more and more to feel that what he had
learned to value was also in part a new sense of spiritual strength.

This strength, or "Power," creatively applied, was by no means
marked by any self-conscious impatience or by any "fallacious
hopes," or ill-advised "passion"; no disproportionate "zeal" was a
factor. Most of all the strength was manifested, he says, through the
quality of "right reason," or as it was imaged through it. Here we find
the truly creative reason: a force which he saw maturing certain
"processes"; this is Wordsworth's term, but it is also one which
Whitehead frequently uses and which is especially fitting to his
insights. These "processes," Wordsworth says, had been matured
through "laws" that have been sufficiently established or that are
fairly to be relied upon. The forces or powers are deserving of
admiration in that through them one avoided being ruled by self-
applause, especially within the realm of the intellect. They are forces,
indeed, that raise one to the spirit of magnanimity, or breadth, and
enable the mind to counteract any intoxication

> With present objects and the busy dance
> Of things that pass away . . . (34—)

In the context Wordsworth was once again seeking to emphasize the importance of a consideration of man as man to which we referred in the latter half of Chapter Nine and thereafter. But he now stresses the fact that the person is of the earth carrying "incumbrances" which we must take account of. We should realize that the human personality, viewed in its reference, or in its "frame" as Wordsworth says— which is both "social and individual"—must be seen in relation to the past, present, and future. That is, it must be appreciated in relation to what "hath been, is, and shall be." Whitehead shows a similar stress. Anyone who has read his works closely will realize that he is extremely sensitive to the past, but this perceptiveness concerning the past is always tied into the present and very specially into the future.

The flow of universal life mentally and physically is constantly in Whitehead's mind. And in it the future has a place. One example will suffice for our purpose, a passage in which he refers to the "insistent present."[2] The danger of an overemphasis upon the past is in his thought, while he also warns us in the next page against a "depreciation of the present." Indeed, the present—which "is holy ground"— may be thought of as being, or it actually *is* "the past, and it is the future." While bringing out a parallel importance of an interrelatedness within time in Wordsworth, we saw that he was expressing the idea of the extremely great power of the imagination. But he was dwelling also on the possible liability, or danger, of a kind of pompousness in "power and action"—a pompousness which stands against or injures the "unassuming things that hold" their "silent station in this beauteous world." Earth is indeed "beauteous" to one who has sought peace, or has "composed" himself and has found both in the external world and, even more important,

> in Man an object of delight
> Of pure imagination, and of love . . . (54—)

As Wordsworth is mentioning imagination again here we must recall his reference to it in the titles of the two preceding books of *The Prelude*, which definitely emphasize the point that this faculty is of high importance to him. His difficulty in dealing with it transparently or lucidly is understandable in view of the fact that it is a troublesome concept even today. In our last quotation he speaks of the human being himself as an object of pure imagination, an idea that recalls Whitehead to our minds in his theory with regard to prehensions. Can one, that is, actually think of man, including both concepts and percepts as well as emotions concerning him? This is difficult but we do it all the time superficially. Insofar as we ever do it in complexity we are viewing man prehensively. Wordsworth's philosophy, like Whitehead's, is a kind of aestheticism, in the best sense.

The use of creative imagination makes it evident that man is a being who, seen variously, cannot be adequately circumscribed within our limited human power of vision. Man is fictive. For Wordsworth he is seen as an object of "pure delight" (he is in this respect an object of the imagination), but he is also an object of love. This last seemingly simple concept concerning love is really no easy concept to understand. But it is very essential to the philosophy we are trying to perceive in the poet's statements in *The Prelude*. It concerns the theory of democratic institutions. Democracy cannot truly exist without love. The problem may be helped in part by attempting to do what Wordsworth aimed at as he grew better able to see life in a well-rounded, many-sided way. For we may notice that he says

> as the horizon of my mind enlarged,
> Again I took the intellectual eye
> For my instructor, studious more to see
> Great Truths, than touch and handle little ones.   (56—)

In the term "intellectual eye" Wordsworth may be referring temporarily to what he regarded as the lower reason, but it is more likely that the term implies what he (like Whitehead also) regards as the higher faculty, for the eye with which he is endeavoring to see includes an enlarged "horizon," a greater consciousness than he had been using previously, in the more or less immediate past. This eye with which he is endeavoring to see includes, as he is explaining, an enlarged consciousness. Actually, it is somewhat like the mental eye of Plato. The poet is seeking, he says, that which is "excellent and right" and he begins to feel that he is coming closer to factors of this nature. He had cast aside plans that were too grossly ambitious, along with the somewhat roseate spectacles which he had formerly been wearing, for example, during his early days in France. What he sought to find now was that good which is to be seen in the "familiar face of life," and it was his hope that within it would be something *not* only for the everyday existence of human beings as passively conceived, with "Rulers of the world" as overlords who could magically shape it to their will. The "Rulers of the world" here could, of course, include dictatorial revolutionists.

Broadly speaking Wordsworth's position now represents the antithesis of the great-man theory of history which was later prominently entertained. Society as a whole, along with cosmic powers, will bring forth the changes that are to come, although strenuous effort by the individual is of course an influence. The allegedly great men, he says, often fail in their purpose even "when the public welfare is their aim"; they lack, in their individuality or self-emphasis, the general thought on which to base plans for a great society, or, all too often, have "bottom'd" their approach to life on false thought processes and a "false philosophy," failing to perceive the depth of things. What are the purposes of "false thought" as they apply to ethics, which is the poet's immediate concern now? The ethics of the great-man theory tends to involve dominance. It does not include an interaction with another personality as a friend, even though all fellow human beings consider friendship as community and as a part of a total life. For Wordsworth and Whitehead we may add there is something in the good itself that moves in the direction of the eternal. Whitehead's ethical theory may be seen somewhat more clearly through reflection on the view of his fellow philosopher G.E. Moore, who held that the good—in and of itself—is not something which is done or achieved for something else.

And for Whitehead, as for Moore, the good is something which is good in itself and not something done for ulterior purposes. An act which is ulterior in purpose may have good results, but it is not then, merely for that reason, in its basic nature, really good. Moore's idea is that good is in a sense an ultimate conception. Both Wordsworth and Whitehead have views that are somewhat comparable to this. Wordsworth, surely, is in a degree concerned for utility. His whole preoccupation with the French Revolution illustrates this. But what would Whitehead feel about Moore's notion that the *ought* is itself connected with utility? The right in itself hardly seems in Whitehead, or in Wordsworth, so close to utility as Moore tends to believe it is. In the poet and in Whitehead a thing is not made right because it has utility; it may have utility because it is right.

Their position is close to that of Norman Kemp Smith when he expresses an opposition to "a morality based exclusively on natural necessities, and a morality conceived as emancipated from all such necessities"[3]; Kemp Smith's idea may be tied in with a thought he has about D.H. Lawrence. Kemp Smith remarks, "The eternal and the infinite are . . . to be found, not by turning our backs upon the immediate, but only in and through the immediate, which is always freighted with something more than simply itself." For Wordsworth and Whitehead the right is decidedly involved with personality, with the social situation at a given time, and also with creativity in a large sense. It reflects something of the constructive or the progressive theme which Aristotle connected not with the utilitarian motive but with the good very largely viewed. Moreover, the good is not independent of all desire, as in G.E. Moore, but is a part of the changing psychology of the self as the person is related to society. This latter is a theme of *The Prelude*. It might be added, however—lest we give too simple a view of Moore—that, like Wordsworth and Whitehead, he holds ethics to be connected not merely with our world but with the universe.

Ethics as applied to national problems of England appears in Wordsworth's comments on the works of "modern Statists" whom he had read and heard and in whom he had often found an ethical "hollowness"; in their works he observes a weakness in contrast to a more "solid" view. The weakness consists of the tendency—ill-fitted to the needs of his time, or we could say also the needs of our time—in which one nation conceives that it could best promote its own advantage by destroying another nation. This destruction could be brought about, for example, commercially. Such a financial, continental approach had been practiced by France prior to the Revolution, though Wordsworth does not mention this. The poet's view is that one person's loss does not necessarily promote another person's gain. A nation's financial disadvantage does not inevitably redound to another country's welfare. Essentially the poet's idea is that there is no wealth but life. The false opposite doctrine leads to international disaster. The unfortunate philosophy of assumed gain through another's loss Wordsworth does not treat in detail, but it had been flagrantly applied in England with reference to her colonies, and it was the chief difficulty she encountered in America.

Napoleon was an eager exponent of such an exclusively self-serving philosophy in the period during which the 1805 *Prelude* was being given its final form. Wordsworth speaks of the "utter hollow-ness" of such a doctrine, and it is clearly insensitive to the conception that the true wealth of nations is in the human beings that make up a world. There he feels the wealth of a nation is "lodged" and it is increased by processes involving interchange between person and person. It is based on an appreciation of the dignity of an individual human being. This interchange he feels would be an expression of a deeply underlying reality of living and growing, rather than a reliance on a "shadow image" of existence which would reduce the affairs of human beings to a mercenary manipulation whereby they are treated like cattle only for the purpose of the cash return that they make possible. The problem, that is, needs to be considered personally and individually, as well as nationally. An important question, further, is whether more that is genuinely excellent for persons than we have thus far attained may be elicited from the individual. There have been ethically and intellectually renowned human beings in various countries, and this prompts the poet to ask

> Why is this glorious Creature to be found
> One only in ten thousand?   (90—)

When we think of excellence in people do we find only one person of great merit in ten thousand? The figures do not matter. They do give roughly, however, a general condition of an assumed rarity of accomplished human excellence. The important point appears in the consideration of this question: What "bars" or stands in the way of bettering people and their circumstances in life, physically and spiritually? Wordsworth is evidently thinking of the condition of the state and the character of people generally. Need this condition be what it now is? We saw in Chapter Nine that thought about natural and civil rights presented problems to him leading to difficulty and confusion.

There are general moral principles which are fitting to matters of civil government. This may be seen in an ethics that is proper to the just settlement of differences that arise in the adjudication of disputes of the citizen with other citizens, as well as in his rights to representation in the franchise. But there are additional concerns which the poet is deeply troubled by, and which are suggested in the term *natural* rights, which he shied away from, or found hard to understand. What, indeed, causes a right to be natural? This is a question which probably continued to trouble Wordsworth deeply. Back of the term there are things connected with history and time immemorial—not to speak of immediate factors related to what is natural, so-called, in the habit of taking a percentage of money when one has made a loan or what is right and equitable concerning a living wage. Various economic practices are deservedly under scrutiny here, including class divisions which may consign one person's life to utter hopelessness. Hope, as we have seen, has an important place in any philosophy which a person may be able to attain. This is the poet's view. A society which makes the attainment of an adequate existence impossible for certain people is not considering them satisfactorily from the point of view of hope and justice.

To return now to Wordsworth's question concerning the "glorious Creature" that the human being has at times been. Here we must consider the "bars," as the poet says, that at present stand in our way and that for him impeded humanity. We may note that these bars, he says, are "thrown" in the way of "hope," and that they need not inevitably be a source of our permanent frustration. If we could master the physical conditions and provide for the "animal wants" that material factors could reasonably meet and take care of, the rest would apparently be the mental, moral, and psychological. These— the "others"—he feels could be provided for or would "vanish into air."

His remark would imply that, mentally, human beings are on the whole not sundered from each other so greatly that little may be done to bring them closer together. It implies that morally those in high places are not so far in advance of the common society that they should be allowed to provide a rule for all in perpetuity. The other factor (psychology) involves custom (use and wont) as well as prejudice. Here is a task that philosophers and psychologists have been working on in our day. Modifications can occur. Change is possible. Certain times are, of course, susceptible to undesirable change—a change which we do not relish. Wordsworth had seen customary use and wont undergo extreme and rapid modification in France. Customs, he knew, can "vanish into air." And this can be either beneficial or noxious. The problem of social philosophers and psychologists, then, is to bring about their changes propitiously.

Wordsworth recognizes that a re-forming of persons is required. This is a need which applies to himself, as to all persons, and operates in a continuing process. He states very directly that he wished to find out "how much of true worth"—he includes "knowledge" in the context—and how much of true "power of the mind" was actually existent among the ordinary class of people in his day. It is necessary that human beings have knowledge (and this he believes can be supplied in supplemental measure where it is lacking), but the factor of the energizing *power* of mind, very consciously directed in the effort at thinking, is also important. Modern psychology has worked on this matter of cognition, but it is notable that the poet wished to inquire whether there was anything favorable or encouraging to be found in the commonalty of men—

> in those who liv'd
> By bodily labour, labour far exceeding
> Their due proportion . . . (100—)

Wordsworth's reference to "power of the mind" deserves careful consideration, but let us now note primarily that the poet thinks with deep concern of one's "due" proportion of the total labor that needs to be done in the world. The essential idea here is that we have no justification to take from another, as our right, labor performed by him which is far out of proportion to what would be considered his fair share on a one-to-one basis. Wordsworth is not demanding an exact proportioning. His whole approach shows that he realizes it is impossible to calculate things of this sort to a fine point. But any such calculation is unnecessary, for very clearly some persons at his time of writing (and in later times) were being unfairly treated. Such a situation is capable of very considerable correction.

Wordsworth goes on to explain that there is "injustice" in this arrangement of life which we as members of society—or through the "composition of society"—impose upon ourselves. The injustice is not delivered to society by a malign universe. Here he advances a social idea comparable to that of Plato that we ourselves very largely make society and that the persons who injure others are injuring themselves as well. The thing that is essential to man is not alone the moral struggle that the single person has within his soul, as some thinkers have held in our own day.[4] The author of *The Prelude* of 1805 does not fussily say that he is interested only in his moral struggle within himself. He does not declare that his own moral integrity is all that is of importance for him in the world. Wordsworth refuses to accept the state of affairs which human beings have inherited. He will not bow before things as they are. He will change them. We are not under fate, chance, or predestination. The poet is thinking of our responsibility along with the fact that society as a total entity suffers, including the very rich as well as the exceedingly poor. This, then, concerns democratic theory.

We have said that Wordsworth's reference to "power of mind"—a kind of cognition—deserves careful consideration, and it is evident that he is thinking of an energizing of the self which is involved in it, and to which our own century, as we have suggested, has given attention. In addition he includes various moral qualities as component factors in the power of the mind, as does Whitehead. Anyone who has read the philosopher's comments on Archimedes or on the energy of mind manifested in history through the seventeenth century and in certain other periods will be struck by his continuing interest in this. But, even as a whole, his works reflect energy, and his philosophy of organism is built metaphysically upon an analysis of spiritual power in relation to the universe. Power of mind is an enormous factor evident in Whitehead's analysis concerning God, but a more obvious example appears in his theory of both university and lower education, where it is power which is to be sought rather than the mere trappings of education. As to this vitally important factor, and its principles, he has in mind, he says, something that can scarcely be defined; he is "hardly even thinking of verbal formulations."[5]

To understand Whitehead adequately one must realize, as he says later, that "the antagonism between the claims of pure knowledge and professional acquirement should be much less acute than a faulty view of education would lead us to anticipate."⁶ He continues, "I can put my point otherwise by saying that the ideal of a University is not so much knowledge, as power." And love is not absent from his thought. Knowledge is of course an essential factor in education, but the "business" of a university "is to convert the knowledge of a boy into the power of a man." He was speaking to boys at the moment. As Wordsworth reflected upon "how much of true worth"and "power of mind" was actually existent among the ordinary class of people in his day, he decided upon an approach something like that which certain early twentieth-century sociologists began recommending to their students—that of going out into the midst of people and observing what one might find there with regard to various problems such as labor unions present. The poet, in attempting to form a judgment about human beings, decided to observe ordinary or even humble persons in their daily way of life, recalling also his earliest "observations" as well as those of "later youth" down to the moment of "that very day."

Wordsworth was not disposed to consider at this point the "throes" or the "tumult" of the world's history. Such factors he felt were not basic. He was concerned with the individual members of a society which any human being could contemplate in respects which were close to himself and his ordinary experience and sympathy. The material he found in his seeking came not only from the countryside where he had been reared but from the metropolis. The city, but for these concerns that he had about individual people, would have been "heart-depressing" to contemplate. He was concerned basically with what he regarded as the "true worth"and the "power of mind"among the commonalty, and he made deliberate use of his wanderings about the lonely countryside, seeking among strangers for the evidence he needed. This latter experience, which was very extended, he tells us he greatly enjoyed. It was second (along with his meditation upon it) only to the joyfulness a human being has of love in youth. At the point where he is considering these things he has a passage of beauty concerning the extent of a precious young love—an experience evidently given in its more ideal form to few.

Perhaps Wordsworth has been thinking also of something comparable to the sense of the power of love to which certain psychologists of our own century have referred, a power which ultimately can be connected with our being or fundamental existence. Strangely, it might seem, he regards as related to the joyfulness of which he had spoken the pleasure one can have in the open road. As he says—

> I love a public road: few sights there are
> That please me more; such object hath had power
> O'er my imagination since the dawn
> Of childhood, when its disappearing line,
> Seen daily afar off, on one bare steep
> Beyond the limits which my feet had trod
> Was like a guide into eternity . . . (145—)

It is the idea of an approach to infinity which is in the background of Wordsworth's mind and which causes him to value this type of road. The reference to the "disappearing line" conjures up childhood's visions, only partly seen because they are "afar off," as he presently says. As he thinks of childhood, he connects the memory of the line to limits that are beyond those "limits" which, because of his extreme youth, he had thus far experienced. Here we find symbolized the restrictions in space to which man must relate "things unknown"; the notion of boundaries and their connection with the possibilities of extendedness is evident. One may find an end, and then, again, another and another—and so on to something like the limits one may perceive in the multiples or the various power of numbers to which we have referred previously. Philosophy of change is involved here.

Wordsworth's thought about limits, distances, and quantities in relation to the infinite (he speaks about the infinite elsewhere in *The Prelude*) may suggest the fact that he was on the verge of an appreciation of the concept of continuous change which is close to the basis of Whitehead's philosophy. This is not to say that the poet was near to a recognition of the importance of the infinitesimal method of calculation to modern constructive thought. Scientists themselves took decades to appreciate critically what might be involved in this method. But what we have commented on here would suggest that the examples given in the past chapters on multiples of ten do have a connection, even if it may seem somewhat remote, with the philosophy he is striving to attain.

Following the references to limits and to infinity Wordsworth speaks of the grandeur surrounding "Wanderers of the Earth" going on their potentially unending journeys. Even the "Bedlamites" and "other Vagrants," although he felt fear concerning their presence, awed and fascinated him. But it was particularly the simple, unpretentious common men that he chose to "watch and question"; here, though in familiar conversation with them, he nevertheless seriously studied them, and he perceived again the mystery of human life in its profundity—that is, in

> Souls that appear to have no depth at all
> To vulgar eyes. (167—)

The commonalty of men—those who "appear to have no depth at all," in the conception of an observer who sees with limited vision—have worth. This is the poet's assertion. What did education do for such human beings as he observed, and what is it doing (despite the fact of a very real progress in certain respects in our methods) today? Whitehead parallels many of the things the poet feels here. He stresses, as the poet does, how little fundamental change society has usually produced through the effects of education. The process has been slow, we must admit even today. Whatever veneer education tends, in the large, to provide for the individual personally, much is lacking in any deeper sense. Whitehead is well aware of this. Like Wordsworth, the philosopher is interested in the individual, but he is also concerned about our reputed civilization. And what he especially notes is a "fading of ideals"[7] which so frequently occurs in modern education. This is a kind of sinking to the level of everyday life "practice." Here "the result is stagnation."

What Whitehead is stressing, and what Wordsworth stresses, is the need of education in humane feeling, or, in the poet's words, "real feeling and just sense"; through our schooling, Wordsworth says, we learn a considerable capacity to verbalize in our "talking world," and this "talking" can be a kind of school in vanity. Is the ordinary man, who has lived a life of gross toil and who has little of this kind of talking, or formal education, necessarily "yoked with ignorance" and a brutalization which is equally gross? Wordsworth is interested in the civilization human beings are trying to build for the future, and this is emphatically Whitehead's interest also. Related to the problem of the growth of civilization, then, is the problem of the commonalty of man. How close are we, one to another? Can we in any wide sense be close to one another? Twentieth-century psychology has given thought to this, we have said. An example that might serve to illustrate the point appears in the statement of Sarason and Gladwin: "It will be our thesis that a heredity determinant of mental capacity must not be assumed to exist"[8] but, rather, that special proof would need to be given in a particular case. The presumption, that is, may be taken to be otherwise than one of condemnation of the individual to a status of basic inferiority.

We have referred to the authors Sarason and Gladwin as quoted in a work by Jane W. Kessler, who goes on to say that a new attitude toward the problem of environment versus heredity "comes from broadening the concept of 'environment' to include the prenatal and physical environment." And she quoted Pasamanick, who talks of hereditary neurological defects and says that "at conception individuals are quite alike in intellectual endowment except for these quite rare hereditary neurological defects." Evidence from other research confirming these conclusions could be cited. The broad problem we refer to here is, however, immensely complex and we would not imply that this is the place to do justice to it. Jane W. Kessler and the authors from whom she quotes need to be seen in full context if their thought is to be understood rightly. They are not inclined, however, to explain individual differences hastily on the basis of mere heredity. This is the important point.

The present question for which Wordsworth was seeking an answer was, as we have remarked, to find how much of true worth (he includes power of mind as well as worth) was actually existent in the large majority of ordinary men of his time. He had tried to look into this matter in various ways and we said he had finally decided to take extensive walks over the countryside, observing people and meditating upon his problem. He had not found among the privileged classes any decided degree of the excellence which he sought. Education, as it was practiced, did not seem largely to produce this excellence. Virtue, he says, appears to be most "hard to rear," even among those who are on the surface most fortunate in background. And "intellectual strength," insofar as it had been developed through the processes of civilization in his time, appeared likewise to be a "boon" which was "rare"; this being the case, he was most happy to find "hope" in his extensive walks and also to find, to his great "pleasure" a sense of "peace" as well as a steadying of his own self-status. Along with these things there came also

> healing and repose
> To every angry passion.   (180—)

Seeking to help others, Wordsworth thus tells how he had found help for himself, comparable to the gain which Goethe refers to in considering similar values. From the "lowly" and the "obscure," Wordsworth says, came tales which did "honour" to them, along with "loftiest promises of good and fair." The doctrine of an elite arbitrarily set apart from other human beings as a whole—a position offered at times today—had no appeal for him. In attacking anti-democratic views, he is presenting ideas that stand in opposition to certain conceptions Coleridge later published and perhaps had expressed by word of mouth in Wordsworth's hearing. The two men, though friends, were very different in their conceptions as to the possibilities of humanity.

Some people, Wordsworth says, suppose that even the "affections" along with "love," considered "by whatever name," come only to those who have grown up with "leisure" and "manners" which have, through elaborations of "elegance," resulted in a culture made exclusively "by man." Such a culture is a factor of importance, Wordsworth grants, but it must be remembered that there are people who have almost no share in it, and who are virtually destroyed by a more or less mechanical society. This destructiveness does something worse, indeed, than the actual killing of people. If his statement seems to the reader exaggerated, it might be enlightening to observe the picture graphically portraying the condition of child labor in our own country a full one hundred years and more after the poet's time of writing—a picture which is well included in a *Time* magazine cover-story concerning America and the mining industry.[9] Wordsworth stresses the handicapping of the individual due to "labour in excess," leaving no time for anything but the daily tasks. He is likewise aware of the disabling of people through their "poverty" which would leave them without hope or the means necessary for self-growth, including

the handicap not only of the lack of schooling but also of lack of
books.

The utter absence of anything like nurture in certain people presents a situation of what might be called nature-in-reverse, or what the
poet regards as an opposing "deeper nature," and it does have in part
a deterministic effect on the person. It has its effects also upon the
human "heart" under such circumstances. This can occur, for example, in the rapidly crowding or misgrown cities, "where the eye" fails
to feed the heart. Under opposite circumstances, the favorable natural effects of environmental surroundings can be of enormous aid.
What the poet learned and deeply felt as a result of his wanderings is
that in our thinking we too often "mislead each other" and that
furthermore certain works that we read "mislead us"; indeed, such
volumes look

> for their fame
> To judgments of the Wealthy Few, who see
> By artificial lights . . . (207—)

Thus it is that the "Wealthy Few" often unconsciously "debase" the
many. It is undoubtedly true that the emotional effect on us of our
self-conceit, as the poet shortly after this says, may affect us. It is
evident from the surrounding context that he well realizes this.
Adverse results of culture are often most pervasively present when we
are least aware of them. They cause us to accept "general notions"
inadvisably, in what is sometimes called the acceptance of labeling or
ticketing. Such notions are made use of

> for the sake
> Of being understood at once, or else
> Through want of better knowledge in the men
> Who frame them, flattering thus our self-conceit
> With pictures . . . (212—)

These "pictures," to which Wordsworth refers, artificially "set
forth" or fix in our minds "differences" between ourselves and our
fellow men. The pictures are false. And here in the falsification there
arises again the problem of appearance as against reality which may

be understood in a deeper sense if we consider these contraries attentively. We must ask carefully whether we are faced with idle constructions, ill serving our purpose of social living. Are there profoundly penetrating artificialities? Such artificialities are "ambitiously" conceived, the poet says: there is ambitious destructive aggression in them which capitalizes on assumed "differences," outward superficialities

> by which
> Society has parted man from man,
> Neglectful of the universal... (217—)

It is by means of the universalizing power, as Wordsworth goes on to say, that man has learned to project himself into other human persons—into many human selves—and by this he achieves an ethics. We stopped short in our last quotation from the poet with the word "universal"; but it is the "universal heart" of which he is thinking. The heart is a source of assertive power by which man operates with psychological and other kinds of energizing. It is the source of what some modern psychologists would refer to as aggressions, in the good sense: the drives toward improved inventions, institutions, creative social relations, and constructive desires including sympathy. Whitehead at times uses the concept of aggression in this way.

But the "pictures" which, according to the poet, man creates may be the means by which he chooses to mark himself in order that he may be set apart from his fellows. Dress, Wordsworth says, is, of course, one of the "outward marks" which men often use as camouflage. But he is struck by the many occasions in which, in his observation, he found evidence of "the power of human minds" revealed in the truly essential character of the person. This revealing of the *essential* character of which he is thinking occurs without the divisive "outward marks"—that is, it occurs in people as they are "within themselves." As Kemp Smith says, it is a mistake to "assume that ignorance of mind and poverty of soul must go hand in hand."[10] Here in the context of Wordsworth as we think of people in their inward nature, we have to judge and consider the inward act and the question of what the concept of judgment itself is. In the end we come to reflection on the social nature of judgment.

We have spoken previously of the "intellectual eye," as Wordsworth calls it. Our knowing is, for the poet, in part our psychological experience of phenomena—that is, our experience of objectified nature. It is also in part mentally created, or is intuited. This may be said of science viewed as objectified nature. The human person is an intuiting maker, whether in the production of science or art. He is, through his acts, objectifying nature, though what he creates into knowing is most often no idle thing. Science when viewed only mechanically presents a somewhat barren, though useful, story. But as a magnificently conceived imaginative construction, neither it nor art can be regarded as a thing of barrenness. This is true for any person who, like a watchman, is constantly and alertly looking beyond the surface of ordinary sight. We are here thinking of the point of view of both Wordsworth and Whitehead. But the conception is also related to the thought of Kant.

Wordsworth had spoken of judgment earlier than in the consideration which was dealt with in our present chapter. Speaking in regard to the social nature of judgment, we have mentioned the inward and the outward features of thought. Judgment may be arrived at too hastily, but, furthermore, there is the difficulty of deciding something when one realizes that the problem ahead involves doing, which should be, presumably, in accordance with the inward act insofar as it is constructive. Hence one often adjusts erroneously the internal judgment in attempting to bring it into conformity with the action that one, perhaps vacillatingly, may in the end only partially carry out. Here we might valuably consider the nature of judgment as it deepens through a consideration of what is good in medieval life and its relation to developments throughout the Renaissance as contributory to the modern world; we might consider, that is, what Kemp Smith refers to as the "transvaluation of the standards of judgment."[11] Of this we shall say more later.

The poet explains that often "high service is perform'd within" by a person who perhaps is very unprepossessing or what the poet calls "rude in shew"; that is, we would perhaps not anticipate that the person referred to would rise to any occasion in the grand manner. On the other hand, people who have had many advantages of person, or of opportunity, seem not to outperform in the field of decent action many people who are regarded as ordinary. The poet feels that the insight concerning the worth of common people is insufficiently valued for what it truly is, and that these people are, by and large, not given the status and the opportunity to live as usefully to themselves and to others as they deserve. He therefore explains that he has made the decision that his literary work will largely deal with problems and human events related to this need within humanity.

Of these things he will sing, if he can only understand them better and "mature" more fully in order to be effective in doing his task. Again his modesty as to the nature of his work is evident. Humility is of importance to his ethics. He declares that, "in truth" and in "sanctity of passion" as well, justice may be done in life and may be shown in a literary man's writing. Thus something of distinct value may be brought to the world. In the two words just quoted—"in truth"—it might appear that the poet is referring to reason in its first function, and the words "sanctity of passion" could be fitted to the poet's theory concerning imaginative functioning. These terms could, however, be thought of more simply. But all along it is ethics and justice rather than art in itself that he is now mainly concerned with.

The deprived people are not to be dismissed in any future he would wish to aid in producing. In general they do have a culture deserving respect. To this culture their religion has to some extent contributed, and books have come down to them, "good books though few"; their religion has been a possible opening wedge to growth for them in the past and it gives promise of bringing values in the future.

Connected with the value of "good books though few" is the doctrine of freedom of choice in what we read, of which one example is the conception of the open Bible with the opportunity toward an expanding liberality of view which it affords. It is the tradition of independent judgment under which the poet had developed. Such people, Wordsworth believes, with their "good books though few" have been given things of value, just as the advantaged people have. Of the two types—the advantaged and the disadvantaged—have those with special privilege made notably better use of their opportunities, as a group, than those who are being contrasted with them? In rare cases the members of the fortunate class have done well morally, but this is very exceptional. Mediocrity of ideal is widespread.

In the portrayal of people which the poet wishes to accomplish it seems to him evident that he will have to present themes of major or minor tragedy, but it is perhaps the constructiveness of the philosophy he is striving to attain which makes him believe that to the reader such tales of love and pain will have the effect within the mind of "Sorrow that is not sorrow," probably because of a kind of catharsis that may counteract it in

> the glory that redounds
> Therefrom to human kind and what we are.   (247—)

To produce effectively the kind of democratic works which Wordsworth has in view will require daring—even adventure—as well as most careful selection of material. He cannot simply tell any story of misery in the hope that it will speak for itself. Thought is requisite, and he plans to follow wherever "knowledge leads" him. For the poet it is a matter of "pride" that he has "dared to tread this holy ground," and he regards knowledge itself as a matter for awe. What he anticipates as a field for work is anything but an area of sentimentality or dreaming. Here he uses in contrast to the idea of idle "dream" the word "oracular," which is more definitely descriptive of that which he wishes to present, perhaps in the basic sense of things characterized by solemnity or high seriousness. But there is also the fact that socially oriented thought is often conceived of as utopian, in the sense of seeming idle or vain. On the other hand, it may be closely related to reality: that is, to changes that are to come and that cannot be overridden.

The relation between Wordsworth's thought and that of the eighteenth century must constantly be borne in mind. Whitehead's friend Kemp Smith, in speaking of the eighteenth century, refers to its preoccupation with humanitarianism as being comparatively independent of "any very real interest in moral ideals."[12] But here as we read, his term *very* should probably be underlined in our thought as well as his word *ideals*. Humanitarianism he traces very largely to classical sources, and he observes the seeming contradiction in the fact that churches should in the main be "so very dilatory in recognizing that the spirit which inspires the demand for the removal of abuses and inequalities"[13] is really "inculcated" in the *sources* of their own religion. For him, the important point, however, is that the modern religious developments and the classical tradition both have something to teach reciprocally. Here he could very profitably have in mind Judaeo-Christian values when thinking of religion. At any rate, we presently see in his thought a thing we have referred to earlier: his conception of the need for what he calls a "transvaluation of the standards of judgment."

Whitehead and Wordsworth have developed ideas that are related to those of Kemp Smith particularly in respect to certain aspects of the modern mind that have a connection with the past. Kemp Smith's article from which we have quoted brings out the point that the modern world can be most profoundly understood in relation to the romantic movement. That early nineteenth-century movement links the past and the present marking "the line of genuine progress—deepening our thought, enriching the emotional and spiritual life, and enabling us more wisely to direct those humanitarian enterprises upon which, thanks largely to the eighteenth century, the modern mind is immovably set."[14]

Organic processes become important here, as in art. For Kemp Smith, as for Whitehead, "The state is an organic growth"; it undergoes alteration according to "laws inherent to itself." This tendency he connects with what he calls a "genuine empiricism." Viewed from the consideration of a large logic, romanticism, he believes, can be seen best in its relation to the very individual character of art. "If all reality be interpreted in this fashion, only a genuinely empirical method can be regarded as adequate." Kemp Smith is here opposing the "sweeping generalizations" as well as "correspondingly wide deductions" of eighteenth century thought.

Whitehead's opposition to the limitations of late seventeenth-century and early eighteenth-century thought is proverbial, as is that of Wordsworth. Parallel to their position is that of Kemp Smith when he resists essentially the tendency toward block thinking. What Kemp Smith makes explicit is a concern for "a visionary empiricism" and the discountenancing of "the uninspired accumulation of mere detail."[15] He would go beyond Bacon and Locke. Here the important thing is what he calls "the *concrete* universal." And in this connection Hegel comes to mind because of his profound effort in the direction of both wideness and minuteness of view as well as in his searching in the direction of a future.

In *The Prelude*, Wordsworth, too, is trying to contribute something to the future, and it has turned out that his contribution does apply to the twentieth century. It takes imagination for a writer to look forward significantly, and we must remember that the poet had at one time conceived his imagination as having been impaired, perhaps irretrievably. But now as he is writing Book Twelve of *The Prelude*, tracing further the factors involved in the effort at restoration of the imagination, he feels that this faculty, as he would conceive it, is coming back even more fully.

The change in his own state is connected with his new confidence in mankind. This, we can emphasize again, is a confidence not in an elite, but in the generality of persons represented in a possible wide human experience. There is no sense of dogmatism here. Rather, there is an inquiry. Wordsworth refers to the fluent speech of many wordly men who become aroused (or "elevated") and who are stimulated "when most admired." They feed on adulation. These people he contrasts with those who do not need such assistance to their elevation. There is an inspiration that comes to a person from something that is within, and where this is true, people are upheld through their earnestness and their genuineness.

We can think here of Goethe's question—How far are you separated "from the others" (*von anderen*)?—which is directed at the danger of conceit and the importance of being prepared to share a common world.[16] Martin Buber faces the other side of the problem in the "solitude" of people "incapable of community."[17] Referring to Goethe, he points out that we can achieve "humanity" in its most general aspect "only by being 'helpful and kind.' "[18] It is in his idea of profound helpfulness and kindness that we find Goethe's thought of value on the central aspect of this issue. He is opposed to any religion which would proclaim a person's "relationship with the Divine Being" while *ignoring* whether that relationship is "based on something common to himself and a community"; he holds that such a religion, maintaining itself as "the only legitimate one . . . must be rejected." This weakness in a non-community religion can be seen in its tendency to emphasize the view that it concerns nobody other than the individual himself, singly, in his relation to the Divine. Martin Buber's thought and Goethe's statement parallel the position of Wordsworth as we have been presenting it.

In *The Prelude* one can find still other references to the cases of men "among the walks of homely life" who are of profound help to others. In quiet contemplativeness, furthermore, they find the inevitable thought or image for an occasion as if a divine force were assisting them—a "God who feeds our hearts" appropriately to his own ends, who knows and loves the members of mankind, even those who "are unregarded by the world." Throughout the context we can find again renewed the poet's reaction against a hierarchy of values which would represent determinism, his conviction that something constructive can be done on the basis of the person's "inner frame" which is the result of his being "graciously composed"; but more, there is "through all conditions" of humanity a "power" available, a kind of consecration, if we will open our eyes to it, which can

> breathe
> Grandeur upon the very humblest face
> Of human life.   (284—)

Is this grandeur in people, referred to here, a consequence of a common nature that we all share as fellow human beings? Is it a thing that is more fundamental than anything that the whole history of class differentiation can demonstrate? Can one attain inward peace through the pursuit of this fundamental, and is it moral in conception? We would do well to think of these things. The appreciation of such a character as the poet has in mind in this last quotation would take a form including both the inward and outward aspects of the individual—that is, his consciousness, his responses to the phenomena about him, and his acts in reference to these things. Wordsworth's other poetry produced in the period of the 1805 *Prelude*, and shortly thereafter, reflects this as does the work itself which we are presently studying. And we cannot refrain from returning here again to the basic spiritual idea of community as it is exemplified in Goethe. Buber declares of Goethe: "He saw no other prospect of mankind's becoming a humanity than through an association of truly human persons, which would irradiate and comprehend all others."[19]

We have spoken of the inward and outward aspects of the individual as having a bearing on the passage from Wordsworth which we last quoted. The human being can consider "outward circumstances," whether of persons or of external nature. The idea of the outer aspects receives double emphasis—indeed triple, if one notes the use of the word "visible" which is an added outward factor. But we see the importance of the inner action in reference to a conscious self and to "passion" in the self, and in "forms" apart from the self, which provide an intermingling with the "works" of humanity. Here we can recall previous contexts in Wordsworth in which an expanded conception of passion plays a part. But the reference in *The Prelude* is not here merely to a conscious self. A passion, operative upon the event, is a factor. That which is outward "intermingles" with that which is within and this occurs

> although the works
> Be mean, have nothing lofty of their own . . . (292—)

In the passage the poet again speaks very modestly of himself. But he refers to the generative factors, or the element related to "genius" that has been implied all along. He suggests that an extreme boldness of creativity is necessary in the uses of the imagination. In it we must follow any lead whatever, of character or theme, to find its latent values. There is humbleness in Wordsworth, but there is a great hope for new possibilities in literature. He contemplates each person "reverentially," and he connects aesthetic production directly with religion itself. Such production is deservedly, he believes, to be associated with the work of the "Prophets"; here he is thinking again of a sense of futurism to which we referred earlier.

The poet is looking forward, as he says, to matters "unseen before"; such is the kind of innovative work to which he would hope to contribute, even though in the end he might turn out to be the "meanest" of the company of creators. We quote his own words here. The "creative" acts that he "might" in the future perform could become—as he must dare to venture—a valuable part of the universe of things, or of nature. The breadth of his conception of nature must be understood. It was in a mood of this sort, concerning the inner and the outer aspects of things, that on one of his extended walks on the roads of England he came to Sarum Plain, where he was without anything to guide him

> along the bare white roads
> Lengthening in solitude their dreary line . . . (316—)

Wordsworth's experience on Sarum Plain emphasizes solitude and reverie, and it is comparable to the experience referred to near the end of the previous chapter as happening in "spots of time" or unusual moments. Now, in a kind of vision of times long past, he saw "multitudes of men" and here and there an isolated Stone-Age "Briton in his wolfskin vest" carrying a "stone-axe" as he walked "across the Wold," while "the voice of spears" could be heard "rattling" in the distance. At this point the poet "called upon the darkness" and it mercifully came to him for a moment, taking away the vision. But soon a second scene followed in this deserted place: a scene with a "sacrificial Altar" upon which "living men" had been placed. He is struck with the thought of a kind of mythic history of man, almost anthropologically conceived, including the worst that man has done.

Nevertheless he does not now pass judgment upon it. He had, he tells us, "other moments" (for he "roam'd" the dreary region three days), and these moments included an appreciation of early man, perhaps also in the Stone Age. Wordsworth is imaginatively perceiving what amounts to mathematical relationships—"lines, circles, mounts, a mystery of shapes"; these take on a form of "intricate profusion" and figure, or describe upon the ground things which constitute an "infant science" that is vividly "imaged forth," though his conception, as he says, may be somewhat exaggerated. But these primitive beginnings, it is no overstatement to say, shadow forth something of which simple men are capable. Continuing, as in a dream, he tells how he

> saw the bearded Teachers, with white wands
> Uplifted, pointing to the starry sky . . . (349—)

Thinking of these men—so close in some respects to the animal, and yet aspiring beings—we may well compare them, in the relation between man and man, to ourselves. Their problems—either savage or reflective—become ours. As we honor these ancient "bearded Teachers" (for we cannot do otherwise), do we not see the folly of any self-exalting philosophy? We can perhaps see the importance of what we can share with our fellow creatures. This is one of the lessons of modern anthropology, and it is to be found, suggested at least, in the poet. It appears also incidentally in Whitehead. For Wordsworth the men in his dream, with their "white wands," are making with their movements over the plain a kind of silent music. This is by no means fanciful, although Wordsworth thinks of it not as a reality, but as a symbol which may be "fancied, in the obscurities of time."

We may note that Wordsworth identifies himself in a spirit of equality with the men of the past; he, too, in "some imperfect verse" (written while he was on Sarum Plain) was exercising through use of "the vulgar forms of present things"—that is, representations of the "actual world"—a "power" which Coleridge, his friend, actually did greet as forward-looking, not a mere repetition of things that others had already sufficiently anticipated or "reflected." This in spite of the fact that he had been looking backward. So he addresses his friend. At any rate, at "this period" Wordsworth seemed to have a vision of concepts that were "new," of

> a world, too, that was fit
> To be transmitted and made visible
> To other eyes, as having for its base
> That whence our dignity originates ... (371—)

Using the poet's words we also wonder from what anthropological source "our dignity originates"; are we to understand, in accordance with an uninspired traditionalism, that we come from one race, and that we have as a common father and mother one Edenic pair? Do we have a God of a single, instituted religion which provides a certification as to the facts concerning our beginnings? Wordsworth does not present any such formulation anywhere in the 1805 *Prelude*. Rather, what he refers to now is a "new world" which at the period some nine years before his present writing he had envisioned. That is, he had envisioned a world "which both gives its being" to one's understanding and provides a "balance" of views and a confidence in the powers of humanity expressed through personal cooperation and sharing. But they are also expressed in an interrelation between the self and outward nature. They provide an "excellence"—indeed the "best power"—of the objects seemingly external to us and to the human "eye that sees."

The book of *The Prelude* which we have been discussing has been concerned with the continuing subject of the imagination and how it may be impaired as well as restored. In Wordsworth's case it had been impaired mainly by his disillusionment and his tendency, as a result, to try to find a center within himself as a single being, apart from his fellows. He had turned to mathematics introspectively perhaps for his own individual delectation and for a very private relief. This tendency could be regarded as a form of personalism in the bad sense. But mathematics, while it may be a distinctly inward preoccupation, can also lead one outward philosophically if it moves toward the infinite as a limit. It can lead some people toward reflection upon the idea of God, and then ultimately back to their fellow human beings.

Over one hundred and seventy-five years have passed since the days when Wordsworth was writing the version of *The Prelude* which we have been examining. The last one hundred years in America and in the Western World have in the main been spent in a life which permits accidental happenings, economically and otherwise, to rule human society—as Michael Harrington has brought out in his volume *The Accidental Century*.[20] Not everything in the past one hundred years of democracy has happened according to accident or chance, of course, but certainly choice rather than chance must become more and more prominent in personal and social life in the future. This concern for a kind of futurism is what Wordsworth and Whitehead share. And the author of *The Accidental Century* is by no means alone in our time in the parallel thesis which he emphasizes in his volume on democracy and its problems. The new century ahead of us must not be another "accidental century."

We have referred to Wordsworth's preoccupation with mathematics at one stage, and his marked shift, later, toward social concerns in the development of a new view of life. Whitehead's philosophy, in a way, is an exemplification of a similar development if we think of his earlier abstract study of mathematics and his later interests which brought him more and more to the concerns of general life and the development of society and civilization. Wordsworth's imagination, in a profound connotation, began to be restored as he considered more and more his relation to persons. And finally it took clearer shape as his thought attained a new direction toward a special democratic ideal, embracing in general all his fellow men, even his fellow creatures.

This is the story of *The Prelude* down to the point which we have now reached. Our next chapter will be concerned with the complex problems the poet faced in reflection on the completion of the poem, among them that of a strange experience he had on Snowden which brought him to a meditation leading toward an approach to infinity and the divine.

Notes

[1] *Essays in Science and Philosophy* (New York: Philosophical Library, 1948), p. 145.

[2] *The Aims of Education*, p. 3.

[3] Smith, *The Credibility of Divine Existence*, p. 409. The essay deals with Bergson.

[4] Certain followers, for example, of T.S. Eliot, stress the single, isolated soul in this way.

[5] *Aims of Education*, p. 42.

[6] *Ibid.*, p. 43.

[7] *The Aims of Education*, p. 45. See also p. 1, on the need in education of "humane feeling."

[8] Sarason and Gladwin as quoted by Jane W. Kessler in an article in *Cognitive Studies*, I, ed. Jerome Hellmuth, with an Introduction by Jerome S. Bruner of Harvard (New York: Brunner and Mazel, 1970), p. 157.

[9] *Time* Magazine, November 25, 1974, p. 30.

[10] Smith, *The Credibility of Divine Existence*, p. 197.

[11] *Ibid.*, p. 197. The essay is mainly on the Middle Ages in relation to the modern world.

[12] *Ibid.*, p. 204.

[13]*Ibid.*, p. 205.

[14]*Ibid.*, p. 210.

[15]*Ibid.*, p. 211.

[16]On the matter having reference to Goethe, see Theodor Reik, *The Need To Be Loved* (New York: Noonday Press, Farrar, Strauss and Company, 1963), p. 207.

[17]"What Is To Be Done?" in *Pointing the Way*, translated by Martin Friedman (New York: Harper and Brothers, 1957), p. 110.

[18]"Goethe's Concept of Humanity," in *Pointing the Way*, p. 79. See also Goethe's poem, "Das Gottliche."

[19]*Ibid.*, p. 80.

[20]Harrington, *The Accidental Century* (New York: Macmillan, 1965); the author acknowledges the help he has received from the Center for the Study of Democratic Institutions, p. 10.

Chapter Thirteen

How Could "The Prelude" Be Ended?

The Prelude is a world. How can we end a discussion of it? We brought our last chapter to a close on a note concerning democratic ideas. Wordsworth had spoken of what is essentially Being, or reality, and we interpreted reality in terms of its relation to a social view of the universe, a point which we find stressed by Whitehead and many other thinkers of the twentieth century.[1] In this connection the poet referred to the endeavor to lift the self to what, for our purposes, is essentially magnanimity or all-inclusiveness. What he is thinking about amounts to a growth in self-identity. In magnanimity we have a character trait that Aristotle emphasized particularly, and a subsequent history of concepts closely akin to it would bring us to a correlated stress upon charity and certain developments even in the most recent decades.[2] What we have just said will serve to bring together some of the ideas of importance in Wordsworth and Whitehead.

Near the close of Book Twelve Wordsworth tells how he had reached a stage in his development in which he had a kind of vision of "a new world" or what might be called a more adequate understanding of humanity and its relation to "pure spirit" manifested in the "power" flowing from the external world ("the object seen") and from the internal faculty of the living person who experiences the so-called objects that appear at first glance to be outside the observer. This new vision which seemed so important to him he now wishes to transmit to others. He is struck by the fact that the "pure spirit" in the universe is the base, or foundation, from which "our dignity"—or that of all men—arises. When we think of "our" status, as Wordsworth uses the term, the I-and-the-thou concept of the twentieth century would certainly apply, for he is thinking of good will toward all mankind, and he is aware, in a sense, of the fact that the *thou* is also thyself— that is, he carries on a dialogue with himself in his developmental attitude toward the "other" who is outside him.

What we have just said will serve as a partial recapitulation of the material we have treated in Chapter Twelve, which concerns itself with Wordsworth's Book Twelve as it is related to Whitehead. A dialectical process is going on in *The Prelude*, in the concern it shows for others and in its recognition of the need for the rise of the emergent person which is within each example of the others. But the *thou* can refer in its modern expression not only to a human person, or, indeed, to persons, but also to a spirit beyond them which is nevertheless part of them—an idea which (without the use of *thou*) is prominent in Whitehead. This, then, may serve for a covering statement concerning the ending of Book Twelve of *The Prelude*, which deals with the restoration of imagination in its relation to character or personality.

Proceeding now, we may observe that at the beginning of Book Thirteen the poet is looking backward, as is so often the case, and he is picking up the thread of one of the "excursions" he had been making as a youthful traveler. These excursions he had alluded to in the previous book. He now relates how he had made a trip in Wales, walking "with a youthful friend" (it was Robert Jones); together they had proceeded at "couching-time," moving westward with the intention of reaching the top of Mount Snowdon. It was their aim to arrive at this height at sunrise. He tells how they reached a cottage at the foot of the mountain and awakened a shepherd who lived there—a man who regularly served as a guide on trips up the peak. Having received "refreshment," the three "sallied forth." The poet brings home to us the "Summer's night, a warm close night," with its wan quality and "dripping mist" which hung low, covering "all the sky"; there is a sense of storm in the air. These forbidding circumstances— along with a gathering fog which made sight almost impossible—did not deter Wordsworth and his companions. But though they were in good spirits each of them had sunk "into commerce with his private thoughts"; in continuing, the poet tells us that he himself saw and heard nothing

> save that once
> The Shepherd's Cur did to his own great joy
> Unearth a hedgehog in the mountain crags
> Round which he made a barking turbulent. (22—)

This detail of homely human interest, in the wild surroundings "at the dead of night," seemed to the men almost an adventure, as simple things often are made to be in the works of Wordsworth. But its homeliness may serve as a contrast to something more momentous that is to happen. Continuing on their curving path thereafter, they wound their way silently, with foreheads inclined toward the ground ("Earthward") as if they were pursuing an enemy. The passage brings to mind a part of a description produced by Coleridge for "The Ancient Mariner" close to Wordsworth's time of writing this portion of *The Prelude*: in the context concerning one who "forward bends his head" while rushing to escape an enemy who follows close upon his heels. In Coleridge, as we see here, the theme is escape; Wordsworth in *The Prelude*, on the other hand, is emphasizing pursuit. Each of the poets, however, is dealing with the cosmos, Wordsworth being concerned with a conquering attitude, not with submission to whatever fate may render to man. Wordsworth, indeed, looking forward, was panting as he continued his way with "eager pace, and no less eager thoughts."

Given over, as he says he was, to an utter solitude of private "musings," he was in a state which might well cause us to wonder:

What were his thoughts? We do not know what went through his mind during the occasion of this ascent, but later, at the time of writing *The Prelude*, his attention is centered upon the interweaving of all things in the universe, and upon vastness. The poem reveals this. For the present chapter we shall have to go into Whitehead's philosophy somewhat more fully than we have done previously. This is fitting because the earlier treatment of it was deliverately aimed at the purpose of introducing his thought in such a way that its breadth could gradually be reached. A possible point of interest for us at this stage—considering the reference to Wordsworth, and his concern with vastness—may naturally be Whitehead's view of the interweaving of all things and their relation to infinity. Here we could well touch upon his theory of physical "societies" that make up all things, and we could also refer to his extension of these material societies into regions beyond material substance.

Recalling what has been said about the "Receptacle" in the chapter on "The Period in London" and in our later discussions, we will now see something of its connection with the thought of Wordsworth and Whitehead. We may again remind ourselves of the fact that for the philosopher in *Adventures of Ideas* the "Receptacle" is a term adapted from Plato's conception of the world and the necessities of its "indwelling shapes."[3] But for Plato, when he considers the universe, it is not merely the shapes of things that he is preoccupied with; he is concerned with *each* entity itself, and its great breadth of application. As Whitehead explains, "It is part of the essential nature of each physical actuality that it is itself an element qualifying the Receptacle"; moreover "the qualifications of the Receptacle"[4] in their turn also enter into the nature of each physical actuality. Here we are speaking of physical objects: the factor of physicality is our primary emphasis, though there is more to the conception of the Receptacle which will later need to receive special emphasis. Our concern at this moment is the physical "societies" which we referred to near the end of the previous paragraph.

When we apply Whitehead's conception of the society to the occasion of Wordsworth's experience while making the ascent toward Mount Snowdon, any given rock in the mountain's crags is a society, and the "Cottage at the Mountain's foot" belonging to the shepherd is, in Whitehead's language, also a society, as in Snowdon itself. All three physical objects involve almost infinitely complex interweavings; Whitehead, as we have noticed, is immensely interested in the interweaving of all things. But here we have begun by explaining his concept of societies as they appear in physical things only. As he says in *Process and Reality*, "Each electron is a society of electronic occasions,"[5] and again, as he later emphasizes, there are "societies of various types of complexity—crystals, rocks, planets, and suns. Such bodies are easily the most long-lived of the structured societies known to us, capable of being traced through their individual life-histories."[6]

Near the beginning of the last paragraph we referred to the occasion of Wordsworth's experience while he was making the ascent toward Mount Snowdon. The term "occasion of experience" is one that is used by Whitehead very often, and the present moment offers a good opportunity to comment upon it. The "occasion" has a relation, in the first or most elementary way, to objects, and these objects are not to be thought of as mere components in experience. This sounds technical, but it may not be too much so in the sequel. An object is not a thing in itself, but rather it is a portion of all things in Whitehead's experience-philosophy. This he points out in *Adventures of Ideas* through a criticism he makes of Descartes, Locke, and Hume and their approach to thought. "It is tacitly assumed," he says, "except by Plato, that the more fundamental factors will ever lend themselves for discrimination with peculiar clarity."[7] A moment later he adds, "No topic has suffered more from this tendency of philosophers than their account of the object-subject structure of experience." We are repeatedly misled by what we regard as things: that is, we are brought to confusion by our notion of the materiality of objects.

For the purpose of Whitehead's analysis, the most minutely short "occasions of experience" are often considered. The fact that an "occasion" is also itself made up in such a way that it involves composite things may serve as a corrective to the notion that an "occasion" needs always to be considered as a tiny split-second affair. The "prehension" itself is thought of as "in" an "occasion of experience."[8] Longer experiences are to be thought of as combinations of occasions. Any "occasion," loosely used in the experience of life, could, technically speaking, be separated into a plurality of occasions. The important discrimination we must make is that the "individual things are the individual occasions of experience"[9]; this distinction in Whitehead is emphasized and re-emphasized in his writings by significant references to "events" which are at times made up of almost microscopic occasions, and by his equating of these events with "actual entities." Here there is a metaphysical principle, involving, as he says in *Process and Reality*, an "advance" which produces conjunctions.[10]

Later in the same volume he comments on the production of a world "built up of actual occasions"[11]; as Whitehead explains his philosophy of experience, he has recourse to an "ontological principle" (or a foundation of reality theory) in which "whatever things there are in any sense of 'existence,' are derived by abstraction from actual occasions." Here there may also be what Whitehead refers to as a "nexus" of occasions, and a plurality of complications of various kinds beyond the nexus. Again this sounds technical, but it will appear less so later, and it has its place with reference to the philosopher's notion of approaches to infinity and the intermingling of all things.

For our purposes all we need particularly to consider now, however, is that Wordsworth's ascent on the way toward Mount Snowdon was made up occasions of experience and, more broadly,, of groups of such occasions in which something of Whitehead's conception of the interweaving of all things may be perceived. Returning now to the notion of "societies" for the moment, we will recall that Whitehead applied this notion to crystals and other very tangible entities, but it needs to be extended to the point where it touches the edge of that which is alive, or living; for example, "consider a living cell. Such a cell includes subservient inorganic societies, such as molecules and electrons."[12] This living cell is in an "animal body"; life—the living force itself—obviously contains societies. Such is Whitehead's way of using the term "societies," and it applies to something approaching infinity.

To come back to Wordsworth, we submit to the reader the fact that the living body of the Shepherd, as he led his two associates on their winding path toward Snowdon, should be regarded also as, in Whitehead's term, "society." Both the mountain and the physical man himself constitute societies. Each, moreover, represents the principle that "the realized nexus which underlies the society," as Whitehead says in another volume, "is always adding to itself, with the creative advance into the future."[13] The philosopher is trying to bring the social more broadly into the universe. The chief character in *The Prelude*, then, is walking up the mountain. Or, thinking in a slightly different fashion of the event and of the universe—enjoying a somewhat widened vision—we can say with Whitehead, "The man adds another day to his life, and the earth adds another millennium to the period of its existence." So time may be marked. These are Whitehead's words concerning the "realized nexus" which "is always adding to itself"; for the term "earth" in the philosopher's passage which we have just quoted we may substitute "mountain," as we think of Snowdon in Wordsworth's lines. But Whitehead, emphasizing the connectedness of man and earth, immediately goes on to say, "But until the death of the man and the destruction of the earth, there is no determinate nexus which in an unqualified sense is either the man or the earth."

Our connecting of Wordsworth's thought in *The Prelude* with that of Whitehead we hope is sufficiently clear. In addition to such mere technicalities as occasions of experience, events, and societies, subordinate or otherwise, Whitehead is also thinking here of the mortality (and immortality) of all things that exist. For him mortality and immortality are intimately connected with eternity. This paradox needs to be considered. But for the moment we cannot stop to dwell on Whiteheads's theory of how transiency fades into the eternal.

What was Wordsworth thinking about so intently as he moved silently through the early-morning dampness and fog when he started the ascent toward Mount Snowdon? It is hard to doubt that, among other things, his mind was concerned with the subject of vastness and mortality. The material that follows in Book Thirteen of *The Prelude* would seem to confirm this. He is in a society in a sense other than the peculiar technical sense of "society" which we have been considering. But for the present we should add that there are Whiteheadian living societies of higher grade than those represented by the bodies of men and animals. There are the living societies of high-grade "occasions" approaching the stage of the mental life of a human being. Man as a perceiver (or an animal as a perceiver according to Whitehead) is a higher-grade of society than the society of the body of a human being. Whitehead puts the matter this way: "A man is more than a serial succession of occasions of experience."[14] And he adds ironically,

"Such a definition may satisfy philosophers—Descartes, for example. It is not the ordinary meaning of the term 'man.' "

We have referred to man as a perceiver and to an animal as a perceiver. The being as a perceiver, we said, is a higher grade of society than the body of a human being. Such a percipient being, whether animal or man, may in Whitehead's philosophy be spoken of as a person. "Thus in one sense," he says, "a dog is a 'person,' "[15] and this would apply, in the ascent of Snowdon, to the "Shepherd's Cur," as Wordsworth somewhat disrespectfully refers to the animal. We see the dog as a percipient being, in his "joy" and turbulence when he unearths the hedgehog. In mere *bodily* nature, however, he is what Whitehead, in the context we have referred to, calls a "non-personal society." The philosopher speaks of man a little earlier and says that, if man is considered merely spatially and temporally as being only a body constituted of "a vast number of occasions," what he is thinking of is something less than a person as in ordinary life we are inclined to view a human being. That is, in some respects the human being is "not a 'person' "; the point Whitehead has in mind here is the spatial and temporal aspect of physical human life.

The interweaving of all things which we find in the Whiteheadian "societies"—and in his conception of the receptacle—is reflected also in Wordsworth's earlier references to the "Receptacle" of London in Book Seven; Cambridge, also, as it receives him in our chapter on his "First Residence" at the college, is a kind of receptacle, as is Paris when he first lives there, and again as he goes to the French city for a final stay after leaving Annette when she was shortly to give birth to his child. Paris at the later stage is a different receptacle from the earlier Paris, by virtue of the further occasions and events of the French Revolution that had been occurring. The city is different also because of the changes that had taken place in the young poet himself during the previous interim at Orleans and Blois.

When we contemplate these many places—and the time that passed while Wordsworth was in them—as well as the time-gap between (when the poet was received into other receptacles)—we can think of them as spreading both spatially and temporally in various ways which involve him. Whitehead's conception of the receptacle, drawn from Plato, is that of a kind of womb, or matrix, into which one is brought for further development. The action of the formative receptacle should be thought of as analogous, in its inward and living character, to the intercellular substance of a tissue in the animal or human body. This substance is capable of producing new, changing, and developing tissue in the vicissitudes of the life that follows the modifications of all organisms. So likewise it is with Whitehead's conception. It is "the doctrine of the unity of nature," he says, "and of the unity of each·human life."[16]

With this we must keep in mind that the "Receptacle" is not only external, but it is internal. It is seemingly both within us as well as outside us at one and the same time, and it represents a continuity of experience split second by split second. Whitehead sees, as he later says, "an analogy between the transference of energy from particular occasion to particular occasion in physical nature and the transference of affective tone, with its emotional energy, from one occasion to another in any human personality."[17]

High-grade occasions of experience are of pre-eminent importance within the Whiteheadian receptacle, for these require mentality— or soul, as he says—in its supreme reaches. Thus, in confirmation of the point we may observe that he remarks, "This personal society is the man defined as a person. It is the soul of which Plato spoke."[18] What have all of these things to do with Wordsworth? The answer is that he was at the very point of entering into an important experience of the soul, as Book Thirteen of *The Prelude* proceeds. Wales, into which Wordsworth had entered for the purpose of one of his "excursions," was, as we have seen, simply another example of the receptacle, along with Cambridge, London, and whatever other places one might mention where he had been. The conception of the receptacle can have a place in a philosophy containing a "stage of provisional realism,"[19] but also in a philosophy which is basically one of organism whether it is seen in Wordsworth or Whitehead.

Wordsworth as we saw him in the ascent of Snowdon had his forehead inclined toward the ground, though he was engaged in a kind of pursuit. His eager physical action, his "eager" pace, was also part and parcel of a mental action, for it included as we have said "no less eager thoughts." As in the philosophy of Whitehead the physical and the mental are here emphatically united; they are emphasized and combined in the repetition of the adjective "eager," which is used to describe both his pace and his thoughts. Note also that Wordsworth's head is inclined to the earth, but his goal is a height: to see a sunrise from a particularly happy vantage position. At this point there arises the problem of appearance and reality, so important in Whitehead, as we have seen earlier. It is important in Wordsworth as well. At first the poet, when he attempts to gaze ahead, can see nothing, but what he does eventually see is a vision. He tells us that at his feet "the ground appear'd to brighten" and, as he took a step or two further, "seem'd brighter still"; he declared that there was no

> time to ask the cause of this,
> For instantly a Light upon the turf
> Fell like a flash . . . (38—)

Looking upward the poet suddenly saw the moon, which "stood naked in the Heavens" at an immense height, and at the same moment he found himself on a shore "of a huge sea of mist"; in a curious figure, this mist, which spread endlessly before him, is referred to as being "meek and silent," while it rests like a living thing at the poet's feet. The event on Mount Snowdon is another example of what may be likened to the peak experience of Maslow referred to in the last chapter. The occasion of experience is really an occasion within an occasion, if we employ the term somewhat loosely. Whitehead, as we have seen, uses the word "occasion" more restrictedly than we are using it here for the moment (he refers to split-second occasions), but the interrelatedness of such experiences is part of his theory with regard to groups in connection with events. The essential idea of the complexity of the interweaving of events is, however, found in the work of both thinkers. This interweaving of events in Whitehead, as we know, may be of high mental order or of no mental order at all, as appearing in human life (at times) or in subhuman life.

What does one mean, or what does Whitehead mean, when he speaks of something of high mental order or of no mental order at all? To answer this question we must first, in a sort of digression, have recourse to a symbol. When we think of symbols (and of a high mental order) we are likely to think of mathematics. But in some respects symbols and mathematics may be related to the use of a low mental order. Whitehead himself says that often in mathematics symbols are used to avoid the necessity of thinking—that is, they may be used in order to move more swiftly (and mechanically) to a given goal. This is true not only in mathematics but in logic. We can illustrate the point by explaining that in our day a rather mechanical symbol could, at times, be used to save the effort of writing six words. These six words (which in writing are to be omitted) could be: "is a set within a set." The mechanical symbol used for these words is a reclining capital U placed in a line of print with the opening to the right. Such a homely illustration concerning symbols may be used, for example, to express the fact that the idea of green apples "is a set within the set" fruit. A capital letter for "Green" and a capital letter for "Fruit" could be used, with the reclining letter placed between the two capital letters.

Thus with the utmost brevity (using three symbols) we could express the idea in its bareness. But for the purpose of acts of high mental order, according to Whitehead, most people prefer to use the symbols of literature. So it is in the Snowdon passage we shall see, as events develop in *The Prelude*, Whitehead used the reclining U (with the opening to the right) in certain technical works, but for his basic philosophy it is the larger symbolism connected with events of high mental order that is needed. Still, the idea of a set within a set is analogous to the simpler aspects of Whitehead's conception of an occasion of experience within a group of occasions. We should remember, too, that a low order of symbolism can sometimes be used in combinations which bring one to a very high order of mentality. This is a different thing, however, from saying that the symbolism of poetry has a relationship to that of philosophy. Whitehead does bring out this last idea when he says that "philosophy is akin to poetry"[20]; there is usually a dim background of thought that is important in both cases, and this at times impinges upon our sense of the endless. In other words, thought about approaches to infinity has a place in many areas which are important to reflection.

Our comments concerning what we have referred to as a lower order of symbolism could have been brought to a somewhat higher order by using any arbitrarily chosen letter in place of the capital letter in the word "Fruit." "Green" and "Fruit" are words that are somewhat restricting to thought. Greater generality can be attained by using a more arbitrarily chosen letter, carrying us beyond a specific color and beyond the concept of the generalized "Fruit" to a wide variety of concepts moving upward in the direction of an approach to infinity. This subject of the infinite we have barely touched upon (in the last half of Chapter Eleven on "Imagination Impaired and Restored") in dealing with Wordsworth's "spots of time," which we compared to peak experiences. The purpose of our present comment on a low order of symbolism was to point up the fact that the abstract idea of a "set" reaches out very widely, as does the very concept of a set within a set; its purpose, further, was in its illustration of the way that both Wordsworth and Whitehead could be interested in symbolism, highly abstract or otherwise. Both, furthermore, were preoccupied with approaches to infinity.

We have referred to a set within a set in its abstract illimitability, which we have suggested is somewhat analogous to Whitehead's conception of an enveloping group of occurrences which contained an occasion of one sort or another within themselves. Such an interweaving may be illustrated by the vision itself on Mount Snowdon, which occurred on the limited occasion within the larger group of occasions constituting the total experience, which Wordsworth calls an adventure: that is, the ascent made by the poet and his friend with the shepherd, and with the "Shepherd's cur" as a kind of fourth person in the party. All this is, on the surface, very mundane, but it is not so as it is placed beside the vision of the mist which is, in our minds, as if alive—along with other factors described immediately by the poet in these words:

> A hundred hills their dusky backs upheaved
> All over this still Ocean, and beyond
> Far, far beyond, the vapours shot themselves,
> In headlands, tongues, and promontory shapes,
> Into the Sea, the real Sea, that seem'd
> To dwindle, and give up its majesty,
> Usurp'd upon as far as sight could reach.   (45—)

The hills are live things with "dusky backs" and are capable of movement, as are the higher forms of animals. The mist is capable of a kind of living pluralism in that it has "tongues," which could almost speak if they would. In the total dynamic picture we have a representation of appearance and reality: the mist, as beheld, usurps the majesty of "the Sea, the real Sea," though the reality of "the Sea" also has a reverse dynamism in its changefulness which gives it the Protean character of dwindling. The feeling of immense distance is included as the ocean is viewed from the height on Snowdon from which the poet looks far "as eye could reach." The moon itself has a vantage point of sight which is transverse, and is not a mere inorganic entity, being full of animated existential significance, as this passage indicates:

> Meanwhile, the Moon look'd down upon this shew
> In single glory, and we stood, the mist
> Touching our very feet; and from the shore
> At distance not the third part of a mile
> Was a blue chasm; a fracture in the vapour,
> A deep and gloomy breathing-place through which
> Mounted the roar of waters, torrents, streams
> Innumerable, roaring with one Voice.   (52—)

Wordsworth's use here of the word "innumerable" (along with his account of the deafening roar of waters) touches upon something experienced that is beyond our powers of definite perception, and these incommensurable things—particularly the use of "innumerable"—may remind us of ideas of an indefinite infinity and their bearing on modern thought. The appreciation of the world of change (and the quantitative is one aspect of this) has an importance in the period of the modern world extending from the half-century prior to Wordsworth's birth to a point roughly a half-century beyond his death. Here we have a span of time which would bring us down to the beginning of our own century. Change was occurring, and the conscious notion of change as a thing worthy of attention was becoming more prominent, particularly in regard to natural phenomena.

The period of time we have referred to here is something more than a century and a half, but it deserves to be extended slightly at both the beginning and the end. In this total time-span the quantitative aspects of the science of mathematics were undergoing astounding growth, and their change affected the whole modern world, including trips to the moon, in ways (apart from science) which are somewhat hard to define—except that the senses of human beings unconsciously underwent gradual modification and thus became somewhat different during this period from what they had been. In the context of the poet's use of the word "innumerable" we may have seemed to speak of mathematics as the quantitative science, but we might better have referred to it, in David Hilbert's words, as the science of infinity.[21] The importance of the quantitative relations of things becomes a factor in the philosophy of Wordsworth, and it is prominently so in the thought of Whitehead in its connection with approaches to infinity as a limit.

In the *Prelude* passage we have last quoted, the voices are innumerable (since actually the streams are thus designated), but the multiple roar of waters becomes constituted as a single thing (as represented by the word "one"); the multiple conception of the "universal" is clearly Wordsworth's. The scene surrounding the poet at the point of his vision on Snowdon has a grandeur within it as people often feel the Grand Canyon has, but it also provides a "dark thoroughfare" which reaches to the spiritual side of man and to the "Soul" of the totality—or the life "of the whole." Thus Wordsworth, using such terms, attempts to express his idea, however imperfectly. Continuing the passage from the poet which we last quoted, we may now in recapitulation observe his lines:

> The universal spectacle throughout
> Was shaped for admiration . . .
> Grand in itself alone . . . (60—)

Following the lines concerning the "universal spectacle" as Wordsworth has just referred to it, he also introduces the inward conception of the personal and of the "Imagination," but we have wished to draw special attention to a part of what we have quoted. As we perceive such a scene as that which presented itself on Snowdon, not without the aid of the imagination which serves as a mediating force between outward appearance and inward reality, we obtain (if the moment is fortunate) an image which is particularly expressive. And we are capable, through the action of time, of adding to the appearance of reality a further reality which is within the new sense of appearance that we come to possess. So it was, after the experience which the poet had on Snowdon, a mediatation "rose" within him, even though the reality of what had been confronting his eyes had "pass'd away"; he had, then, that night, a second vision. In it what came to him was "an image of a mighty Mind"—a mind such as a person might himself attain, providing that he had become one who "feeds upon infinity"; along with this he had a feeling of "an underpresence" of a divine character.

The upshot of Wordsworth's vision on Mount Snowdon (which is to be thought of as partly appearance, partly reality, and partly "Imagination") is that the "Soul" for the moment receives focal emphasis. He had started out in the dead of night with the intention of seeing the sunrise from the peak, we will remember. But nothing is said whatever now or later concerning the *achievement* of this initial goal. For him the scene in the mist became an image or emblem important in itself. All he says after this is that he continued in "meditation" on that occasion, and, to sum it up, he declares that the scene

> appear'd to me
> The perfect image of a mighty Mind,
> Of one that feeds upon infinity . . . (68—)

We shall refer in a moment to the mind "that feeds upon infinity," which we have mentioned, but observe, first, the word "image" in the passage. The expression (which we have earlier equated with the idea of an emblem) should be thought of in relation to the idea expressed in the term "Imagination" appearing in the beginning of the preceding paragraph. The emblem, Wordsworth says, images forth something concerning "Mind" and the idea of feeding upon infinity, along with the feeling of an underpresence, a "sense of God"; in this fashion it is possible to see influence exerted "upon the outward face of things," and to see this influence in a process. And in that process the self, through its contact with nature, "moulds" and "endues" things (we will quote this again later); it

> abstracts, combines,
> Or by abrupt and unhabitual influence
> Doth make one object . . . impress itself
> Upon all others and pervade them . . . (79—)

The function of these action words ("endues," "abstracts," "combines"), for the purpose of *The Prelude*, is like the functions of similar words for the philosophy of Whitehead in its interweaving, as we may say again, of all things in the universe. Whitehead also uses all three of these quoted terms. Wordsworth speaks further of the thrust upon the senses coming from the world outside. He speaks of its strength, which he likens to that of the correlatively involved use of the imagination. He is thinking of the effect of these thrusts upon every object in the universe and of the accomplishment of transformations as well as of the capacities of the human being. These capacities through the use of the imagination enable him to entrap or bring into being an existence involving proportions of permanence and change. But we are anticipating matters to be discussed later. Essentially the poet would suggest that aspiration and devotion are present when human beings build great things. And some accomplishments arise from very small, we could say almost infinitesimal, perceptions.

We planned to comment on Wordsworth's statement concerning a mind "that feeds upon infinity"; what can be indicated about such a mind, or about a person who has an inclination toward such an action? Newton might serve as an example of one who "feeds upon infinity"; earlier (in Book Three), the poet spoke of the "great Newton's own ethereal self" and made reference to the eternal silence of his thoughts, suggesting infinity; in a subsequent revision for the later *Prelude* he included lines concerning Newton's mind "for ever" traversing "strange seas of thought," which might well apply to the limits of the infinitesimal and the projections of the infinite which Newton pondered. Recalling the fact that Whitehead makes frequent references to "eternal objects" (and sometimes by way of clarification refers to them as "transcendent"), we may observe that the notion of the eternal appears even in concepts such as that of shape.[22] Here it may also be helpful to think of his reference to Wordsworth's "enduring permanences" in connection with the observation of things in the universe and his explicit statement concerning the poet to the effect that "eternal objects are there for him"[23]—that is for the poet—as he attempts in his poetry to deal with the world.

At all events, Wordsworth now, in Book Thirteen, refers to the sort of mind that "feeds upon infinity"; certain things that parallel this may be seen further in Whitehead. But the problem is an involved one. Whitehead refers to an abstractive hierarchy which may be "called 'infinite' if it includes members belonging respectively to all degrees of complexity."[24] As he continues, he says that it "may contain any number of members, finite or infinite."[25] Then there is the idea of the infinite within the mind in "the concept of eternal space in which the world adventures."[26] In a note of correction (about ideas in which he felt he had earlier been mistaken) he speaks of "infinite events"[27]; for him the abstract concept of importance itself "is derived from the immanence of infinitude in the finite."[28] One might feel at times that Whitehead was almost obsessed with aspects of the seeming infinite. The pervasive importance in his philosophy of things which are persisting or enduring (in contrast to those which are passing) can be felt in the frequent references which he makes in a variety of volumes to objects which are eternal.

The little things, however, which often may be overlooked, are at times of considerable significance in relation to theory about infinity. For example, if a single number "is in some sense exempt from the flux of time"[29] and is a more complex concept than most people think, as Whitehead believes, so also is the process of elementary division. In the fourth-grade stage of the subject of division we have the "gazintas" of which children, to our amusement, sometimes speak: three "gazinta eighteen" and so on. As to this matter, the Greeks in their early days could not speak of the divisions which we present as fractions, but "thought of this subject rather in the form of ratio, so that a Greek would naturally say that a line of two feet in length bears to a line of three feet in length"[30] a certain ratio, which is two to three.

The process of division which at times seems so elementary may, in instances of it which involve fractions, become very confusing to people, and this was true especially in the historical development of human beings. The matter of ratio and proportion is one of those things which are deserving of very careful and highly imaginative treatment when we are young. The confusing aspects of division may occur, for example, if angles or circles are under consideration. In a half-revolution of a circle one hundred eighty degrees are covered. A curved portion of that circle equal in length to the radius "goes into" the half-circle three times approximately. The number of times is not three and one-tenth or three and one-seventh (as we sometimes use the figure practically, though inexactly); the precise figure concerning the relationship between the radius and one hundred eighty degrees (or between the diameter and the entire circle) cannot be computed. Here in the act of division, or in angles, we have the problem of the seemingly endless in the incommensurable, as, indeed, we do to a certain extent even in various simpler instances of division. In a sense, number is at the base of the world.

An amazing extension of the mind of man touching upon infinitude has been remarked by Whitehead: that which occurred when decimal fractions were invented. This deserves stress in our minds because, having learned of the decimal process shortly after studying division, we tend to assume that the whole thing must have been familiar to people for a very long time. Actually, this was not the case. As Whitehead makes clear, the use of decimals "was not accomplished till the seventeenth century."[31] This was in the century prior to Wordsworth's birth. To Whitehead such an advance was an "almost miraculous result" of an increase in man's ability to use a new kind of notation, in which the decimal point enabled him to perform with relative ease formerly difficult operations of division. We have mentioned earlier, in another connection, the importance of the decimal system (and of powers of ten) in relation to an approach to infinity.

To return somewhat more abstractly to the subject of the quantitative in relation to approaches to infinity we may note that Whitehead's feeling about the importance of change is markedly stressed in a metaphor which he presents: an avalanche. As he considers developments in connection with quantitative relationships, even looking back to beginning stages of certain developments at the time of Fermat, who died in 1665, he thinks of the unloosing of a great mountain of snow as a representative of what was happening. The date given here is a little more than a century before Wordsworth's birth. While men later than Fermat have had the good fortune to produce cataclysmic final ideas, Whitehead says, this does not mean that they truly excel their predecessors; "it is both silly and ungrateful to confine our admiration with gaping wonder to those . . . who have made the final advances . . ."[32] Here we see in essence the democratic aspect of Whitehead.

To Whitehead, Fermat is an example of a forerunner who helped in loosing the avalanche concerning changes in quantitative considerations, especially in the rates of change. Certainly all that we have said about division (and about ratio and proportion in its relation to infinity) was quite available to the general meditation of people even at the time of Wordsworth's birth—and, indeed, if some effort were made, was readily available a century earlier. If it might seem that infinity, after all, is rather simple, or that we have been stressing small or obvious things unduly, Whitehead's statements concerning difficulties which mathematicians have had in finding their way in their chosen area may well be remembered. One example of this is his following remark: "The great mathematicians of the seventeenth and the eighteenth centuries misconceived the subject matter of their studies. For example, in respect to the notions of infinitesimals, of the necessary precautions in the use of infinite series, and the doctrine of complex numbers, their discoveries were suffused with error."[33] So far as error is concerned human beings are not as far from one another as is often supposed.

Everyone makes errors. If we come back to the division of angles, we have a problem of extensiveness, especially if we think of the number of central angles which could be formed within a single circle, which at once seems endless. Even the use of the word "any" when we speak of "any angle" or "any number" reaches out to the innumerable. The same is true of the use of the word "example"; for Whitehead, algebra itself is based on "the notion of *any* example of a given sort, in abstraction from some particular exemplification of the example or of the sort.' "[34] The unending character of the concept "any" appears also in geometry; indeed, Whitehead relates algebra specifically to geometry in this respect.[35]

Similarly, then, in trying to measure angles (and need we repeat that Wordsworth says in *The Prelude* that he was interested in geometry), we find a connection with the idea of the infinitely extended. Thus one useful way of measuring angles (if we may be very concrete) is by considering the radius of a circle as if it were a stick moving from the top to the left backward until one has a central angle of thirty degrees or—going further in the backward rotation—until one has an angle of ninety degrees, and so on to an exceedingly obtuse angle, prior to reaching the point of one hundred eighty degrees, or the paradoxical straight angle.

Division of angles may occur here, as Whitehead explains, in that the angles thus formed may be considered generally in reference to the lengths of their arcs—that is, the curved lengths of the arcs which are intercepted by the sides of the angles as the sides are extended to the circumference of the circle. The length of the arc which is intercepted may be thought of generally, and this "'arc divided by radius'" forms, in Whitehead's statement, the highly abstract conception of the measurement of "the magnitude of an angle . . ."[36] Whitehead was concerned, then, with the highly abstract or universal conception of the measurement; here division in the extreme of ideality is the point he is making. The statement should cover *any* case, and, in doing so, touches once more upon the innumerable. This question, like that of the incommensurables referred to earlier, is connected with Wordsworth's thought about the person who, if he has made a sufficient effort in development, "feeds upon infinity"; as Whitehead says concerning incommensurable ratios, "from the time of the Greeks onwards a great deal of philosophic discussion"[37] about them has taken place.

The same can be said, Whitehead declares, almost in principle, concerning even the arrangement of "the whole series of real numbers"; as to this he says, "We are here in fact touching on the fringe of the great problems of the meaning of continuity and infinity."[38] The matter of the abstract measurement of an angle is related to the problem of the incommensurable in another way. In the measurement of such angles we have two variables, the arc and the radius—the values of which, since they could be many, may remain unnamed for the sake of increased generality. The size of the circle (as well as the size or length of the arc) may change correlatively. The value of the one (as it changes) may be determined from the value of the modification of the other. One is thus the function of the other, in the sense that we might say that the degree of melancholy which Coleridge, for example, suffered was the function of his neuralgia, or of his having or not having a job and, with it, an income. Correlative changes may serve as simply another illustration of the importance of what Plato was working toward in his refinement or revision, as Whitehead explains, of the "doctrine that number lies at the base of the real world."[39]

We have been considering incommensurables, the measurement of angles, and series of numbers in their relations to approaches to infinity. But our main topic is connected with the fact that the appreciation of the quantitative relations of things (the recognition of the importance of changes of magnitude) has a profoundly significant place in the development of human perspectives from a period starting, as we have said, half a century prior to Wordsworth's birth to a period extending some fifty years beyond his death. Our own century, coming immediately after this span of time, is of course affected by what had occurred in connection with these seemingly quantitative considerations. And yet, curiously enough, it is rare to find individuals in our day who give much thought to the subject of infinity. The main point, however, is that both Wordsworth and Whitehead were concerned with the subject.

Still, our own time has seen an acceleration of the importance of the abstract relations of quantities in various avenues of thought. Change is a factor here, and the notion of the world as involving change and process (for better or for worse) has been increasingly in people's minds throughout the span of time from the point some fifty years before Wordsworth's birth to the present moment in our own lives. One evidence concerning this is in Wordsworth's reactions to occurrences in the French Revolution. The rate of change of social phenomena in France was very much in the poet's mind during the period of his thought about revolution generally. This was not a matter of high-level abstraction. But he was interested not merely in change in institutions and men as these modifications were taking place in France. He wondered about the rapidity with which general republicanism or democracy could be brought about.

Rate of change is one thing and "feeding upon infinity" is another. But rate of change, in its relation to seemingly infinitesimal units (as in the slow springtime acceleration of a glacier) and to very vast modifications in aeons, has its connection with theories in regard to the eternal. Such theories involve an entertainment of a doctrine "in respect to the infinitude of circumstances to which it is relevant," which according to Whitehead constitutes philosophy itself.[40] In any event, Wordsworth refers to one who in a context of the seemingly endless feels "exalted by an underpresence"; in his vision concerning the "mighty Mind"—a vision which occurred after the mounting of Snowdon—he had a feeling that, to recapitulate,

> One function of such mind had Nature there
> Exhibited by putting forth, and that
> With circumstance most awful and sublime,
> That domination which she oftentimes
> Exerts upon the outward face of things ... (74—)

Nature, then, puts forth a *domination*, exhibits a *function* of such a "mighty Mind"; we are tempted to say that a change occurs at times in the face of the earth as a result of a force within a universal mind and that the change takes place correlatively to the dynamic movement which gives rise to it. It might seem, almost, that this is what is being represented in *The Prelude*. If it should be true that this is represented in the passage, what can be said about the concept of rate of modification here? Can there be present any such conceptual connection? The word *conceptual* may seem too large for the situation before us. However, the change which had occurred was, according to the poem, awe-inspiring—indeed "sublime"; a "domination" had occurred which was without exaggeration gigantic. This is what happens in "peak moments," in the view of people who believe in them. Such was the experience of Pascal in the momentous "spots of time" that he underwent. The phrase is Wordsworth's, but it applies very well to the great moments that led to Pascal's shift in point of view from a stress upon changes in mathematical contexts to an emphasis upon what he regarded as the vast distance between body and mind (see his famous Pensée 792) and "the infinitely more infinite distance between mind and charity"; the expression quoted may not seem one which would naturally be expected from a mathematician, but it shows a side of Pascal's nature whereby he felt that there was something divine which made its appearance in the human achievement of charity.

In Wordsworth too, when he spoke of infinity—in the passage on which we have commented perhaps all too fully—there is indicated an immediate and explicit connection with the divine. But before we make certain observations on the subject of the divine, we should remark that his seeming recognition of changes that occur correlatively (when he speaks of the "function" of a "Mind" which had been shown in an awe-inspiring way) perhaps receives further confirmation in a number of expressions that echo terms we find in Whitehead. It should be admitted, first, that the poet may have used the word "function" very literally. But aside from a possible literal use of the term, the idea of correlativity is present in various respects in the whole passage. This may be granted from points that we have already mentioned. At any rate the "mighty Mind" which had been as Wordsworth says "exalted" (by a power beyond itself and with the help of nature) somehow exerts domination, as we may quote again,

> upon the outward face of things,
> So moulds them, and endues, abstracts, combines,
> And by abrupt and unhabitual influence
> Doth make one object so impress itself
> Upon all others and pervade them so
> That even the grossest minds must see and hear
> And cannot chuse but feel.   (78—)

If we notice the last word here—the word "feel"—we may think of it as used by the poet in the sense of feel *prehensively*, in Whitehead's fashion. But the importance of feeling (especially in connection with perception) in Whitehead's whole philosophy should be recalled now. Feeling is as emphatically present in the philosopher as in Wordsworth. Furthermore, in the lines quoted, the manner in which "impress" is used, as well as the word "pervade," and indeed the whole passage itself, suggests a variety of contexts in Whitehead, especially those which present his view with regard to the "togetherness" of all things.

Other expressions in Wordsworth's context could be singled out, among them the poet's use of the term "abrupt" as we think of the parallel in Whitehead's contexts in which the word is employed, for example his use of "abrupt realization" in connection with "eternal objects,"[41] as well as his concept of "abruptness" in his chapter "Abstraction" which precedes that which deals with abrupt realization. There is also the possibility of considering his conception in *The Function of Reason* with regard to "flashes of novel appetition" which he contrasts with "tedium" or with what he calls "the Way of Blindness,"[42] which is connected with "relapse." Wordsworth and Whitehead are both in opposition to "tedium" or inertness, whether in the individual or in the culture. But this we may regard as minor.

We have pointed out that when Wordsworth made his remark concerning infinity he brought it into immediate and explicit connection with the divine. The presence which is beneath all things, and which he connects with infinity, is a "sense of God," whether "dim" or otherwise. When we consider Wordsworth's use of the word "dim" in connection with our vision of this "underpresence," we may recall Whitehead's thought in a similar context of his own. The conception of an "underpresence" of God may be contrasted with the idea of a dictatorial overpresence (or what Whitehead would call a barren absolute condition) of the deity which is very commonly held, but which Whitehead repeatedly tries to avoid and which Wordsworth is here avoiding. Moreover, an "underpresence" is something concerning which our vision is "dim," as in the poet's expression. In Whitehead also we find a parallel: "However far our gaze penetrates," he remarks, "there are always heights beyond"; these heights "block our vision."[43] He is modest here, but he nevertheless presents his insights, as he says later, though they may be "inadequate."[44]

For him God is to be conceived as existing from the very beginning: in one sense, "he is the unlimited conceptual realization of the absolute wealth of potentiality." But there is a second side to the nature of God which Whitehead feels must never be forgotten, a side which goes beyond the primary or elemental. God in addition to being "primordial is also consequent."[45] He must be thought of "in unison of becoming with every other creative act." The emphasis upon every creative act is striking. Here we have the concrescent side of the action of the great underpresence which is God. What we have dealt with in the foregoing has to do with the subject of feeling in Wordsworth and the subject of prehension in Whitehead, as referred to a short while back.

We shall resume now our comment on the last quotation from *The Prelude* which ended on the "Power" of all human beings, at whatever level, to "feel." Wordsworth senses the universal principle of feeling and imagination. The universality of this principle in Whitehead's philosophy refers in its functional character to people of every class and condition. Now a person's tendency toward a diminishing of his own feeling may be a function of his emphasis upon the world of disparate physical objects. If the one (that is, the diminishing of feeling) becomes the function of the other (preoccupation with separate material things), a person holding such a view would be removed as far as the poles from Whitehead's process philosophy and from Wordsworth's thought as well. This "Power" to feel which Wordsworth has mentioned is part of a potentiality of everyone whereby "transformations" may be sent forth; the potentiality is most noted, however, when it comes by fortunate chance to those who may seem to be exceptional and who at any rate give forth something which appears to parallel the transformations that are presented to man by the universe; that is, in Wordsworth's lines,

> They from their native selves can send abroad
> Like transformations, for themselves create
> A like existence, and, where'er it is
> Created for them, catch it by an instinct;
> Them the enduring and the transient both
> Serve to exalt . . . (93—)

In the last two lines presented in this passage both the "enduring" and the "transient" are emphasized as features of importance when "transformations" occur. These two principles receive similar stress in Whitehead in like contexts. The poet's use of the word "transformations" should be especially marked. We may think of one meaning of the word as involving changes in the form of something without essentially modifying its value. That meaning we would expect to find and do find in Whitehead, because of his interest in mathematics. But more important is the kind of meaning which involves change in that which does the modifying as well as in the thing modified. Thus Whitehead points out, with reference to God, that his essence is "the realization of the actual world in the unity of his nature, and through the transformation of his wisdom."[46] But the whole passage we have quoted from *The Prelude* at the end of the last paragraph, along with its references to the "enduring" and the "transient," may be related to important lines of development in a variety of Whitehead's books. We might almost think, in reading his pages, that he had derived many of the elements of his thought from the poet. But this need not necessarily follow.

What we should especially note, however, is that the philosopher himself is conscious of the presence in Wordsworth of certain things that he regards as very significant, as we can see in a quotation which we will give. In it Whitehead stresses how deeply Wordsworth in lines of his poetry was influenced by the enduring factors in life—"the enormous permanences in nature."[47] The poet in such lines considers the factor of the transient in its relation to the enduring element in living experience. "For him," Whitehead says, "change is an incident which shoots across a background of endurance . . ." What has been stated here could very well be made to apply to Whitehead himself, just as it applies to the poet. The enduring and the transient, working together, act upon both men, and, in regard to their ideas related to God, serve them in such a way that they are exalted by a kind of philosophic penetration.

A while back (by way of anticipation) we mentioned the thrust upon the senses coming from the outside world or nature, as Wordsworth conceives things. The strength of the sensory implications which he holds is hardly less than the force of the imagination, though the latter is to him a supremely glorious faculty. Wordsworth thinks of the effect of these two forces on every object in the universe and of the accomplishment of what he calls transformations. In addition, he has in mind the talents and capacities of a person to bring into being new existences—that is, to entrap or "catch" an existence which may be marked by endurance or transiency. In other words, he would seem to employ what Whitehead has in mind with regard to permanence and change in his various references to appearance and reality and their relations to each other. Men by these means—by the sensory, Wordsworth says, or that which is thrust forth "upon the senses" and by "the glorious faculty" of the imagination—deal with the universe, and in the end, if they are willing to apply themselves,

> build up greatest things
> From least suggestion, ever on the watch,
> Willing to work and to be wrought upon . . . (98—)

Thus interactionism is present. We have spoken of the word "function" and we may say that the poet's reference here to one's willingness, in a sense, to work should be correlated to one's willingness to be a recipient of influences from the outside. There is a functional relationship between these two factors: willingness to make an effort has a functional relation to readiness to accept what can be obtained from the world of external things. But we have a further remark to make upon function in that we might have given as an example of it the fact that Coleridge's happiness on a certain occasion (and the point is pertinent here) was a function of his thinking about his friend's production of *The Prelude*. Contemplating or meditating upon the whole work Coleridge was moved to something like religious awe. His awe we might say was a function of his continued, almost breathless, meditation upon it. We do not wish to suggest that such a response is to be expected from each reader of the poem. We wish now only to make a comparison concerning the use of ideas that are functionally related.

Whitehead speaks of the transient and frequently expresses transciency through the related idea of "the fluent"; he also brings out this idea in relation to the concept of the enduring or the permanent. He sees a correlative connection between them. That which is marked by "fluency" is in the relationship of a function or duality to that which is marked by duration: "the problem as double," Whitehead says, needs to be considered; it cannot be thought of "as single."[48] We cannot assert that there is "the mere problem of fluency *and* permanence. There is the double problem: actuality with permanence requiring fluency as its completion," as well as actuality with flux requiring the eternal or the enduring for its completion. Whitehead in his process philosophy relates this double problem to dual situations with regard to the conception of the divine to which we have already referred. Thus he shows from his point of view how the God existing from the very beginning is related to the idea of his sequential nature looking forward through the present and on into the future.

This, as he explains a moment later, we may see exemplified in part in "the completion of each fluent occasion by its function of objective immortality, devoid of 'perpetual perishing' "; in being *devoid* of perishing it is " 'everlasting.' " Once again in his passage Whitehead emphasizes the "double problem" which must be understood as correlatively significant. In the same page he makes clear that "the consequent nature of God is the fluent world become 'everlasting' by its objective immortality in God." As we think of the flowing world and of Whitehead's physical things (or a world of death), we may reflect, by way of contrast, upon those to whom Wordsworth pays tribute for their interactionism (or process) in the lines

> in a world of life they live
> by sensible impressions not enthrall'd
> But quickened, rouz'd, and made thereby more apt
> To hold communion with the invisible world. (102—)

The "sensible impressions" referred to here are important in Wordsworth, as we see in passages of *The Prelude*, and notably in "Tintern Abbey," but their relation to the "world of life," the dynamic, is most notable in the passage we have just quoted. The "world of life" enriches the sensory experience. It is that portion coming from "the invisible world" which the poet is here emphasizing. This relation to the "invisible" can come into being, can happen, in the ordinary, day-to-day existence in which, as Wordsworth says, we "need not extraordinary calls" to bring us to a decidedly living experience. We can, that is, do much for ourselves out of our own inward energy. Here there is interaction. Can we then say that our minds, if we give them a chance, "are truly from the Deity," as Wordsworth puts it; can we establish a natural theology without benefit of dogma? Indeed this is the situation which Wordsworth is in.

Leaving aside the question of the "Deity," can we, along with a constructive society which could presumably help us, somehow enable our minds to grow more beneficently, and thereby attain an inward and "quickened" sense of responsible, enduring self-identity? We have used certain of the poet's words here. For Whitehead the term for self-identity is endurance or stability of character, as we shall see more fully later. We need not necessarily put aside, however, Wordsworth's use of the word "Deity"; Whitehead, too, uses it in such a context, inspired in part by another modern philosopher: in contrast to "the static necessity of each form of interwoven existence," that is, "Deity expresses the lure of the ideal which is the potentiality"[49] carrying us beyond that which is immediate. To be carried beyond that which is immediate applies to the cosmos, but it is also, for Whitehead, the essence of character or of identity.

And Wordsworth, like Whitehead, is concerned with the essential or fundamental feature in character. The problem of the kind of character which endures through time—that is, in the extended life of the individual—is very important. This is the self-identity which gives definiteness of personal outline whereby, to speak figuratively, one is king over oneself. It is very important to us in our own world today. Indeed, it has been suggested that people in our time are often inclined to lament, "I don't know who I am," or to use equivalent terms. But Wordsworth almost exactly a century and three-quarters ago used virtually this expression in Book Thirteen of *The Prelude* when he explained that it is profoundly comforting to be able to give an answer to the question of one's own personal identity when there is a need for a feeling of a certain strength of self. His own words about people who have such psychic energizing are given in a statement in which the problem of human "Powers" receives mention. His words, that is, about such people are that

> the highest bliss
> That can be known is theirs, the consciousness
> Of whom they are . . . (107—)

Reference here to "the highest bliss," which Wordsworth says is "infused" through all images, comes with a sense of inner selfhood. This suggests that the poet is concerned with something that is a very profound aspect of consciousness. But such profound consciousness we may feel is not steadily present. We are thinking of inner matters now, but the external self is a factor that needs also to be reflected upon. We are reminded of Whitehead's philosophy here in that he warns us not to "identify our more vivid perspectives" of the outside world "with ourselves." This is commonly done. He does not literally admonish us, but he sees as one example of this the almost universal danger of identifying ourselves with our bodily condition. Our bodies—which he says are "part of the external world"[50]—should not be identified with our deeper selves, though both our bodies and our more profound selves work together. The identity, also, between the baby that you were in the cradle and the adult at thirty years of age may in *certain* circumstances sink into what Whitehead terms "a metaphysical irrelevancy"[51]; this would perhaps be true for a situation in which as an older person you might be directing a moon rocket. The irrelevance of the cradled baby to this later situation seems on the bare surface to be evident.

In addition there is the problem of your self-identity under emotional disturbances—for example, in the event of a series of earthquakes or "revolutions in social habits"[52] (such as the bussing of children to produce racial desegregation, to cite one case); again, an individual may become quite another person during a violent electrical thunderstorm, depending upon the background in which he was reared. Wordsworth, as we know, became a seemingly new person when the guillotine was being put to use during his visit in Paris. Whitehead thinks that in such situations of disturbance a sense of order is of great importance to the conception we have of ourselves. But the essence of existence is in transitions, apart from order. Herein lies the essential "process of self-determination."[53]

The question of identity may be subtly connected with an establishment of some kind of relationship of a person to the divine, but identity can be profitably considered apart from this. Whitehead's own very broad "understanding of the world consists in the analysis of process in terms of the identities and diversities of the individuals involved."[54] A few sentences later than the words we have quoted he continues with his very extensive insight concerning "passage from experience of individual fact to the conception of character." In the first instance he does not think of "character" as connected only with human beings or even with animals. The generality of his view is striking. But he does reach the point of the human situation, and this is implicitly present when, as he continues, he says, "Thence we proceed to the concept of stability of character amidst the succession of facts." The context is not a simple one to follow when on the next page he proceeds to the view that the idea of "potentiality is fundamental for the understanding of existence"[55]; this point is made particularly with reference to his process philosophy. But it is very clear that he is struck by potentiality. As he says near the end of the paragraph from which we have just quoted, "Hope and fear, joy and disillusion, obtain their meaning from the potentialities essential to the nature of things."

Whitehead's context is not simple, we have said, and that is especially true because it needs to be supplemented with a reminder of his view of the divine as related to his conception of character. He tends to focus first not merely on the enduring feature of personality as applied to self-identification, but as applied to what we might call *futures* (Whitehead is greatly interested in what lies ahead); he is concerned with the self not only in reference to the responsibilities that as we grow in maturity we need to assume. He is concerned, also, not alone with responsibilities which may involve a painful process, but with the self-freedom that comes with accepted responsibilities. There is in addition the self-maturity which we obtain as we move more completely into high-level abstraction, or philosophy. The importance of everyone's immense though often unpracticed potentiality arises here. And once again we may return to the fact that self-identity, for Whitehead, tends to bring out the relationship of man to the divine. As we indicated in a passage we have partially quoted before, we are thus brought to the conception of the "Deity" as expressing "the lure of the ideal which is the potentiality beyond immediate fact."[56]

A statement from one of Whitehead's other volumes will help clarify his conception that we possess not only "central direction," which is suggestive of our sense of being as persons. Our sense of immediate awareness of self is important. As he says, "Our own self-consciousness is direct awareness of ourselves as such persons."[57] But he adds a footnote here indicating: "This account of a living personality requires completion by reference to its objectification in the consequent nature of God." With regard to the necessary completion, further material may be found, as the philosopher suggests, in a later chapter. This later chapter is entitled "God and the World"; but Whitehead's additional development of the point we cannot deal with here. Nor can we touch upon the question of whether a person has a soul (a problem which could become more burdensome than is now necessary) or indeed whether, if a human being is to have character, he needs to be very distinctly individual.

But there are further pertinent relations between Whitehead and the poet, with reference to identity, which we must now mention. Our present concern is for persons who do not know (or for characters who do know), according to Wordsworth's phrase, "whom they are"; the extreme of self-assertive individuality is not an essential here. On the contrary, the tendency of persons to accept being pushed around—or being told what to do or to be until they reach the stage of bewilderment—is the problem. Integration of self is thus important, and if this need can be positively met, it may be that the other matters concerning the soul can also tentatively receive answers.

We have spoken figuratively of a person who is king over himself. The term is not used by Whitehead, though we do find in essence the expression "president" of oneself in a slightly different connection. His view of one who has persisting character implies, however, that such a person is more than merely a "president" over himself, though we do find at times the use of the image of "presiding" in respect to attaining the centrality of control that is necessary in selfhood. Hence he says with reference to the brain that "a peculiar richness of inheritance is enjoyed now by this and now by that part; and thus there is produced the presiding personality at that moment . . ."[58]

Whitehead thus refers to "personality" as expressing itself in a "moment," and we can here see how it has at times erroneously been thought that for him character is a matter which finds expression in split-second occasions only, and that therefore he lacks any sense beyond this of a conception of an enduring self. This is not an adequate notion of Whitehead's position. Far from conceiving character as basically a thing of fractional occasions such as an occasion of a tenth of a second or half a second, Whitehead does not even accept the idea of "matter 'at an instant.' "[59] The important point is process, which is continuous. But even if he regarded character as making its appearance in short occasions of experience, there are enough split seconds in a life to constitute a complex being. One's act of presiding over the self is, however, not necessarily brief or a thing of utter spiritual isolation.

Hence, even more important in Whitehead than the concept of "presiding" is his view of "The Psyche" (he uses capital letters for the phrase), which, connected with the self, plays an important part in his philosophy in its relation to the thought of Plato. Our next chapter will involve, to a certain extent, the "Psyche" concept. It is very pertinent, however, to mention here a point finding reflection in Wordsworth, but which for the moment we will center in Whitehead. The philosopher feels we are most ourselves—and possess personal self-awareness most emphatically—when we are attempting to penetrate profoundly into something, and this may be connected with Pollock's more recent development of the view that "the concept of a person cannot be defined in terms of other purely physical concepts."[60] The way we realize a sense of self in consciousness is important. "My thesis," Whitehead says significantly, "is that when we realize ourselves as engaged in a process of penetration, we have a fuller self-knowledge than when we feel a completion of the job of intelligence."[61]

Whitehead would not deny the significance of completion experiences or of an act of completion. But what he has to say here is essential to self-identity or a sense of being, and it is vital to the concept of the awareness of one's own being in relation to reality. Growth is involved in acts of penetration. Stability of character, or of self, need not negate the significance of certain kinds of transformations of the self. In Whitehead we feel the importance of one's inner consciousness which parallels the modern idea that authentic being is attained through increased and profound self-understanding. Such knowledge is not, of course, the only source of an understanding of being. Still, it is very important, and it has a connection with the mental health and well-being of the individual, as recent developments in the broad field of psychology indicate.

Wordsworth, too, in his work is referring to personal identity in relation to the health of the individual. The whole *Prelude*, we saw, tells how he dropped into loss of hope and how he rose from the depths of despair to a new attitude toward life and toward his own being. What Whitehead emphasizes in connection with the growth of one's personality (in the very next sentence following the one which we last quoted from *Modes of Thought*) is that we find mere completion itself includes the presupposition of a "relation to some given undefined environment, imposing a perspective and awaiting exploration."[62] There is a wide reach of generality again behind this suggestion, a generality which includes personality. The generality concerns our expanding, extensive world, psychological or otherwise. It could apply, Whitehead believes, even to our knowledge of colors, as we can see if we consider the lifelong activity of a landscape painter. But it applies to everyone, for everyone has a veritably huge "knowledge of the colour 'green.'" And this knowledge, Whitehead adds, relevant as it is "to definite unexplored immensity," cannot be understood adequately "by its relevance to alternative immensities." It is beyond man. Here again we are back to Wordsworth and his immensities. Infinity, or something akin to it, is around us everywhere.

This same feeling with regard to immensities will once more come to mind if we consider Whitehead's distinction between general sense-figures (sight-figures of actuality would be one example) and abstract geometrical figures. Notice that in the following, in which he is quoted, he thinks of the concept of *any*; that is, the minute we pass beyond "generalising from a dark-blue figure to a sight-figure, we pass to the relation of any sense-object to the volumes of its situation."[63] Thence, in moving through high perceptive capacity to the "concept of a figure in which any particular sense is lost sight of," we are also making a transition of immensity, requiring penetration attained through the long history of the human race.

Related to this long history is Whitehead's belief, expressed in another work, "that we are part of an infinite series and since the series *is* infinite, we had better take account of that fact, and admit into our thinking these infinite possibilities."[64] A high generality again is clearly present here. In other words, if we now go back to a consideration of the point of obtaining what Whitehead called "a fuller self-knowledge" (through "penetration"), we are touching the problem of an approach to infinity. In Wordsworth also (and here we wish to bring out another parallel to Whitehead) the context which refers persons to knowledge of "whom they are," as the poet expresses it, involves a relation to the problem of infinity. The sense or "consciousness" of self-identity indeed, is inward and it is

> habitually infused
> Through every image and through every thought,
> And all impressions . . . (109—)

In these lines concerning the fact that self-identity is an inward thing and "infused" in a complex way with "every image" and tied with virtually "every thought," as well as "impression," the poet is using language which significantly calls to mind Whitehead. The stress on consciousness is important here. Moreover, Wordsworth is leading up to the statement "hence religion"; that is, religion grows out of human beings whose "Powers" (the poet's term) are most distinctly human or, as Whitehead would say, operate under conditions in which change is an incident.

Whitehead himself speaks of Wordsworth directly concerning change. In his view, such change, as it appears in the poet's thought, is "an incident which shoots across a background of endurance," and to illustrate this fact of change he quotes a passage from Wordsworth about a sound which arises against "the silence of the seas"[65] in the Hebrides Islands. The "Powers" which exist under these conditions (in which change is an incident) require, we may suggest, the use of Whitehead's "eternal objects"; in modern terms, we try to use in "relation to space-time" those things or objects which are "eternal."[66]

But the consideration of complexities in connection with the self should not result in a loss of emphasis upon matters that are central. The aliveness of the intuitive is prominent in Wordsworth and in Whitehead in connection with one's dominance over the self. Here we are keeping in mind the social nature of the self in the sense of the I and the Thou. Personal self-dominance does not mean the domination of others. What Whitehead calls central dominance within the self is connected with mental soundness and health, but it is hard to attain and it never can be completely attained; always, he says, "central dominance is only partial, and in pathological cases is apt to vanish."[67] This point is strongly brought home by Whitehead in the climax of a chapter. It parallels the idea concerning a strong sense of personal identity in Wordsworth's reference to people who seek to give thought to "whom they are."

But to return for the moment to the complexities of personality, we will consider Whitehead's statement about "the relation to space-time" of things which are "eternal"; these eternal things as related to space-time are, in modern terms, necessary. They are necessary, that is, before we can "pass to the consideration of the things that endure."[68] But the inclusion of our incidental thought about space-time here is not so very far from the conceptions Whitehead himself sees in Wordsworth. In any event, the language Wordsworth used concerning the inwardness of self-identity (referred to earlier) has religious implications. This language about self-identity being not only inward, but "infused" in a complex way with "every image" and tied up with virtually "every thought" as well as "impression," has special implications. It has special implications because it leads to the poet's words "hence religion," in a statement he makes which is exceedingly forthright. The word "religion" he connects with "faith" and "endless occupation of the soul," both of which involve problems which present difficulties to any thinker.

But it is the topic of religion, not faith, with which we must next deal, for religion is given precedence by the poet. A striking passage in *Process and Reality*—which we will need to consider again later—can serve now to contrast the processes which emphasize the "physical" with those of intuition which he regards as a form of "conceptual origination."[69] Here a decidedly favorable or constructive sense of the word "intuition" is given emphasis by Whitehead, and reference is made to the fact that intuition, viewed in a wide context, may undergo a transformation "into the notion of a 'positive prehension'"; he almost at once adds: "A recurrence to the word 'God' is still necessary" in order to provide a mediation "between physical and conceptual prehensions . . ." This "recurrence," however, is to be resorted to in no "crude" way. He is cautioning the reader against overly simplistic views of God. A page later he brings in the need for "some restatement of Platonic realism, modified so as to avoid the pitfalls which the philosophical investigations of the seventeenth and eighteenth centuries have disclosed."[70]

Whitehead's reference to God will serve to bring us back once more to Wordsworth's emphatic "hence religion," which, as we have seen, follows upon the poet's reference to the problem of personal identity. The self-integration which people achieve, the sense of "whom they are," as Wordsworth says, leads very evidently to what his conception of religious understanding means. It is related not only to the development of the self but also to the growth of religion within the self. Religion thus undergoes growth and process.

From this we can see again that Wordsworth's view of religion is not the conventional one. For Whitehead also, religion grows from within the person. In a famous statement (in which the word "does" should perhaps be emphasized) he remarks, "Religion is what the individual does with his own solitariness."[71] This remark, which would seem to accord with Wordsworth's view, has received certain criticisms. It has been at times thought that, according to this statement, Whitehead's religion is both undynamic and unsocial. Actually, the opposite is the case. For him, as for Wordsworth, religion is decidedly dynamic and social. Had Whitehead italicized the word "does" in the passage, perhaps he would not have been misunderstood. Still, no one should in the long run misconceive his expression of his idea because he makes himself clear in certain other things that he soon says.

Whitehead's basic ideas make evident the direction of his thought. His activity philosophy is explicit in other contexts. The great religions, which he values, developing as the outcome of active "religious consciousness,"[72] are universal, and they have had widespread consequences. The point Whitehead makes is that they are great because they are not limited to their "immediate surroundings." They are agencies. They are still enormously potent in their influence, though we might hope that their influence for good could be greater than it is. They bring about what Wordsworth and Whitehead both regard as transformations. In this process the higher or creative imagination plays a part. For both men the higher imagination is in itself religious. Like Wordsworth, Whitehead is impressed by the factor of transformation, as we have seen, and he uses variations of this word several times. To the philosopher, religion is a dynamically "transforming agency."[73] Agency suggests action. Indeed, as he says, "Your character is developed according to your faith. This is the primary religious truth from which no one can escape." Development involves action. It is true that in the page that follows he states that religion is not "primarily a social fact." Here, for the sake of clarity, perhaps the word "primarily" should have been italicized.

Whitehead's point is that he feels religion is basically a metaphysical thing, though it has great social consequences. What is important to the philosopher in this respect appears in his later reference to "supreme religious moments in history."[74] This statement may bring to mind Wordsworth's conception in regard to spots of time, which we discussed in the previous chapter and to some extent even before that. If we wish to see a further view of religion in another volume by Whitehead we may note that for him religion involves a "creative advance into novelty."[75] All creativity involves action. His social interest in a religion of activity is evident in a still-later volume where (with reference mainly to slavery) he pays tribute to the insights and actions "of Catholics, of Methodists, of Quakers."[76]

Here Whitehead also includes the value to society of the fine work done by "sceptical humanitarians" whom he regards as essentially religious in their functioning, quite apart from their reluctance to submit to dogmatic creeds. His willingness to accept as religious much excellent work done by sceptics whose point of view is man-centered parallels certain ideas becoming prevalent more recently, as seen for example in Michael Novak's *Belief and Unbelief* (1965) and in a later volume, which he edited, *American Philosophy and the Future: Essays for a New Generation*, as well as in his work *A Time To Build* (1967). Whitehead's conception is related, likewise, to that of the Quakers, who admit into their meetings people with no creed whatever, and who are willing to listen to distinctly and restrictively humanist reflections contributed by visitors to the regular church services, as we see in the earlier pages of *The Quakers* by John Sykes. Such tendencies, and other examples could be given, may be related to the broadening ecumenism of our day.

A very liberal natural theology, apart from the direct worship of nature, is now more and more to be seen. It will be remembered that Wordsworth speaks of a seemingly simple worship of nature in a period prior to his composition of the work we are considering, but through *The Prelude* and his subsequent writings his position represents a new growth. For Whitehead a crucial point is reached when people of different creeds attempt to draw close to each other. "They can learn from each other, borrow from each other ... Above all, they can learn to understand each other and to love."[77] And love, for the philosopher, is not a matter of passivity or mere inertia.

We may recall now a reference earlier in this chapter to a passage from *Modes of Thought* in which Whitehead spoke of the Deity as expressing "the lure of the ideal which is the potentiality beyond immediate fact."[78] It is in the context of this idea that, when we have mere fact (without a consideration of "Time"), "there is," in his view, "no meaning for purpose, hope, fear, energy." If there is no such meaning, then we would have "no historic process"; that is, when everything is simply "what it is," without process, we have "mere fact." All life and motion, he believes, would then be "lost." Similarly, "Apart from Space, there is no consummation." Through the means of time and space the universe receives expression in such a way that transition in its essence is achieved. In the end "there is Deity," Whitehead says, "which is that factor in the universe whereby there is importance, value, and ideal beyond the actual."[79] This is what is meant by "the lure of the ideal" expressed by the Deity, to which Whitehead earlier referred.

As we think of the word "lure" here, it may be helpful to consider it in regard to the complexity of our mental operations. Such inner complexities Whitehead chooses as an equivalent of the word "mind" in its relations to the make-up of actuality. Using the word "mind" with this meaning, he is able in some contexts to exclude consciousness from it; that is, he may include in it "subjective ways of feeling"— which are "not merely receptive of . . . data as alien facts," but which "clothe the dry bones with the flesh of a real being, emotional, purposive, appreciative."[80] To illustrate this he cites the example of the four-winds miracle of creation "described in the vision of . . . Ezekiel," wherein the prophet brought forth "an exceeding great army."

For Whitehead, there are astounding things which the lure of feeling actually can do. To such feelings we may connect what Whitehead elsewhere calls "the intuition of holiness, the intuition of the sacred, which is the foundation of all religion."[81] Here, then, is the basis of religion, for him, whether seen in the Hebrew prophet Ezekiel or in the Greeks or in Buddhism. But it does not mean inertness. The place of this "lure" in Whitehead's philosophy parallels the importance of feeling in Wordsworth, which is related to the imagination, and to "the Deity," as well as to "powers" that the human being has within the self. Out of these come a variety of things: the poet's sense or "consciousness," we may emphasize again, of personal identity or character which is profoundly inward, as well as certain infusions through "every image" one encounters and "every thought" and "all impressions"; these things are combined with a sense of religion, or in Wordsworth's own statement in summary:

> hence religion, faith,
> And endless occupation of the soul
> Whether discursive or intuitive . . . (111—)

As we see again from the last word we have quoted, the intuitive is important to Wordsworth's sense of the religious, and in thinking of the subject of religion we may recall that Whitehead employs the doctrine of "The Psyche" not only in connection with psychological self-identity (discussed earlier) but in relation to the dawning of the human mind. That dawning, he says, occured in a period covering three thousand years (a rather long dawning) down to the present age. In that period the Psyche as the "active grasp of ideas" conditioned impartially "the whole process of the Universe."[82] Such an active being or activity includes anticipation and effort. This *active* "grasp of ideas" becomes an essential feature in Whitehead's philosophy, when it is reconciled with a modern reinterpretation of the seven main notions of Plato which he lists.

The active grasp we refer to is an essential feature of Whitehead's world-view, at least in so far as, according to the Platonic approach, man can himself radiate toward and be radiated upon by a kind of Receptacle such as Plato had in mind. The philosopher thinks of this as in tune with the conception of "God, according to Leibniz," which has a place of importance in "cosmological theory."[83] Here he brings in reference to Newton's thought and the "Leibnizian God." The association between Newton and Leibniz is brought out in regard to the seemingly empty space around us, or in connection with "the 'sensorium of God' "; Whitehead next brings into juxtaposition "a formidable display" of thinkers as to this, ending with "Newton and Leibniz." He has been speaking of general principles. And he ends his paragraph with a reference to another "problem, derivative from these general principles" and "of major importance for human life"; this is "the doctrine of the spirit of man in the scheme of things." The spirit is not static. That is, in Whitehead's view, the psychological structure of man enables God to relate himself to man. Whitehead feels strongly that Plato can be helpful to us here. As he says, the adaptation and the "interweaving" of the "main notions"[84] in Plato are important to man today. The adaptation of these seven notions needs consideration. It would be of value to us not only in relation to personal identity (as applied to The Psyche) but also as we try to relate Plato's conceptions about religion to the present time—a thing which it may be possible to accomplish partly through Whitehead's philosophy itself. For this, purpose is essential.

Thus, for the present, we end the discussion of Wordsworth's Book Thirteen on the note of religion and its relation to the ideas of the philosopher we have been considering. We shall next have a number of further and very special things to say about Book Thirteen, touching upon the problems of the seven main notions of Plato, as well as upon faith, the discursive, peace, foresight, and certain moral questions. These we are reserving for the chapter that follows.

Notes

[1] The point mentioned here is brought out notably, for example, by Heidegger, Karl Jaspers, and Paul Tillich.

[2] See, for example, the fine essay "The Traditional Pragmatism," Chapter 17, in Michael Novak's *A Time To Build* (New York: Macmillan, 1967), pp. 323-336.

[3] *Adventures of Ideas*, p. 156.

[4] *Ibid.*, p. 171.

[5] *Process and Reality*, p. 139.

[6] *Ibid.*, p. 155.

[7] *Adventures of Ideas*, p. 225.

[8] *Ibid.*, p. 227. Note his statement that "individuals" as used in application to an "occasion" are composite things. For comparison, observe also that an atom is also composite.

[9] *Ibid.*, p. 228.

[10] *Process and Reality*, p. 32.

[11] *Ibid.*, p. 113.

[12] *Ibid.*, p. 262.

[13] *Adventures of Ideas*, p. 262.

[14] *Ibid.*, p. 263.

[15] *Ibid.*, p. 264.

[16] *Ibid.*, p. 241.

[17] *Ibid.*, p. 242.

[18] *Ibid.*, p. 267.

[19] *Science and the Modern World*, p. 93. See also the passage "The concrete enduring entities are organisms . . ." on p. 115, and p. 151 on "primary organisms as being the emergence of some particular pattern . . ." The receptacle is not referred to, however, here or on p. 115.

[20] *Modes of Thought*, p. vii.

[21] Whitehead says that infinity is introduced early in algebra; see *An Introduction to Mathematics*, revised (Oxford, 1948), p. 7. He speaks of the quantitative relations as being involved in the traditional notion of mathematics, but he would not confine his definition to the quantitative. His expansion of the subject may be seen in "Mathematics," *Essays in Science and Philosophy*, p. 201.

[22] *Science and the Modern World*, p. 134.

[23] *Ibid.*, p. 127.

[24] *Ibid.*, p. 242.

[25] *Ibid.*, p. 243.

[26] *The Concept of Nature*, p. 177.

[27] *Ibid.*, p. 198.

[28] *Modes of Thought*, p. 28.

[29] *Science and the Modern World*, p. 41.

[30] *Introduction to Mathematics*, p. 49. Note, however, the lack of "reference to creation" in ideal Greek ratios. "These ideal forms are for them motionless, impervious, and self-sufficient—each representing a perfection peculiar to itself." *Modes of Thought*, p. 111.

[31] *Ibid.*, p. 40.

[32] *Ibid.*, p. 162.

[33] *Modes of Thought*, p. 94.

[34] *Essays in Science and Philosophy*, p. 80.

[35] *Introduction to Mathematics*, p. 176.

[36] *Ibid.*, p. 134.

[37] *Ibid.*, p. 50.

[38] *Ibid.*, p. 55.

[39] *Science and the Modern World*, p. 42.

[40] *Modes of Thought*, p. 233.

[41] *Science and the Modern World*, p. 254.

[42] *The Function of Reason* (Boston: Beacon Press, 1958), p. 20.

[43] *Process and Reality*, p. 519.

[44] *Ibid.*, p. 521.

[45] *Ibid.*, p. 523.

[46] *Ibid.*, p. 524.

[47] *Science and the Modern World*, p. 125.

[48] *Process and Reality*, p. 527.

[49] *Modes of Thought*, p. 139. Whitehead makes reference to Samuel Alexander here.

[50] *Ibid.*, pp. 29-30.

[51] *Ibid.*, p. 129; p. 146 also refers to this complexity.

[52] *Ibid.*, p. 130.

[53] *Ibid.*, p. 131.

[54] *Ibid.*, p. 135.

[55] *Ibid.*, p. 136.

[56] *Ibid.*, p. 139.

[57] *Process and Reality*, p. 164.

[58] *Ibid.*, p. 166. He speaks of body and brain.

[59] *Modes of Thought*, p. 121. Descartes and Newton do erroneously so conceive matter, according to Whitehead.

[60] John L. Pollock, *Knowledge and Justification* (Princeton, 1974), p. 249.

[61] *Modes of Thought*, p. 60. We could relate the point concerning "penetration" to Whitehead's theory about discovery; see, for example, in another volume, "The type of Truth required for the final stretch of Beauty is a discovery . . ." *Adventures of Ideas*, p. 343.

[62] *Ibid.*, p. 60.

[63] *An Enquiry Concerning the Principles of Natural Knowledge*, p. 193.

[64] *Dialogues of Alfred North Whitehead*, p. 237.

[65] *Science and the Modern World*, p. 125-126.

[66] *Ibid.*, p. 126.

[67] *Process and Reality*, p. 167.

[68] *Science and the Modern World*, p. 126.

[69] *Process and Reality*, p. 78.

[70] *Ibid.*, p. 79. The conception of prehension in the earlier quotation is developed partly under the influence of Descartes.

[71] *Religion in the Making* (New York: Macmillan, 1926), p. 16.

[72] *Ibid.*, p. 47.

[73] *Ibid.*, p. 15.

[74] *Ibid.*, p. 52.

[75] *Process and Reality*, p. 529.

[76] *Adventures of Ideas*, p. 29.

[77] *Ibid.*, p. 220. The emphasis on love here in some measure recalls the thought of Martin Buber. Note also, however, in *A Believing Humanism*, trans. Maurice Friedman (New York: Simon and Schuster, 1967), p. 193, Martin Buber's emphasis upon experience and the "here and now."

[78] *Modes of Thought*, p. 139.

[79] *Ibid.*, p. 140.

[80] *Process and Reality*, p. 131. See Ezekiel, XXXVII.

[81] *Modes of Thought*, p. 164. An entire book could be written on Whitehead's philosophy of feeling.

[82] *Adventures of Ideas*, p. 189.

[83] *Ibid.*, p. 172. But see Gottfried Martin, *Leibniz Logic and Metaphysics* (New York: Barnes and Noble, 1967), p. 178.

[84] *Ibid.*, p. 188.

Chapter Fourteen

Further Reflections on the Latter Part of the 1805 "Prelude" and on Whitehead

The present chapter will include reflections on Plato, faith, peace, and other topics, all of which are connected with the outlook of Wordsworth and Whitehead. We ended the last chapter on the subject of religion in its relation to some main notions of Plato as selected by Whitehead, who adapts these notions to his own philosophy. This philosophical adaptation, despite its involvement with the ancient past, emphasizes experience, life, and activity. In Plato's late period, according to Whitehead, there is a development in which "life and motion" replace an earlier stress on a static absolute. The concepts of life and motion are prominent in Wordsworth's *Prelude*, but were also present in the poet's thought seven years before the completion of the 1805 version, as can be seen in his poem "Lines Composed above Tintern Abbey." In the "Tintern Abbey" poem he makes reference to a "motion and a spirit" and to "thinking things," and to "all objects" considered as universally interrelated to life. The poem in addition gives the reader, through the word "flows," a sense of the fluent energy of the world such as one sees in Whitehead. Activity is, however, more prominent in the later work.

The main notions of Plato we have referred to are, as Whitehead says, "The Ideas, The Physical Elements, The Psyche, The Eros, The Harmony, The Mathematical Relations, The Receptacle."[1] Whitehead capitalizes these seven main terms for the purpose of emphasis, as we shall do also for the moment. All of them are connected with his religious outlook upon the world. "The Ideas," first of all, have a connection with religion in that for Plato the highest of these ideas is the conception of the Good. A second point we would make is that in Whitehead's use of "The Ideas"—and in Plato's also—the importance of abstraction is pre-eminent.

And yet abstraction can be sadly misused, as Whitehead explains in a section of *Modes of Thought*. Abstraction can take us far from the world of actuality and can lead to an unfortunate absolutism. But in this work he also says that our very "growth of consciousness is the uprise of abstractions."[2] Indeed, on the positive side, again, the self makes its appearance very largely as a result of this considered "uprise" of generalized thought. One example of a significant abstraction in relation to "The Ideas" is the "continuity of nature" which Whitehead finds illustrated in "non-sensuous perception"[3]; his illustration here of the "non-sensuous" as continuity is of course not one which would be readily recognized in ordinary thought.

The second Platonic notion which Whitehead lists, involving "The Physical Elements," was chosen by him doubtless because, in its emphasis upon the physical, it reflects the deep concern for science which along with abstract philosophy was one of his abiding interests. Moreover, the importance of the physical is one of the features of Plato's thinking which is likely to be overlooked by the hasty reader.

The third of the notions—"The Psyche"—we wish to consider particularly, and along with it we will make special comments on the fourth of the notions, "The Eros"; the two terms together Whitehead referred to as presenting difficulties, but they are nevertheless in his view vital. The Psyche Whitehead equates with the soul. The Eros (which we tend to associate with love) he designates as "supreme"; it is related to the divine, but it does not constitute all of the divine. It is constantly present in the occurrences of each fractional moment in the world, and it acts as a determinant for every future development. The conception, as it is related to love, has some links with a number of features in modern personal psychology and with the divine. In Whitehead's philosophical language it must be thought of as "incarnating itself as the first phase of the individual subjective aim in the new process of actuality."[4] Here he is very abstract, but his word "new," as applied to "process," emphasizes the ever-changing dynamic quality of the world. An additional statement concerning the ideal will put his basic thought more tersely: "The Eros is the urge towards the realization of ideal perfection."[5] Here we see its connection with the divine in the word "perfection."

The Eros, then, for Whitehead necessarily includes conscious insight and purpose because of its operation in the person through the Psyche. The reference we have given (drawn from *Adventures of Ideas*) parallels to a certain extent his suggestion which we mentioned near the end of the last chapter, that the "Deity" is "the lure of the ideal"; this "lure," or urge, which he speaks of—as a factor in the "Eros"—may be placed beside a suggestion in another context in which he refers to ideals as tied in with the "impulse of energy."[6] Here, in energy, we see a metaphor drawn from the physical sciences. But he goes on at once to say of this impulse that it operates through religion: "It is the religious impulse in the world," that is, "which transforms the dead facts of Science into the living drama of History." In this case his use of the word "impulse," which may be viewed correlatively with his feeling for Plato's "Physical Elements" (the second of the main notions), implies something that *impels*. Can we see a relationship here between science, modern religion, and the Platonic notion of the Psyche selected for emphasis by Whitehead? Modern religion tends to see the importance of reconciling itself not only with science but with the physical, and it recognizes also the value in a wide overall psychological view, not omitting the ideal.

The urge toward perfection and the lure of the ideal, then, are not rightly understandable, in Whitehead's philosophy, except as they involve an interaction between the Psyche and the Eros. As he says a moment after speaking of the soul and the Eros (and after stressing the importance of life and motion), "If we omit the Psyche and the

Eros, we should obtain a static world. The 'life and motion,' which are essentials in Plato's later thought, are derived from the operation of these two factors."[7] Whitehead found an immense inspiration in Plato.

We come now to "The Harmony," the fifth of the Platonic notions here being considered. The importance of this fifth item has been implied in our whole earlier discussion of Whitehead. Certainly the idea of "life and motion" which he refers to twice has relationship to it. Parallel to this we may notice that Wordsworth in "Lines Written above Tintern Abbey" speaks of "an eye made quiet" by "harmony, and the deep power of joy" which under a reflective meditation enables a person to "see into the life of things." The poet has been speaking here of external factors (sights and sounds) which in their relation to the internal are involved in harmony.

External matters are related to internal ones, likewise, in a passage from Whitehead's chapter "Nature Alive" in which he says, "Consider the types of community of body and soul, of body and nature, of soul and nature, of successive occasions of bodily existence, or the soul's existence." We need to take account of these types of what he calls community, which represents a kind of communication. Whitehead proceeds and says, "These fundamental interconnections have one very remarkable characteristic."[8] He would attempt to indicate what this characteristic is, and he says, "Let us ask what is the function of the external world for the stream of experience which constitute the soul." Here he doubtless had in mind the word "experiences," or else he was thinking of the *streams* of experience which constitute the soul. But in any event in all this a "harmony" is evidently involved. This is what Wordsworth also is considering in the "Tintern Abbey" poem and in certain portions of *The Prelude*.

The words of Whitehead include expressions much like those which might have come from the poet. These terms of the philosopher are leading the way to the doctrine of duality (or of a twofold unity) as well as of immanence; they are suggestive of a remark that Whitehead makes later, "We are in the world and the world is in us."[9] Here we are thinking of central or crucial things referred to in the volume *Modes of Thought*. The soul, being in the world, helps to constitute the world in mutuality. This is not a cold matter of the intellectual or of the conceptual "entertainment of alternatives."[10] It springs from life and from occasion after occasion of experience each of which is as he says "an activity of concern, in the Quaker sense" of the expression.

The word "concern" is a troublesome one, here and elsewhere in Whitehead. It has to do with activities of immanence that are going on deeply within us when it is difficult to see them clearly. We can say also that it has to do with transcendence, with the actual world, and with the subject, or self, which perceives the world. This is our explanation. But Whitehead himself goes on to explain his meaning after speaking of an "activity of concern," such as one finds among Quakers. "It is the conjunction of transcendence and immanence." This point with regard to transcendence is what Whitehead is seeking in part to suggest by the title of the chapter "Nature Alive"—the chapter from which we have been quoting. In the entire actual world and in the subject—and even in the act of perception—there is included "The Harmony" which Whitehead honors. On this we shall have more to say later.

Is there a connection between "The Mathematical Relations" and the discussion we have just given of the "Harmony"? The expression "The Mathematical Relations" is listed as the sixth of the seven Platonic notions which Whitehead adapts for the purpose of his own philosophy. What we have said in earlier chapters about approaches to infinity would apply here if we keep in mind Whitehead's rejection of the static element in a philosophy which would conceive transition as an occurrence applying to rigidly limited forms. Whitehead's own approach requires, in contrast, far different and exceedingly active "forms of transition." As he says, "The modern concept of an infinite series is the concept of a form of transition"; that is, in his view, "the character of the series as a whole is such a form."[11]

Here we have the abstract idea of the live "character" of a series, when taken in its potential entirety. And we must recall something further: the fact that he has also been touching upon infinity, which we have previously in part discussed. It is necessary to include the abstract idea of the "character" of the total series as constituting a "form." This form is dynamic. The idea Whitehead presents is that of activity as applied to an indefinitely long series. It is part of a larger discussion of activity.

These very abstract conceptions are brought out in Whitehead's chapter entitled "Perspective" in the second division of *Modes of*

Thought. The whole second division of the book is given an overall title of "Activity," covering a concept which has a relation to the idea we are developing here. He is concerned with perspectives that reach into a great variety of other perspectives. Our modes of thinking, mathematical or otherwise, involve penetration into matters that are dynamically characterized. Whitehead, in continuing, speaks of the "sum" of such a series as we have mentioned; we usually think of a *sum* as it is marked by a thing which is static: two hundred and ninety, three hundred, or whatever. But Whitehead refers to "the sum of such a series" as an active issuance in a "transition." We may usefully consider the word "transit" as being central in the term "transition" here, as, for example, in the numerous moving cars in the transit system of a great metropolis. What he tells us is that the "sum" needs to be regarded as "the notion of a final issue indicated by this form," which is not altogether static, but which is a "transition."[12]

All along Whitehead is telling us these things because he wishes us to see the importance of our most complex perspectives to the understanding of the world in our own difficult day. The perspectives have some of the qualities of being alive. The chapter itself in which these ideas appear represents a more advanced development of a section on abstraction in his earlier volume *Science and the Modern World*. In this earlier discussion of abstraction he was trying to prepare the way (through a discussion of the abstract ideas of "relational essence") for a later chapter entitled "God." All of the Platonic notions stressed thus far—even "The Mathematical Relations"—have a connection not only with activity and philosophy but with religion.

We come now to the last of the seven important notions in Plato, "The Receptacle"; this notion we have treated in an earlier chapter and to some extent in successive pages. Whitehead does not conceive of "The Receptacle" as a simple container of material things. Wordsworth also uses the term, in speaking of the whole city of London with all its vibrant, social, living character. This we have referred to in Chapter Seven. For the present the important point, however, is that in Whitehead's view modern man can make use of the notions of Plato we have enumerated because, he says, "all philosophy is in fact an endeavor to obtain a coherent system out of some modification of these notions."[13] His feeling toward Plato is seen in the remark that "while we note the many things said by Plato . . . which are now foolishness, we must also give him credit for that aspect of his teaching in which he was two thousand years ahead of his time."[14]

Near the close of the last chapter we suggested that it would be of use to consider the subject of faith and certain other topics mentioned in Book Thirteen of *The Prelude*—all of them having been referred to successively by Wordsworth following his mention of religion. Can we see any connection between the subject of faith and Plato's outlook, which we have examined as Whitehead thinks of it? Plato was two thousand years ahead of his time, Whitehead believes. Confidence in long-range insight and *faith* in oneself is required, it would seem, if one is to have such far-reaching anticipatory views.

When in Book Thirteen Wordsworth uses the word "faith," in a sequence subsequent to his reference to religion, some readers of traditional inclination might wonder why he did not invert the order of terms, placing faith first. But from the poet's point of view in *The Prelude* the primary task, it would seem, is to generate a religious outlook and, from this consciously held spiritual world-overview, to attain, if possible, a faith which has a fitness with what that overview suggests. Faith would not eventuate *necessarily*, however, as we see, by comparison, in a quotation from Sartre, who tried, ultimately, and with extreme difficulty, to save himself through "work and faith."[15] What Sartre required and what Wordsworth also needed, it would seem, was faith in life. In recent times many people find this difficult to attain. Perhaps Whitehead could be a help to the modern world in this situation.

The final word in the *Prelude* passage, quoted near the end of the previous chapter, referred to religion in relation to the "intuitive"; and the conception of the intuitive is important to our present discussion. It is important in Wordsworth, as we will emphasize again, in that it is related, he says, to "endless occupation of the soul," including not only intuition but other factors which, taken together, present a very difficult area to circumscribe. As Whitehead also says, emphasizing his own point of view, "Language halts behind intuition." The intuitive appears in the fact that one's "understanding outruns the ordinary usages of words."[16] And it is in this connection that philosophy has its poetical side.

Without now attempting actually to survey the intuitive, we may connect it with the matter of our most direct relation to the world of actuality. Here the faith and directness of certain aspects of Santayana's thought come to mind: its forthrightness in some contexts was a quality which Whitehead well appreciated. Such a direct relation to actuality Whitehead stresses strongly in his philosophy. In considering it we could well include, by extension, the problem of whether it is possible to have faith in both the cosmos and the system of society in which we live, regarded as part of the cosmos.

This aspect of faith presented itself to a certain extent in an earlier chapter when we pointed out that Wordsworth was facing revolution both in the world outside and in that which was within himself. Now the focal center is the relation between the sense of the self, the matter of faith, and a social religion which does not involve a loss of self (as we have already emphasized)—or a submission to something that would impose upon us from the outside what we should do or be. It is not a literal faith in a crucified God betrayed by men, which some modern people seem to feel the need of. Nevertheless it is an attempted answer to fear or despair.

The skeptical extreme of the modern world has one of its origins in the acute critical analysis made by Hume in the eighteenth century, but in the twentieth century Santayana's earlier thought has been cited most often as illustrative of reasons for skepticism and doubt. The most extreme problem occurs when we come to the danger of a loss of belief in time, as well as of a belief in space and even personal identity. Whitehead recognizes this danger and speaks of Santayana as making "a vigorous and thorough insistence, by every manner of beautiful illustration, that with Hume's premises there is no manner of escape from this dismissal of identity, time, and place from having any reference to a real world."[17]

But Whitehead would insist that we *must* find an escape from such a "dismissal"; what we need is faith which permits us to retreat from the distorting abstractions which would negate self-creative activity and would stress a static location of physical objects as fundamental to philosophy. In opposition to this he takes recourse to the "givenness of experience" which "expresses the specific character of the temporal relation of that act of experience to the settled actuality of the universe which is the source of all conditions."[18] His complete argument concerning this cannot be summarized here. Given in capsule form, Whitehead's faith is closely related to "the primitive functioning of 'retreat from' "[19] things which give rise to fear or terror, and an expansive growth toward such salutary matters as serve one's needs of "love" and "massive enjoyment," as well as of kindred things which are primal. Self-expansion of a benign sort rather than capitulation is prominent here. His whole life work involves the expansion that is a result of faith.

Whitehead's tribute to primal emotion appears in another work when he says, "If we allow the term 'animal faith' to describe a kind of perception which has been neglected by the philosophic tradition, then practically the whole of Santayana's discussion is in accord with the organic philosophy."[20] Here with a slight reservation he identifies Santayana's position concerning faith with his own faith in a philosophy based on organism. But he has a criticism. Viewing Santayana's philosophy somewhat differently, he sees that there is also a danger in the acceptance of the "phenomenal veil, a primitive credulity associated with action and valuation,"[21] which many readers, along with Whitehead, have been troubled by. At a still later date, Whitehead suggests that "most philosophers do intensely mean what they say, and all of the great ones do. With Santayana's philosophy, I have a feeling that he is merely playing with ideas"; the basic difficulty or weakness, it appears, is that "he is lacking in sincerity."[22] Faith would seem to require a somewhat more complete sincerity than Santayana shows, and it is here that skepticism such as Santayana's is at a disadvantage in connection with our topic of faith.

In both Wordsworth and Whitehead, sincerity is central to ethics. Faith, likewise, has its place in this sphere. To some readers this connection between right and faith might seem far-fetched. We know that the questions of ethics and morality (for example, those connected with loyalty) are, of course, very complex. But this is not to say that they do not exist or cannot be resolved to a degree. And their resolution is involved with faith in circumstances in life which are antecedent to those connected with the fully developed human person. Such a faith is prominent in Wordsworth, as we have seen, and it is prominent also in Whitehead. For both, faith in life is almost a function of ethical experience. For Whitehead, questions of right and the good existed "*before* man"[23] came into being. At least in very young children, when they have to make a choice "between the good and the less good," the questions often arise.

We will add a note from Whitehead concerning younger persons and their susceptibility to "appeals for beauty of conduct."[24] It is of ethics that he is thinking. Youth, he says, "understands motives which presuppose the irrelevance of its own person." Motives which Whitehead has in mind here would presuppose faith in life and even in death. A few sentences later Whitehead attributes "the harmony of the soul's activities with ideal aims that lie beyond any personal satisfaction." For him this harmony is connected with "Beauty" in the world, which, on the whole, is self-justifying. This self-justifying quality "introduces faith, where reason fails to reveal the details."[25] Here Whitehead's faith goes well beyond the animal faith of Santayana.

All that has been said about "faith" needs confirmation through consideration of topics such as religion, which previously have received attention, as well as through the "sovereignty within" which Wordsworth in his *Prelude* calls for. Like the poet, Whitehead also feels the need for self-sovereignty, and for him it applies definitely to faith. The problem of fact arises significantly here. How can we achieve a faith if we are utterly confused in regard to the problem of fact? What is fact and what is not fact? Are the two as readily isolated as we are inclined to suppose? Here the danger arises of being limited too much by dictionary meanings. The dictionary gives us a start, but only a start. With reference to fact, Whitehead suggests that an error sometimes occurs in that a person may believe that things are connected in a fashion in which each thing is "understandable, apart from reference to anything else."[26]

But this would give us no sensible or adequate approach to the question of fact. For Whitehead, "the perspective for a factual occasion involves the elimination of alternatives in respect to the matter-of-fact realization involved in that present occasion"; it also includes "the reduction of alternatives as to the future" because "that occasion, as a member of its own contemporary world, is one of the factors conditioning the future beyond itself."[27] These words may sound complex, but the vital point is that facts are never connected in a way in which each is understandable as an isolated thing. Here we can again see the importance to faith of the consideration of the nature of facts. In regard to them we have to face what in another context Whitehead calls the "difficulty in relating the static immediacy of fact to the historic process with its past and its future."[28]

A rough illustration of this can be given if we point out that the thought of a significant early religious leader (for example, Christ) may be distorted by another leader of very considerable stature who speaks in a new voice in different times and under other conditions.[29] The facts with regard to the early religious leader undergo change in the course of time. This may be bad, good, or neutral. We may also add Whitehead's belief expressed in another work in which he indicates that "Hellenic thought has a way of becoming whatever the people who receive it are themselves." The tendency to impose one's self-orientation upon another person or culture is a continuing obstacle for every human being, but this tendency of interpretation does open the way for change and advance in creativity.

A difficulty in connection with our present topic, faith—and indeed with some of the other topics we shall deal with in this chapter—is that ideas in the one area presuppose, or intermingle with, ideas in another. We have seen earlier, for example, that self-identity is closely allied to faith. An intermingling occurs to a certain extent in the ideas of every thinker, but it is notably so in both Wordsworth and Whitehead. We mentioned in the last paragraph the dubiousness caused by the static immediacy of fact narrowly understood, and must reiterate now the point that for both men the resolution of the problem of fact and faith was not easy. In the *Prelude* passage mentioning faith, which we have quoted, the intuitive finds a place. And we know that what is supremely important for both men, after initial thought concerning religion, was somehow to attain faith in life here on earth—a very difficult undertaking then and, we have granted, for many in our modern world.

In this enterprise concerning faith on earth Wordsworth would have us find a place for love. So likewise what Whitehead emphasizes is the extreme claim of love "where the potentialities of the loved object are felt passionately as a claim that it find itself in a friendly Universe."[30] For Wordsworth, too, the notion of a cosmos which is not altogether alien to man is very important, and, as in the case of Whitehead, it has a relation to the good, or more specifically to moral judgments. It is faith that Whitehead is basically thinking of in this context, and, like the poet, he is considering it as consequent to the development of a structure of religion; hence, it is not an unthought-out faith. It involves a "deep ultimate" conviction "that through and through the nature of things is penetrable by reason."[31] In this respect he is going beyond the usual conception one would expect of him—he is beyond mere faith, though he uses the word "faith" in the context.

We are faced now with the subject of the discursive, to which Wordsworth refers in connection with various "occupations" of a person who has made an effort to attain a religion that would lead him to faith in life. What can we make of Wordsworth's reference to the discursive? In the "discursive," as we may be reminded, one proceeds by limited reason, or by step-after-step argument based on isolated factor after factor having no part in any large intuitive form. It is associated with a restricted view of science.

Wordsworth, nevertheless, shows a tendency to appreciate the discursive as part of the continued "occupation of the soul," and we may well remind ourselves of parallels to this which are in Whitehead. We should recall the nature of his emphasis on the discursive (in contrast to the creative); this was brought out in our Chapter Twelve in reference to his book *The Function of Reason*. Or again, there is the passage previously quoted in which he speaks of "the various categories of physical and conceptual origination."[32]

The physical here, on the one hand, would be connected with science narrowly considered (that is, the discursive), and conceptual origination, on the other hand, would have reference more largely to the intuitive. The scientist Galileo, as Whitehead views him, is an example of a person having the discursive talent in that he was "a supreme experimentalist"[33]; he also, however, possessed eminent, though lesser, intuitive talent. Whitehead makes many references to what in substance is the discursive without employing the word, though he is explicit when he uses the phrase "the superficial play of discursive ideas."[34] He is even more so when, in speaking of the limitations of certain uses of propositions, he says: "The bare 'truth or falsehood' of propositions is a comparatively superficial factor affecting the discursive uses of the intellect."[35]

It is not to be supposed, however, that Whitehead, in this remark upon the discursive, takes truth or falsehood lightly, and we know the seriousness with which Wordsworth viewed them. The very emphasis in *The Prelude* on the "endless occupations of the soul" in the areas of thought reveals the degree of the poet's concern for truth. Whitehead often seems to be almost engrossed with the problem of truth; in one volume he devotes a whole chapter to the subject. But here we have been following the sequence in *The Prelude*, including a variety of conceptions in Book Thirteen, down to the mention of religion and the discursive which we have treated, all leading to the words

> Hence sovereignty within and peace at will
> Emotion which best foresight need not fear ... (114—)

A person's sense of his self-sovereignty—which Wordsworth has in mind in the first line here quoted—leads, as he has explained, to a sense of "peace"; and it is this inward peace which is to be our next topic of discussion. Peace involving such self-sovereignty is more than mere detachment. Similarly Whitehead, when he thinks of "Peace," does not have in mind detachment—though the latter idea *may* at times be profound; nor does he intend us to think of peace as impersonality[36]—which he explicitly excludes from his concept. He makes plain, furthermore, that by peace he does not mean anesthesia. In his remarks he explains that through peace he is "in a way seeking for the notion of a Harmony of Harmonies, which shall bind together" various qualities, among them truth, beauty, and art. These, taken together, in his view constitute the Platonic Harmony. For Whitehead spiritual "Peace" involves "a grasp of infinitude, an appeal beyond boundaries." Writing in another work he reinforces the importance to his thought of the doctrine of harmony, and he adds the fact that "the notion of harmonious conjunction is derived from the concept of a monistic universe."[37] He sees, however, the danger of unduly monistic views. On this point his writings are eloquent. What is needed within the self is a balance between unity and activity, effecting peace.

The peace which Wordsworth mentions grows, we have said, from a kind of sovereignty within, which brought with it equanimity. This equanimity was important to the poet. It evidently comes "at will" if one is properly prepared for having it, and may be connected with the kind of long view Wordsworth associated with the seeming endlessness by which he felt attracted in an ordinary country road. Contemplation of the right sort, associated with his lone wanderings, brought spiritual peace. That is, contemplation provided a state of self-equilibrium when it was needed. Is the same true for the philosopher? His interest in balance of the self is shown by the fact that in *Adven-*

tures of Ideas he has written a chapter on the subject of inward peace.[38]

Thought about inner peace may recall to one's mind the popularly understood doctrine of Stoicism and of right, but for Wordsworth the sense of peace is by no means that of the resistant Stoic, nor should we expect this of a poet who has warm social purpose. Peace, in his thought, is also nondestructive in contrast to so many things that are destructive in life. Its essence likewise in Whitehead contains a variety of constructive elements and purposes. If a whole society could contain many members who participate in these qualities, it would for Whitehead be called truly civilized. Wordsworth's self-sovereignty or "peace at will" could be best understood by saying that, if you call upon it (peace), it is there; surely this is a state of the self for which one would devoutly wish. Peace, or equanimity, includes what Whitehead describes as "the removal of the stress of acquisitive feelings arising from the soul's preoccupation with itself."[39] The nonacquisitive is profoundly a part of Whitehead's philosophy (though in no absolutistic sense), and we will see that Wordsworth's case represents an emphatic parallel in a later introspective passage beginning "Oh! who is he that hath his whole life long," which we will have occasion to discuss in another connection. In the passage the poet levels a strong criticism against an exaggerated and self-directed acquisitiveness. He is striving for what to him is an ideal. As we turn to Whitehead, his term "Peace" might seem to be a strange word for the quality of character he is describing, which is very evidently moral and fruitful in that it is centered in "that passion whose existence Hume denied, the love of mankind as such."[40]

While striving for inward peace—through a struggle which is a growth in self-civilization—we are moving toward an ideal which is a matter of direction of travel, rather than a specific goal of attainment. Before we can have an effective sense of this direction of our movement (within the self), we are likely to learn what tragedy means in the world. Whitehead relates the sense of inner peace to the penetration into the nature of tragedy—a penetration which needs to be appreciated—and he seems almost to be thinking of Sophoclean drama when, speaking of the eventuations of life, he says: "The tragedy was not in vain."[41] Actually he is thinking here of the reconciliation of one of the complexities in life as against another before the

"Peace" can be attained which amounts to the kind of self-civilization we have mentioned.

Wordsworth's concept of peace may seem less specific than that of Whitehead. This is surely true. But the attitudes of both on the matter are mutually illuminating. Peace in Whitehead is a philosopher's ideal which appears, in his own words, as a thing founded upon an "ultimate intuition" which extends "the influence of the source of all order."[42] Does the "source" of all ultimate "order" suggest an overarching religious mental structure? It does include a "moral code" and, as he says one sentence later, involves in its essence an "attainment of Truth"; here we come back to harmony. Hence Whitehead explains that he means the following: "The intuition constituting the realization of Peace has as its objective that Harmony whose interconnections involve Truth."

Harmony is limited inevitably in so far as there is a deficiency in truth of this sort. Of course, there is always some degree of deficiency in the experience of every human being. Harmony comes to one with a certain degree of vagueness. Whitehead therefore does not in the passage have in mind the truth of mere propositions ("a comparatively superficial factor" as he has emphasized before), which for his present purposes would be of insufficient avail. What he does contemplate in the quest for peace is the effort of a person on a given occasion to bring his notions of appearance more closely into conformity with facts of reality. Here we have the great problem of appearance and reality, wherein that which is perceived may be at times largely erroneous. We do not have total reality.

In the context from which we have quoted, Whitehead is speaking of the essence of a welcome inner truth demanded by peace. This inner truth includes not only "the reality from which the occasion of experience springs—a reality of inescapable, stubborn fact," but also "the Appearance with which the occasion attains its final individuality—an Appearance including its adjustment of the Universe by simplification, valuation, transmutation, anticipation."[43] Obviously we do have to simplify things when we attempt to understand or to grasp them. What seems an adequate grasp brings with it a good state of mind. In brief, it is an insight into truth as well as right that is necessary in the attainment of peace, and this grows from the reconciling of the seeming opposites before us in our notions, as well as from the realities that our notions strive to represent. The problem of appearance and reality requires a recognition of the importance of the adjustment of mutually interfering variations in behavior. But our recognition of the difficulties in the question of appearance and reality need not involve inevitable discord. Oppositions or contraries may contribute to concordance. Oppositions or contraries need to be resolved to the best of our abilities.

Yet discord is prominent in our day, and this needs to be considered. As we think of certain social activists, we wonder about the education they may have received; at times emotion altogether rules them, and they may be given to violent action. It seems that such persons need to learn to strive doughtily, as Whitehead might put it, to bring appearances which are within their minds to some sort of equivalence with reality. To the violent activists the doctrine of straining or stretching the appearance (with an effort), until it is brought into conformation with reality, seems far-fetched. Their "appearance" is to them reality. But Whitehead's idea about straining or stretching will be less far-fetched if one looks ahead and realizes, for example, that a new enterprise which seems almost ideal will have its human limitations: the first appearance, that is, has to undergo modification, which comes after an alert sense of realism. Things will not, then, appear exactly as they had at first appeared.

Perhaps Wordsworth had something related to this in mind, in view of his interest in appearance as in opposition to reality. He does, however, give evident stress to the values of emotion, and this might seem to conflict with an adequate sense of reality. He qualifies his endorsement of emotion distinctly, and in trying to understand his position it may be an aid to think of the problem in a setting contemporary to us. That is, it could be helpful to think of the feelings that are aroused in certain nuclear physicists in the pursuit of their work and in their moments of notable discovery. These are feelings which are "worthy of trust" (Wordsworth's term), doubtless because of the background of ideas and the energizing force that they bring into being.

At any rate, very shortly after Wordsworth refers to a state of peace within the self (along with his reference to emotion which need not be dreaded) he makes mention of foresight. The problem of foresight will be the topic which we next discuss. It is not simple. Foresight is a quality which a person needs if he is to possess an adequate feeling for the world of reality which surrounds us. As to foresight, Wordsworth is thinking of the fact that sanguine appearances all too often rule our vision to our own detriment. This is a point which Whitehead also emphasizes with careful analysis. The fact that the poet uses the term "best foresight" shows that he too saw that the problem foresight presents is not simple.

Likewise in Whitehead the complexity of this quality of character, with its anticipatory nature, becomes evident when he connects it interrelatedly with intention, and then makes some further observations to which we shall refer. In Wordsworth, too, we have the idea that, if one has founded his thought upon a sense of reality, it would seem that intention and purpose would follow, along with foresight. Whitehead presents the problem effectively when, in *The Function of Reason*, he speaks of "the conduct of human affairs," and adds that it is "entirely dominated by our recognition of foresight determining purpose, and purpose issuing in conduct."[44] Further observations that Whitehead makes in another work show his recognition that the matter of foresight is not simple. In these observations he stresses the importance of developing qualities of character which bring with them the capacity to anticipate eventualities and contingent circumstances. Examples of these qualities are the "clarity and orderliness" of mind which "enable the possessor to deal with foreseen situations."[45] But "transcendence" is also needed. Thought concerning foresight needs to be connected with the balance between other qualities, but this balance is especially important in relation to the imaginative impulse and the gift of penetration which involve a wise solution of the difficulties arising, as we will say once more, in appearance and reality.

For both Wordsworth and Whitehead the concept of foresight, we should imply again, is related to their trust in life. Such a trust is not likely to involve terror when the person is confronted with vicissitudes of experience ordinarily befalling man's lot, provided that he has attempted to foresee them. Terror occurs only in unusual circumstances which habit cannot control. An example will be helpful. Whitehead indicates his position by explaining that we have a drive to carry on our intellectual speculations, which may be "disturbing" to received opinion, and this drive or "urge" comes from a conviction that "reason"[46] is a deeply underlying factor in the universe. And we should recall also his view that the word "reason" has for him a double character (including a decidedly creative element), which is covered in our Chapter Twelve. Terror may at times of course be involved in independent thinking, as we see in the case of Faust.

Reason can be made to have the purposive activity which has its helpful relation to foresight in the thought of Whitehead. Such purposiveness has profound connections involving the inner reality of the self, and it is, indeed, tied in with social change in long epochs of human effort, as well as in short moments involving "independent activities." The important point is that our "understanding of the Universe requires that we conceive in their proper relations to each other the various roles, of efficient causation, of teleological self-creation, and of contemporary independence."[47] In connection with the quality of foresight we have to think not only of design, or the "teleological self-creation" Whitehead has just mentioned (and its possible validity), but also of the limitations of science. Teleological self-creation is *design* of self-creation.

Whitehead, we have made evident, saw foresight in a many-sided fashion. Technology and science, as he often mentions, are tremendously important, but because of the nature of the transforming processes of the world (and religion is a key factor here so long as it is not an instrument of obscurantism), "the dead facts of Science" must not must not rule us. Here the word *dead* should be emphasized. In science we do not find the highly personal quality that the inner thought of foresight can give us. "Science can never foretell the perpetual novelty of History."[48] What Whitehead constantly seeks is a superior foresight comparable to that which Wordsworth includes in his philosophic effort toward balanced conceptions. For the philosopher, feeling has its place here, and in the whole scope of his thinking. We would not wish to strain the parallel between the two men unduly. But for Wordsworth emotion must be regarded as having a use if it has been preceded by the kind of thinking *The Prelude* had represented. Such emotion, then, has a value; it is a thing, as we have indicated earlier, which there is no reason to

fear,
Most worthy then of trust when most intense. (115—)

We have criticized emotion earlier, however, in its connection with violent activities. Such an emotion, according to Wordsworth, *would* need to be feared, as we may judge from his observations on his French Revolutionary experience. His statement is no prescription for impulsive action, though he has given stress to the value which emotion has for man. Feelings (as well as emotions) have their relations, however, to trust in life; they can operate beneficently, bringing a kind of vigor of activity into being whether in a scientist, a poet, or a person of any other vocation. But now we have to stress the fact, presented in Book Thirteen, that out of the foregoing— including a wise foresight and an adequate use of emotion—we may, according to Wordsworth, enjoy the boon of

> truth in moral judgments and delight
> That fails not in the external universe.   (118—)

What do we mean by such "moral judgments" as Wordsworth mentions here? In this case the Stoics may come to mind, with the contribution they have made concerning principles of right. It is evident that we cannot expect rightness of judgment to come without an effort. We have spoken in a previous chapter of Wordsworth's realization that the problem of judgment is no easy one. Whitehead also is concerned about this: he analyzes truth, for example, as related to judgment and to the relation that these factors have in connection with what he calls "judgment-feelings"[49]; thus he would seem to be bringing what Wordsworth calls emotion "which we need not fear" into relationship with judgment. Some emotions we need to fear.

A better and less abstract example, perhaps, may be given in Whitehead's very wide view in reference to the motives behind aspects of personal *growth* which could have judgmental value generally. For the moment, however, in the passage that we shall quote, he is thinking of growth in connection with the development of insights into science, including "judgments as to the beauty of the structure" of the matter under consideration, "or as to the duty of exploring the truth"; he adds a further factor, "the satisfaction of physical wants."[50] Appearing here, and basic to Whitehead's theory of reality, are (1) the requisite of "structure," (2) the requirement of seeking or "exploring the truth," and (3) the necessity of "satisfaction" meeting more mundane needs.

These three requisites (applied to science, but applicable also more generally) do not seem far afield from the "judgments" which Wordsworth values. The motives exemplified—through the aesthetic (which is of course also important to the poet), through "duty," and through basic satisfaction-needs—give a generally adequate coverage of the deepest human experience, presented by Whitehead under his conception of essential reality or what we would regard as the existential. He refers to this as being connected with judgments which are ontological and presupposed in the three types of acts which have been indicated. They concern existence.

The first of these—the aesthetic—may be illustrated by recalling to mind Wordsworth's climbing of Mount Snowden in the middle of the night, with the intention, after he should reach the top, of seeing the first rays of the sun coming over the remote horizon below. He speaks of this in *The Prelude* (at the beginning of Book Thirteen) as an example of one of his "excursions," and we might ask ourselves whether he was, by any chance, interested in essential reality of existence as related to these excursions insofar as they were connected with beauty. The sight from the mountaintop was evidently important to him.

The vision, if he reached the top of the mountain just as the first faint rays of light appeared, would be very different from the vision he might imagine he would see at the very same moment from the inn, far below in the midnight valley. Being in *another* geographical circumstance (at the top of the peak) he would have a feeling of overtaking time, and of sensing reality somewhat differently as the result of his movement, or journey, up the mountain. Reality seems a strange thing at times, as, for example, under the circumstances of jet travel, which in a very few hours can carry one through and past three or four time zones. The beauty of the world near dawn of day, similarly, seems strangely different under such differing geographical circumstances as occur at various stages in climbing a mountain. You may have a sense of having overtaken time or of time overtaking you. In any event, we know Wordsworth did not take his excursions lightly.

Whitehead's position as to the general topic concerning what basically exists may be made more definite, perhaps, by comparing it with the position of Bertrand Russell, who, after abandoning his youthful idealist philosophy (which had some affinities to Wordsworth's views at a certain stage), was preoccupied with the abstract matter of "relations" and a Platonic view about statements. We are told that at this early stage he was seeking "to establish the irreducibility of relations and a Platonic theory of propositions which would render them independent of mental activity."[51] His position is expressed here somewhat intricately (he personally approved the statement), but what it comes down to is that he was struggling to attain a fundamental theory of reality in its foundations so far as it seemed to him possible. He was at that stage perhaps less down-to-earth than Whitehead is in the foregoing explanation we have given of the triple motives (see the enumerative mention of them) related to a person's fundamental sense of existence. Both were influenced by Plato, however, in their efforts at analysis.

Returning to Whitehead's thought, and the triple motives, we may observe that, regardless of the many possible motives related to theory of reality which could underlie scientific activity (motives roughly covered under the three divisions he had indicated), "without judgments of value there could be no science." He is thinking mainly of the three divisions here, which we have noted earlier, and the problem of what he calls "moral judgments"; accordingly, he follows the words we have quoted with an idea that he regards as most important: he makes reference to "moral judgments" which he connects in his mind with his theory of reality or of the things which ultimately exist. As to the necessity of these ultimately existing "ontological judgments" Whitehead says, "They are in fact presupposed in every act of life: in our affections, in our self-restraints, and in our constructive efforts."[52] Though the reference by the philosopher here has been to scientists, the general theory concerning the items that we listed earlier, using the enumerative method, may be made to apply to artists and indeed to all men, and it certainly relates to Wordsworth in its triple application.

If we would connect Whitehead with Russell once again, we may observe the latter's concern about the nature of the existence of matter and his despair as to any way of indicating what it is. For Russell, "Idealism and materialism are too dogmatic in their interpretation of matter ..."[53] When Russell comes to deal with the mind (the other existence which he recognizes), he thinks of the self "which is aware of things in sensation and of universals in conception; and it is also that which believes and thinks and desires: in short, it is *con-sciousness.*" This is a rather elaborate way of thinking of mind in relation to the self, and including the equating of it with consciousness.

As far as Russell goes in these matters, however, he is close to Whitehead. This is the Russell of *The Problems of Philosophy* volume. He does not, however, touch with any degree of closeness Whitehead's philosophy of organism, some sense of which may be felt in certain previous paragraphs on interrelatedness and in many places earlier in this chapter. Whitehead's basic emphasis (as it contrasts with Russell's) may be seen by comparing with other aspects of his process philosophy his ideas in *The Aims of Education* from which we have quoted above. Russell tends to emphasize less the interconnectedness in all experience. He likes to take things apart analytically. Hence it is almost surprising to find that he is greatly concerned with the ontological wholeness or the ultimately existing nature of things. He is paradoxical. Russell is unendingly paradoxical.

All along in our present discussion we have intended to stress the importance of value, ethical or aesthetic—or indeed value more nearly ultimate. In one of Whitehead's works he has important references to judgments which "involve the ultimate notions of 'better' or 'worse.' "[54] These references bring us closer to Wordsworth than we have been in our thought about Russell. The judgments Whitehead refers to spring from our dynamic "internal activity" and give rise to "Valuation," which Whitehead explains as "one meaning of the term Judgment." Judgment, he goes on to say, is "a process of unification. It involves the necessary relevance of values to each other." We should stress the word *unification.*

Some of the insights Whitehead has concerning that which is moral are interconnected, as we might expect, with the sense of peace we have already presented as forming a part of his philosophy. For him philosophic peace is "a quality" of firmness which steadily relies on a conviction "that fine action is treasured in the nature of things."[55] It involves a "trust" in beauty as being capable of justifying itself in the long run when connected with action and goodness, including—as we have had occasion to quote before—a "faith where reason fails to reveal the details."

What concerns him is covered in a statement he makes elsewhere about "the real motive interests of the spirit"[56] in contrast to the motive which appears on the bare surface of things. Youth, though it is often shortsighted, is very responsive to beauty as it appears in conduct. And beauty in conduct has its relation to philosophic peace. This may be partially seen in that youth, as we have quoted earlier, "understands motives which presuppose the irrelevance of its own person."[57] In Whitehead's view mere general moral precepts are on a lower level than that of the ethical character (of the person); this we can see in the concept of "Peace" as he defines it. We can recall Martin Buber here. Nevertheless, according to Whitehead even moral precepts themselves "express the doctrine that the perfection of life resides in aims beyond the individual person in question."[58] Here a reader may find that the use of the word "perfecting" in place of "perfection" will fit more helpfully the conception that is being discussed.

But we often learn more from an example than through many words. And in this respect the poet Wordsworth is at times very effective. The case of Wordsworth's associate Beaupuy, as he is revealed in the middle of Chapter Nine of our book, will serve as an illustration of what may be brought to humanity through "aims beyond the individual person" and any private purposes such a person may have for his individual life. Here we have exemplified the moral view of Wordsworth, which is decidedly like that given expression by Whitehead. In a sense, the moral character (as a person) may be thought of as a true adventurer in life, but not as an adventurer having the quality of restless egotism. Both Wordsworth in *The Prelude* and Whitehead in *Adventures of Ideas* show calm benignity rather than egotism.

We all need what Wordsworth has called "truth in moral judgments"; there is a universalism in his approach which tends to share or to level itself morally with all men. The inclusiveness of Whitehead's approach appears on the page from which we last quoted when he cites as an example the case of Regulus, for whom the Roman Republic meant so much that he placed his life on the scale for it, thus transcending "his individual personality"; he "achieved magnificence," by his conduct, in a way that the world refuses to forget. "The Roman farmers agreed; and generation after generation, amid all the changes of history, have agreed by the instinctive pulse of emotion as the tale is handed down."[59] Regulus has become a symbol of the nobly regulated life. For Whitehead the moral codes of mankind do not in their generality carry the immense weight of such an action as is effected in the deed done by this basically simple man.

In the process of attaining an ethical character, more, as we realize, is necessary than the sounding of numerous shibboleths and precepts. Many inward qualities of character need to be developed, and among them the mental quality which we have seen Whitehead chooses to name "Peace"; here one moves beyond selfish love and "the narrow self-regarding motives."[60] It is in this connection that we would quote from Wordsworth's famous introspective passage beginning "Oh! who is he that hath his whole life long," to which we have made allusion earlier when we were presenting the topic of peace. In this *Prelude* passage the poet refers at first to an inner freedom which, he feels, comes as a consequence of the capacity to order our lives in accordance with the explicit and just "moral judgments"; upon these we have tried to make comment.

The freedom which is within the self is for Wordsworth, then, the only "genuine Liberty"; in agreement with this we may grant at once that to some extent we must preserve a profound liberty within the self despite the outer circumstances we encounter. But this self-satisfaction may be only that—a self-satisfaction merely or an illusion. External conditions must also exist which are not altogether illusory if we are to have "genuine Liberty"; and surely what Wordsworth in this expression has in mind is not merely illusoriness. For Whitehead, if we think of him in comparison with the poet, freedom involves creative ideas which we may have, and the opportunity as well as the trained capability of putting them into action.

The idea of freedom as "patent" is mentioned by Whitehead, and comment should be made here on this view. For Whitehead freedom is not a *patent* (as one might have a patent on a mechanical contrivance); in former days a member of a profession or an institution often had such a "freedom," or license, or "patent" to act in a certain way. In some colleges town and gown were isolated from each other so that students could behave unsocially or even illegally with complete immunity to the wishes of the town administrators. But this would be very far from constituting Whitehead's idea of freedom, nor would it cover Wordsworth's conception, though he, with other students, had enjoyed something of this feeling at Cambridge. Certain people would refer to this Cambridge feeling as an arrogant assumption of a patent on impudence.

The important point of Whitehead's doctrine is that freedom essentially involves socially constructive and personally constructive ideas which one strives to put into action. The seeming intricacies of Whitehead's view might cause one to prefer an idea of "freedom" which contains a greater element of license. But a different attitude may arise if his view of purpose is considered. License or "patent" is far from this.

Prior to the discussion of our present topic—freedom—we spoke of purpose in its connection with foresight. In Whitehead it is so connected. But now, when we think of freedom, purpose deserves renewed consideration. Purpose is central to Wordsworth's famous introspective passage beginning "Oh! who is he . . ." Wordsworth in this passage is thinking of the type of person who has the right amount of freedom, and this is a matter of measure. We may think here of Aristotle's view of a character trait possessing balance. The idea in Wordsworth is brought out in a kind of self-analysis, though for our purposes we may regard the introspective as subordinate to the presentation of the philosophy. His point as he thinks, "Oh! who is he," is that such a person as he refers to in Book Thirteen does not "tamper" with himself from the point of view of an exclusively self-aimed purpose, nor is he, at least in any of his hopes,

> the dupe
> Of selfish passions . . . (133—)

The question has been raised—Who is such a man as we have described? And the answer is that a human being of this sort can be found, and can carry out a life appropriate to such an ideal. Throughout history, we know, there have been many leaders of thought (Socrates, for example) who have striven to make progress in this direction. The fact of purpose, which is here evident and which is essential to Wordsworth's and to Socrates's point of emphasis, is in itself a mysterious thing, and the sense of it we may take to be referred to by the poet as coming in "visitations" which at an early age he did not fully appreciate for what they were. He cannot here deny that he had been "careless" of the boon that was "given" to him. Now, with the hope of following up these "visitations," he speaks of something which will require meditative consideration. And "suffering," too, which comes to man, is necessarily involved. Purpose itself is something of a mystery, as is personality. Our reference to the mystery of purpose applies to the higher levels of human activity, but for Whitehead it is a part of all life.

What we have presented here has been an outgrowth of our references to inner freedom, a freedom which is attained largely by the rejection of self-regarding means. Wordsworth in effect has been suggesting, in his famous introspective passage, that he had made what amounted to a conscious effort in the direction of sterilizing his prejudices, as we today would express it. What he did in Book Thirteen was to make an attack on the limited vision accompanying the sense-oriented approach to life and to shrink from

> every combination that might aid
> The tendency, too potent in itself,
> Of habit to enslave the mind . . . (137—)

We have considered in this chapter the fact that Wordsworth refers—though somewhat rapidly—to a number of topics such as faith, the discursive, the intuitive, sovereignty within, peace at will, emotion which may be such that it need not be feared, foresight, and truth in moral judgments. Without question, as he mentions these things in Book Thirteen, he considers each of them important, and this has been evident in our discussion. It has also become evident that many of the topics are, for him, interrelated. Virtually all of these topics appear importantly in Whitehead, and are for him also interrelated. One might almost imagine that he had read the references to them in Wordsworth, and, having pondered them—whether he recalled the fact that they are all in Wordsworth or not—decided to write about them in his own way as the occasion arose. Such a surmise cannot be proved, and, even if it were true, it would not detract in any degree from Whitehead's original creativeness as a thinker. It would only indicate once more his wisdom in using a stimulus wherever he might find it.

We closed our main discussion in this chapter upon the note of Wordsworth's reference to the tendency which "habit" has "to enslave the mind"; on this thought we shall open the next chapter, and proceed to a further discussion of a number of additional topics of *The Prelude*, Book Thirteen, which are vital to the poet, among them the matter of self-identity treated once again, the place of sense-experience in the world, the conception of the divine, and the place of love in a carefully meditated philosophy. All of these topics, and others to be dealt with, have a place of importance not only in *The Prelude* but in the intricately interconnected meditations of the profound philosopher we have been considering.

Notes

[1] *Adventures of Ideas*, p. 354.

[2] *Modes of Thought*, p. 168.

[3] *Adventures of Ideas*, p. 236. We may feel the author's sense of the importance of this high abstraction in that it appears in a short sentence constituting one complete emphatic paragraph.

[4] *Ibid.*, p. 256.

[5] *Ibid.*, p. 354.

[6] *Modes of Thought*, p. 142. The lure of the ideal is mentioned on p. 139.

[7] *Adventures of Ideas*, p. 355. The double reference to life and motion is important here.

[8] *Modes of Thought*, p. 223.

[9] *Ibid.*, p. 227.

[10] *Ibid.*, p. 229.

[11] *Ibid.*, p. 112.

[12] *Ibid.*, p. 113.

[13]*Adventures of Ideas*, p. 354.

[14]*Process and Reality*, p. 145.

[15]Quoted in Michael Novak, *Belief and Unbelief* (New York: Macmillan, 1965), p. 12.

[16]*Modes of Thought*, p. 68. Wordsworth's reference to the "intuitive" is in the 1805 *Prelude*, Book Thirteen, 1. 113. In quoting we have added a comma after *fear* in 1. 114; see the latter part of this chapter.

[17]*Symbolism*, p. 33.

[18]*Ibid.*, p. 39.

[19]*Ibid.*, p. 45.

[20]*Process and Reality*, p. 215.

[21]*Ibid.*, p. 216. Whitehead, it is to be also noted, associates Locke's "simple ideas" of sensation with "Santayana's 'intuitions of essences.' "

[22]*Dialogues of . . . Whitehead*, p. 266.

[23]*Ibid.*, p. 194.

[24]*Adventures of Ideas*, p. 371.

[25]*Ibid.*, p. 368.

[26]*Modes of Thought*, p. 90.

[27]*Ibid.*, p. 91.

[28]*Ibid.*, p. 138.

[29]*Dialogues of . . . Whitehead*, p. 307.

[30]*Adventures of Ideas*, p. 373. Here we may recall Martin Buber, referred to near the end of our Chapter Twelve in footnote 77.

[31]*Ibid.*, p. 137.

[32] *Process and Reality*, p. 78. See also pp. 406-412 on "Higher Phases of Experience."

[33] Whitehead, "The First Physical Synthesis," in *Science and Civilization*, ed. F.S. Marvin (Oxford, 1923), p. 162.

[34] *Adventures of Ideas*, p. 368.

[35] *Ibid.*, p. 377.

[36] *Ibid.*, p. 367. He also includes in Harmony the quality of adventure.

[37] *Modes of Thought*, p. 73.

[38] *Adventures of Ideas*, p. 366.

[39] *Ibid.*, p. 367.

[40] *Ibid.*, p. 368.

[41] *Ibid.*, p. 369.

[42] *Ibid.*, p. 377.

[43] *Ibid.*, p. 377.

[44] *The Function of Reason* (Boston: Beacon Press, 1958), p. 13. Whitehead has a whole chapter on "Foresight" in *Adventures of Ideas*.

[45] *Modes of Thought*, p. 108. Transcendence is also strongly emphasized, p. 109.

[46] *Adventures of Ideas*, p. 137. This point with regard to reason has been emphasized earlier in the discussion of the topic of *faith*.

[47] *Ibid.*, p. 251.

[48] *Modes of Thought*, p. 142.

[49] *Process and Reality*, p. 396.

[50] *Aims of Education*, p. 229. Compare this and what we say later with

Kant's threefold factors: aesthetics, ethics, and logic—or, put differently, feeling, willing, and knowing. Note also the relation of abstract principles of right to Stoicism in *Science and the Modern World*, pp. 16-17, and *Adventures of Ideas*, pp. 16-17.

[51]Morris Weitz on "Analysis as Ontology" as practiced by Russell, in *The Philosophy of Bertrand Russell*, 4th ed., ed. Paul Arthur Schilpp (LaSalle, Illinois; Open Court, 1971), p. 59. The title of Weitz's article is "Analysis and the Unity of Russell's Philosophy."

[52]*Aims of Education*, p. 229.

[53]*The Philosophy of Bertrand Russell*, p. 63. The words quoted are by Morris Weitz. It would be tempting to go into Russell's later neutral monism here.

[54]*Essays in Science and Philosophy*, p. 62. Note the word *ultimate*.

[55]*Adventures of Ideas*, p. 353.

[56]*Ibid.*, p. 368.

[57]*Ibid.*, p. 371.

[58]*Ibid.*, p. 373.

[59]*Ibid.*, p. 374.

[60]*Ibid.*, p. 371.

Chapter Fifteen

Later Topics in the 1805 "Prelude" Connected with Whitehead

Near the end of the last chapter we spoke of Wordsworth's concern about the "tendency" of "habit" whereby it brings about an enslavement of the mind. The tendency of habit "to enslave" a person—if genuine enslavement occurs—gives rise to a change within the self or what amounts to an injury to the self: this we could fairly call a disintegration (or at least partial destruction) of such personal identity as one might have. The whole *Prelude* is of course an effort to put together what is involved in the attainment of the self, and this necessarily includes many difficult factors. The underlying purpose of the poem all along includes the problem of development and self-creation.

Whitehead's conception of the self presents a parallel to this in that he stresses the importance of self-creation. This is a continuing problem also in Book Thirteen of *The Prelude*, the discussion of which we wish now to carry forward. What we find in both Wordsworth and Whitehead is a conception of the self as living and creative as opposed to one that is completely determined and noninitiating. Basic in this view is a conviction of the functioning in our lives of a mode of perception which at given times is not sensuous; such a perception, as Whitehead believes, is one aspect of the "continuity of nature."[1] This is part of the problem of the relation of the subject, or self, to the object which is perceived. These two should not be branched or separated into distinct divisions.

Whitehead, in the whole discussion of this matter, fears that his point of view may seem a part of an unfortunate revolt against dualism, and he later explains that he has "endeavored to put forward a defence of dualism, differently interpreted."[2] We all believe in dualities of various kinds. But the danger is that aspects of our view of life may be unfortunately split. Whitehead approaches the matter psychologically. Dualisms such as are to be found "in the later Platonic dialogues," as well as in Descartes (for example, in "the Cartesian 'thinking substances' and the Cartesian 'extended substances' "), need to be somewhat modified. He seeks greater integration—less of a biforked tendency. It is not our purpose here to trace such matters as seen in the history of thought, but Whitehead himself mentions them, and he gives Locke as another example of the tendency he is referring to (involving bifurcation), which Whitehead feels needs to be modified in the interests of a more organic theory. The excellent tendencies toward a dualism of a kind are to be found— as modified organically—if we look, Whitehead says, "within each occasion of actuality." We are led toward a philosophy of organism then by life itself, if we keep our attention upon the dynamic actual.

What Whitehead wants to avoid is an unreal dualism which would take abstraction for an *ultimate* actuality. He has at times been called a pluralist, and this fact may help one to see that his answer to the difficult problem of dualism represents a resolution of the matters we have mentioned through the fact that "the universe is *many* because it is wholly and completely to be analyzed into many final actualities"[3]; in the sentence following, he explains that the oneness of the totality is the result of the "universal immanence." The dualism in Whitehead, then, appears in what he calls "this contrast between the unity and multiplicity." Here he is attempting to face the problem of uniformity and variety, that of the one and the many in the world. A humble illustration of it is that the individual is one person but he encounters a world of many troublesome actualities that need to be coped with. And to some extent the individual succeeds in bringing things together, or he could not live from the psychological viewpoint. Wordsworth, like Whitehead, is consciously interested in this developmental task which everyone should attack with some definiteness in order to clarify the elements that the person is bringing together. *The Prelude*, as we have said, represents Wordsworth's development.

There is an important difficulty (which Whitehead later takes account of) in relation to the immanence of the future in the present. The future, as he considers it, is part of our present existence. "The difficulty," he says, "lies in the explanation of this immanence in terms of the subject-object structure of experience."[4] Whitehead's treatment of the problem in *Adventures of Ideas* is not simple, but the important thing for our purpose is that the future is part of the very essence of what is here now; it "belongs" to the present, as he says later in the volume.[5] We, as persons, are thus projected forward into futurity. Moreover, this is a part of our independence as selves. Even two occasions of experience have "vast causal independence" and these occasions are "preservative of the elbow-room within the Universe." This quality is also part of our own independence and our personal "self-consciousness." What we refer to here is our consciousness of the self, even though there *is* danger in an undue self-concern. "Our claim for freedom is rooted in our relationship to our contemporary environment."

For Whitehead we are in nature and we are also a part of nature, but through it we are given "a field for independent activities." We need to learn adequately, in this sense, an "understanding of the Universe," and such understanding may be attained through recognizing the relationships of aspects of immediate causation as well as sensing designs for the future and becoming aware of the fact that we enjoy a considerable degree of "contemporary independence." In the sentence following that from which we have already made quotations of certain expressions, he goes on to say, "This adequate conception requires also understanding of perspective elimination, and of types of order dominating vast epochs, and of minor endurances with their own additional modes of order diversifying each larger epoch within which they find themselves."[6]

Our personal or individual structure, then, constitutes a wholeness, though it is part of the totality of nature. This wholeness of the self, this personal unity, is important; it is a part, we will say again, of a total unity, and here we must go back to Whitehead's earlier discussion of this unity. In that presentation he indicates the total unity in summary by using "such terms as 'personal unity,' 'events,' 'experience,' and 'personal identity' "[7] in place of certain related terms that Plato uses. Our personal identity, as Whitehead says, "is a perplexed and obscure concept," and in trying to explain his point about the self he adapts a passage from Plato's *Timaeus*; from Whitehead's adaptation we have quoted for our purposes certain fragments. Our own inner selfhood, or any outside person's inner selfhood, is not easy to understand, although by an act of simplification we make an attempt at understanding it.

The obscurity of the conception of the self also runs through the efforts that Wordsworth makes in *The Prelude* to understand his own self-identity. It is such efforts to reach an understanding of his own selfhood that cause the poet to reflect that, although he was at times guilty of committing wrongs, he at any rate, in doing such acts, did not "tamper" with his more profound being. So he tells us in the famous introspective passage to which we made allusion in the middle of the previous chapter. He had not allowed grosser aims of the "self" to take such things in charge willfully (Wordsworth's expression of the idea is somewhat old-fashioned), nor had he permitted habit to make him its slave. In a word, he had continually made an effort to give "the mind" due respect. He has some embarrassment, and hence difficulty, it would seem, in discussing this subject. What he means to suggest in Book Thirteen is that he did not at any time oppress the mind

> by the laws of vulgar sense,
> And substitute a universe of death,
> The falsest of all worlds, in place of that
> Which is . . . true.   (140—)

It is hard to doubt that Wordsworth has made a sincere effort toward idealism in the popular sense, as this portion of his introspective passage indicates. There is always a danger, he feels, that the mind may become a victim of "the laws of vulgar sense," which are oppressive in their effect upon the deeper self. Is there a parallel between his statement here concerning the dangers of "sense" (with an attendant "universe of death") and the views of Whitehead?

Just as Wordsworth is directing a criticism against an overemphasis upon the interpretation of the world on the basis of the sensory, so we find Whitehead objecting to the sense doctrine which has been very commonly present in the twentieth century and earlier. For him the emphatically directed sense approach is deficient in that it results in a kind of nonharmony in one's structure of the world, and it is also destructive of the development of individual and creative selves. We are interpreting Whitehead to a certain extent here, but the interpretation is close to his views when, along with a statement about individuality, he says that "in recent times, with the predominance of the sensationalist doctrine of perception, modern views of the Harmony characterizing a great experience have reached their lowest point."[8] He was making this judgment in 1932, during the Depression, when what he regards as hopes for greatness were not high.

According to Whitehead the trouble in general is that the sensationalist doctrine leads to a tendency toward "experience comparatively barren of objects of high significance."[9] Thinking of this barrenness he says, "The complex to which the term Harmony is applicable is conceived as a mere spatio-temporal pattern of sensa." Such limited spatio-temporal patterns of sensation can in part produce a seemingly complex experience which in a fashion could be called a "Harmony," but only one of a "debased" type, lacking in valuable elements of "intention." The experience of such a pseudo-harmony can excite us only "by a sense of strangeness." This occurs when we are relatively fortunate. "At the worst, it fades into insignificance." Today we may feel that there are many cases of such insignificance in our lives, represented, for example, in the stories of suburbia.

We come now to a consideration of what Wordsworth says when in Book Thirteen of *The Prelude* he brings out, in contrast to the idea of "a universe of death," the conception of a universe which is "true." Near the center of the passage of several lines which we last quoted from Wordsworth we see him referring to the danger to our thought when we find that in effect we are substituting "a universe of death" in place of a universe which is "true." In the idea of a "true" universe he has in mind a universe in our consciousness which is made up, not of a dead nature, but of a nature which is alive. Likewise we find in Whitehead that in many of his volumes the prime purpose he has in mind is to replace a universe of death by a universe of life. He says, for example, "a dead nature can give no reasons." And a moment later he adds, "A dead nature aims at nothing."[10] In this statement he is thinking of value and its aims. From his point of view life and movement should substitute for the static form, and this substitution gives rise to active process.

Whitehead emphasizes our liveness doubly in one short passage: "We can shut our eyes, or be permanently blind. None-the-less we are alive. We can be deaf. And yet we are alive."[11] There is a gladness, almost an exulting in his voice which the reader may feel here in the passage, as there was in his living voice. Elsewhere, when he speaks of science, his major interest is to save it by giving it life. The contributions of Newton and Hume, though they have basic use in a limited scientific reference, are in a larger view "gravely defective."[12] They have value, but "they omit those aspects of the Universe as experienced, and of our modes of experiencing, which jointly lead to the more penetrating ways of understanding."

Applying his thought to the situation in our country in 1932 (when thinking, again, of the Depression), he says, "The Hume-Newton modes of thought can only discern a complex transition of sensa, and an entangled locomotion of molecules, while the deepest intuition of the whole world discerns the President of the United States inaugurating a new chapter in the history of mankind." It is a whole living world that needs to be considered, Whitehead feels, including, as he implies, the life of the people. Throughout the chapter in which this thought is presented he is moving from what he calls "Nature Lifeless" toward a new chapter in his book, a chapter entitled "Nature Alive."

In another volume the thing that he is greatly troubled by, as he explains it, is a "mechanism of matter" which is a "monstrous" issue of "limited metaphysics and clear logical intellect."[13] This monstrosity is what he refers to in indicating that a "work of clearance" needs to be done—in our terms what might be called a kind of bulldozing action. The monstrosity of materialism was manifested most fully, he indicates, in the eighteenth century.

A few passages later than the passage which we have quoted,

Whitehead relates Wordsworth by way of contrast to this developing "scientific materialism." Its first "triumph" had occurred in the period prior to that of the poet, and Whitehead explains that "Wordsworth in his whole being expresses a conscious reaction against the mentality of the eighteenth century."[14] The reaction by Wordsworth was, in the view of the philosopher, a "moral repulsion." A moment later Whitehead adds that Wordsworth "felt that something had been left out, and that what had been left out comprised everything that was most important."

Does Whitehead feel that the poet's reaction of moral distaste was nonintellectual? It might seem so to some readers, but it would be difficult to conceive a truly moral reaction—especially in Wordsworth—which had no element of the reflective mind within it. The tribute to Wordsworth given by Whitehead covers broadly the objection that both men felt toward a mechanistic interpretation of life. Whitehead's opposition to the mechanism of matter may be seen in greater depth if we consider an atomic theory which he later mentions—that of John Dalton, who was born four years before Wordsworth's birth. This advanced atomic theory, which Whitehead has in mind, was introduced in the same period as the "living cell" doctrine.[15] But "nearly half a century after Dalton had done his work," the *fruits* of the living cell conception appeared more fully in the work of "another chemist," Pasteur, and this later work, Whitehead feels, is very helpful to us in understanding the significance of an opposition to a mechanical interpretation of existence. That is, the pronouncedly living aspects recognizable in Dalton's period were "carried over" more clearly to the later time.

As Whitehead develops his own view, he explains that "the cell theory and Pasteur's work were in some respects more revolutionary than that of Dalton." Certainly, by common consent Dalton's contribution has been considered supremely significant in its time, but what Pasteur later "showed" was "the decisive importance of the idea of organism at the stage of infinitesimal magnitude."[16] This infinitesimal may be interestingly compared with what the astronomers had lately shown as to the new and increasing immensity of the interstellar universe. We have here a suggestion, like the idea of the microcosm as opposed to the macrocosm.

Wordsworth's thought was in process of moving in a profoundly important direction, as Whitehead himself realizes in the tribute he pays to the poet. But we have not sufficiently covered the character of the developments which we have been considering. For Whitehead, life and activity have a place, not merely in the history contrasted with the school of Dalton. They form a part of the Platonic notions which Whitehead had found so profitable to his theories, even in the case of Plato's "Mathematical Relations" that we referred to near the beginning of the previous chapter. As to Whitehead's life and activity doctrine, in its relation to mathematics, Leibniz is a foreshadower of later developments. He may serve as an example of a figure who is important to the evolution of the theory of form as process.

What we should probably think of here is not form (in the singular) but forms in process, in that the idea Whitehead sees through the approach of Leibniz is curiously reminiscent of a tendency toward an appreciation of the use of a slightly complex curve (which one could draw on a blackboard) as a representation of the form which is expressed in a given equation. This reference to a slightly complex curve may seem to some persons an understatement, but curves such as we refer to could be somewhat complex or very greatly complex, depending upon what is represented by them. The challenge to the mind of any forms which approach infinity (or as a counterpart may approach the infinitesimal) does have an important place in the thought of Leibniz, as well as in that of Whitehead. Many examples of this could be given. But here we are thinking only of the fact that an equation may be thought of as having form, and that we may think of a variety of related equations as representing forms of various kinds. The fact that these can be related, one to another, may seem somewhat technical, but it is suggestive of certain aspects of what the philosophy of organism is working toward.

The significant point that Whitehead has in mind is that a curve (which we can imagine as drawn on a blackboard) is in one sense a "static form," though it nevertheless expresses an "active process." Similarly there is the active process in history which Whitehead compares to this. "There is an analogous difficulty," as he says, "in relating the static immediacy of fact to the historic process with its past and its future."[17] But the general historical problem has to be faced in spite of its complexity, and it is helpful to see it symbolized in order to understand better the activity, or process, in the new many-sided world which is confronting us even today.

All along we have been dealing through history and in other ways with the conception of a "universe of life" or activity in contrast to "a universe of death," which Wordsworth felt was the "falsest of all worlds"; the universe of life (which Whitehead refers to in the words "nature alive") may be seen further by extending somewhat the notion of the curve—which, we said, could be drawn on a blackboard—as it is related to active process. Whitehead in many of his works criticizes the static Newtonian cosmology. One example of his criticism appears in his objection to "a bit of matter occupying" a particular "region" at a "durationless instant."[18] We will, however, center upon his criticism more simply. "Velocity and momentum," he says, "require the concept that the state of things at other times and other places enter into the essential character of the material occupancy of space at any selected instant."[19] The Newtonian conception does not meet this test, and it is therefore "inconsistent."[20] This problem can be somewhat clarified further by relating it to the concept of function in the sense we have previously indicated: that is, with reference to the idea that Wordsworth's change from a state of misery to one of happiness was a function of the increasing clarification in his mind of certain philosophical matters.

Our statement concerning the poet here is given not for its own sake but in order to make somewhat clearer a point about Whitehead's thought. The assertion as to the increase in Wordsworth's happiness is not altogether correct because his change of state (in leaving behind his condition of misery) was not, of course, in an exactly correlative or precisely functional relation to his increasingly great insight into philosophical problems. But this *actual* fact is not to our present purpose. Our point is related to the idea that Whitehead had been giving thought to "a bit of matter" as being placed in a certain spot statically. The static view of matter seems to him impossible. Matter cannot, then, be thought of as occupying a particular space at a durationless instant. His opposition to this idea, as we have in part explained, is that, with such a belief, velocity would make it necessary for "the state of things at other times and other places" to become a part of the fundamental nature of the physical existence in a specific spot "at any selected instant."[21]

Newton's view, we have said, cannot meet what Whitehead requires. The problem will be seen best, perhaps, if we note that this material occupancy of space is analogous to or "corresponds to the value" of an endlessly changing mathematical function, or correlation, but merely has this effect "at a selected point."[22] This occupancy of space makes no allowance for activity; it depends entirely upon "the limit" of the mathematical operation at one static moment. Process is absent in this view and, with the absence of process, life is necessarily absent. Whitehead is unable to proceed in his philosophy except by abandoning the Newtonian view and by introducing "the concept of Life"[23]; this he does in the chapter which immediately follows the pages from which we have drawn his statement. Here and in the foregoing we have had to devote attention to concepts that involve a certain amount of abstraction.

But central in Wordsworth and also in Whitehead (as we look beyond the abstractions) is the matter of aliveness. The passage of several lines which we last quoted from *The Prelude* was not given in full, we can now say, because we wished to place emphatic attention upon what Wordsworth regarded as a false philosophy. Now, providing a slightly different emphasis, we shall point up the fact that the quotation, as we will indicate a part of it again from Book Thirteen, concerned criticism of the substitution of a lifeless universe,

> The falsest of all worlds, in place of that
> Which is divine and true.   (141—)

Here for the purpose of our discussion the key word which the poet employs is "divine" as applied to the universe, though it is a term which would be rejected as quite out of consideration by those who accept a mechanical interpretation of life. Whitehead, like Wordsworth, finds a place for the expression of the divine, as we may see in his remark that Plato "proclaimed that the divine persuasion is the foundation of the world"[24] despite the difficulty that has been in the world because of the presence of "brute forces" which limit the action of the divine force. We find Whitehead on the next page again declaring that "the divine persuasion" continues to hold "its old power," and indeed "even more than its old power, over the minds and the consciences of men." As an example of this he cites the response of the whole world to one of the actions by Gandhi in cooperation with other people. So far as Whitehead's own thought is concerned, he feels one can select from "intimate human experience" and from "general history" certain basic factors "to exemplify that ultimate theme of the divine immanence, as a completion required by our cosmological outlook." What he is referring to here is his own view, which involves the rejection of a static condition of affairs anywhere in the universe.

Whitehead's purpose in his discussion of "the divine" here is to call for a new reformation in religion which he thinks could be accomplished among human beings if a harmonizing "metaphysical theory" could be provided. This new reformation could become a real possibility even though people would necessarily have to disagree "in various explanatory formulations." As he continues his discussion he refers to "the divine" in various contexts, revealing its immense importance to him.

Whitehead relates this element of his philosophy to intellectual work that has been done upon Hebrew or Old Testament backgrounds and upon Augustine. He is very wide in his religious sympathies, including in them "Wycliffe and Huss, Luther and Calvin . . . John Wesley, Erasmus . . . the Socinians, George Fox," and other figures.[25] For him the divine element is not an arbitrary dogmatic power but a "persuasive" action in the universe.[26] This idea of the "persuasive" is related to a comparable view in Plato which is in opposition to the tendency to treat honorifically "a coercive agency."

Far more than need be, mankind has taken recourse in the coercive; as civilization advances such a factor can become less prominent than it has been. Here orthodoxy is called into question, but Whitehead's opposition to it elsewhere goes beyond an implied criticism of prominent religious views to an attack, also, on "scientific orthodoxy undisturbed by much thought beyond the conventions."[27] Such an orthodoxy in science can also be exceedingly misleading.

At this point, as we consider the action of coercive forces—and the necessity of replacing them by something that is more nearly benign—we find arising the difficult problem of whether the single individual person or entity can be thought of as really existing as set against, or in opposition to, a plurality of individual persons or entities; the main difficulty is centered in the question of the static unity of all things, which Newtonianism and certain other doctrines would require. In regard to the matter Whitehead draws again upon Plato for inspiration (while recognizing that this inspiration cannot be followed unreservedly); he indicates his own view, adapted to modern times, as a solution exhibiting the plurality of individuals as consistent with the unity of the Universe, and furthermore as "a solution which exhibits the World as requiring its union with God, and God as requiring his union with the World."[28]

So much, then, for the parallel in Whitehead to the view in Wordsworth as to the element of the divine which both men strongly feel that the universe contains. Our last quotation from Wordsworth, as we saw, ended with the word "true." What can we say about the conception of a universe which, as humanly conceived, can be regarded (in Wordsworth's sense) as true? Here we are dealing with a very large and general observation on the part of the poet—including as it does a generality which presents the kind of difficulty that is characteristic of most of the major problems of philosophy.

The very large use of the term "true" which appears in Wordsworth occurs also in Whitehead. As Whitehead thinks of this word "true," however, he ordinarily begins with a restricted approach rather than a universal one. In a certain passage, for example, he considers whether an idea is in accordance or not in accordance with the actual state of things. He is concerned initially with our experience in the midst of so-called actualities, and in a sense he is contemplating the relativity of our truths.

But relativity in his thought is a two-sided conception. It is connected with the need for an interrelation of persons (in contrast with an isolated individualism); he is concerned, further, with our connectedness with ideas which do not play us false, as would a pseudo-friend who is not "true" in the sense of the faithfulness of Bunyan's character Faithful. We can count on these true ideas.

Such a view may be understood best if we recall the principle of loyalty as applied by Royce to the stress in our lives which we *should* give even to our philosophy. One should be generally faithful, or loyal, to one's philosophy unless something is lacking in the philosophical perspective. The problem of the "true" presents various complexities, both in thought and in action. It concerns, for example, the way Newton saw things (at times grossly, according to Whitehead), but the fact that Newton saw certain things inaccurately (untruly) also helped him to see more clearly other very important things that he needed to focus upon. Had this not been the case "the world might still be waiting for the Law of Gravitation."[29] Thus the problem is complex in unexpected ways. More nearly final truth would have caused Newton to see less truly certain striking factors.

Thinking of this, it is well to consider that the thing that is "true" in one sense may be unsuitable for what is required at a given epoch in history, or at some moment of experience. As to the latter—*personal* experience—a photograph taken by a private investigator could be a true photograph, we may feel, but it might give rise to a false appearance within the mind of someone who interprets its configuration. Again, one may consider extremists unintelligent, but is it well to barnstorm about the country making speeches to emphasize such a conception? Will the truth be best served by such an action? Whitehead does not give this example, but it is illustrative of his theory. Still, for Wordsworth, the Newtonian concept of the universe is simply not true if we are to think of things in a large perspective.

We have explained that Wordsworth is concerned (in the passage we quoted) with a very large and general conception about a universe which, as humanly conceived, may be regarded as true. A similar large and general conception appears in Whitehead when, in referring to "the truth-relation between the Appearance and the Reality," he tells us that there is "the truth-relation between the Appearance and the Reality . . . of the Essence of God."[30] In the context he refers to "National Relations" and to war. Is the conception here so large that it would be impossible for man to deal with it? Whitehead does not think so. As to Wordsworth's large and general use of the word "true," we can see that the poet is thinking less of the uncertainty of our knowledge than of that which he believes is divine within human beings, including fortunate and profound insights that we may at times have.

Is truth sometimes close to evil? In a chapter entitled "Truth and Beauty" Whitehead contends that a truth-relation at times "may be evil."[31] Is this kind of thought in Whitehead difficult to reconcile with the views that are most characteristic of Wordsworth? The poet does realize that the world contains discordant occurrences. The fact of the discordance may be helpful to an understanding of the idea that a truth-relation may be evil, because in the context we have referred to Whitehead discerns discord as an evident factor in experience. In connection with the modes of "Beauty," for example, he says, "Some admixture of Discord is a necessary factor in the transition from mode to mode." Discord is at times connected with the true. Discord even has its advantages, as for example sometimes in music as well as in thought. It "may take the form of freshness," and it has other merits; for example, it may appear even as hope. On the other hand, it may take the shape of "horror or pain." The whole problem of the true is for Whitehead an involuted one involving multiple discords. But nothing we have said concerning his conception of the matter is inconsistent with Wordsworth's basic view of things.

Another of Whitehead's contexts which might at first seem somewhat remote from Wordsworth's reference to the true concerns truth as "a discovery and not a recapitulation."[32] Whitehead is thinking again, for the moment, of truth in its relation to beauty, an area which should have great importance in connection with the art of poetry. But Wordsworth also sees the importance of discovery. His penetration into the lives of unusual characters illustrates this. He wishes to see them truly. He suffered calumnies because of his poetical interest in characters ordinarily regarded as humble or even "low" in a most extreme sense. Close to the conclusion of the chapter in which Whitehead refers to the importance of truth and beauty, he speaks of a "function" of art "in human experience when it reveals as in a flash intimate, absolute Truth regarding the Nature of Things."[33] This again definitely represents a very wide view.

Discovery, in addition to being a factor in truth and beauty, is related to what Whitehead calls "Adventure," and in a later chapter than that on "Truth and Beauty" he suggests, with reference to "Adventure," not only that we cannot have a static perfection, because of the very nature of process, but that—and here he says he is indicating an important metaphysical principle—"every occasion of actuality is in its own nature finite. There is no totality which is the harmony of all perfections."[34] He is referring here to the limitation of natural human life.

Truth and "Adventure" have a connection here. If we bring one thing to realization, this fact of the realized actuality "necessarily excludes the unbounded welter of contrary possibilities." The welter will not lead one to truth. The human adventurer must get out of the welter. We must not be deluded by the yearning for any inoperative "might have been"; here we are quoting Whitehead's words. We are surrounded by finiteness, and some things—for example, in art or in politics—simply cannot be brought to realization jointly. This is the nature of the world. Evil arises when (even though we are seeking an ideal) we find ourselves attempting to accomplish something that is simply not compatible with what is aimed at by another group of people of good will. This point with reference to the philosophy of incompatibility is important even in regard to the "divine nature."[35] We have to recognize that "a process" is necessary to "God's nature, whereby his infinity is acquiring realization."

This latter idea is aptly developed in the chapter entitled "Adventure"; in it we see that, for the philosopher, there are cosmic or metaphysical reaches to the experience of that which is truly adventurous. Later, in the final chapter of the volume from which we have been quoting, he relates the "attainment" of what he calls "Truth" to the quality of a profound "Peace."[36] The accomplishment whereby we may reach Peace involves his modification or adaptation of the principle of "that Harmony whose interconnections involve Truth." And he explains emphatically in the page from which we have quoted that he is not thinking of truth with reference to the assertions that appear in propositions.

Correctness or falsity in a propositional formulation is "not directly to the point" for Whitehead's purposes in dealing with various large conceptions. This deserves re-emphasis. The idea would seem to apply also to Wordsworth's conceptions concerning a universe which is to be regarded as true, so far as man in his finite limitations can try to perceive it. Propositions, Whitehead says, are related to the conflicts of contradictoriness and to "bare" or naked statements. We see this strikingly in dogmatic thinking, which proceeds from sweeping generalizations and arrives through a continued emphasis upon deduction at ever narrowing and restricting conclusions. Whitehead's distinction regarding propositional thinking has been brought out earlier—for example, in previous chapters in which we touched upon the "discursive" operation of the reason—but the point is so central in Whitehead's philosophy that it has needed special emphasis. Propositions are related to the conflicts of contradictoriness and to "bare" or naked statements. Whitehead's wish is to avoid the "superficial factor"; what he is concerned with as he speaks of the factor which is superficial touches upon "essential truth" such as "Peace demands," which, as we have implied, is related more ultimately, in a metaphysical way, to his philosophy.

In all this Whitehead has a largeness and generality that would fit in with Wordsworth's statement about the conception of a true world-view which he held in contrast to the one he regarded as false. But neither Whitehead nor Wordsworth would present categorically such ideas as to truth. Their approach is investigative and speculative. In the passage from the poet to which we have been referring he doubtless means that the conception of the live world he has in mind is more true than its alternative, which is machine-like. The alternative, if held, would play one false, to use an illustration given earlier, as would a friend who is not true. We think of *true* here in the sense of being profoundly faithful. It is hard to doubt that Wordsworth would understand the substance of Whitehead's philosophy touching upon the uncertainty of man's ideas concerning the truth.

We have taken note of the fact that our last quotation—of two lines from *The Prelude*—ended with a reference to the "true"; thereafter Wordsworth confronts us with the difficult problem of "fear," which it seems he wishes to resolve. Apparently he has thought of fear as important to one's belief in a philosophy of spirit (as contrasted with a death-philosophy), but he quickly follows up the fear-reference by emphasizing the importance of love. We may judge that fear, initially to Wordsworth, is a necessary part of man's condition; after all, it is only natural to experience this emotion under special circumstances. But fear in general, he seems to feel, is the result or lack of or *absence* of love. It is resolved, according to *The Prelude*, when we learn that love is "first and chief" because "there fear ends"; it may be difficult to grant acceptance to this. Can we say, after careful reflection, that fear can be cancelled out by love? Further understanding of his thought may be found in a consideration of fear as it is related to pain, which we see in his statement about the polar

> principles of pain and joy,
> Evil as one is rashly named by those
> Who know not what they say.   (147—)

Pain has its necessary place in life, many philosophers have been prone to say—especially those who are interested in religion. And certainly the terrible fact of the existence of pain, sometimes in acute form, must be recognized as heartrending so long as the problem remains unresolved. Indeed, we are all inclined to identify with ultimate evil our many pains and disadvantages. Whitehead himself, in thinking of various things he had said about evil at an earlier point, explains finally with characteristic modesty that the view he had given was too "simple-minded."[37] He would nevertheless hold "the fundamental position that 'destruction as a dominant fact in the experience' is the correct definition of evil." There is an inevitable "intermingling of Beauty and Evil," he believes, coming about through "metaphysical principles"; importantly in this connection even "mental functioning introduces into realization subjective forms conformal to relevant alternatives excluded from the completeness of physical realization."

Aside from the technical details we have given here, the essence of Whitehead's position is that we have to move on despite the destructions that we indeed encounter. Wordsworth's *Prelude* shows him doing just this. That is the importance of the context in his work from which we have quoted concerning, not the simple-mindedness, but the rashness of people who, as they consider evil, do not realize "what they say." The temperateness of the poet's statement is notable in that he is not contemptuous. We are rash, at times, when we reflect upon evil without seeing things widely enough. We have granted that for many philosophers pain has its indubitably tragic place in life; this is true according to both the poet and Whitehead. In the words of the latter, "As soon as high consciousness is reached, the enjoyment of existence is entwined with pain..."[38] And yet for Whitehead there is a comforting factor available for man in what may be reflected upon concerning "the intuition of permanence."

The reconciliation of Whitehead's seeming opposites is accomplished, once again, through the mental faculty of peace. The problem of evil is a very wide one impinging upon joy, as we saw it does in Wordsworth's juxtaposition of the two features "pain and joy"; the position of Whitehead on the matter becomes somewhat better clarified when he explains that "the culminating fact of conscious, rational life refuses to conceive itself as a transient enjoyment, transiently useful."[39] We may notice the word "enjoyment" here and remember Wordsworth's use of "joy and pain" as seemingly "adverse" or polar principles. The correlativeness of such factors is present frequently in both men.

Both Wordsworth and Whitehead are approaching the problem of evil by trying to clear the ground of a certain superficiality: the too hasty polarizing of particular forces in the world. In a page that follows the one from which we last quoted it is evident that Whitehead by no means minimizes the problem he has confronted, for, as he says, "ultimate evil in the temporal world is deeper than any specific evil."[40] A few sentences later he adds that "the struggle with evil is a process of building up a mode of utilization by the provision of intermediate elements introducing a complex structure of harmony." These words from *Process and Reality* sound rather formal to anyone who has acutely suffered a bereavement. There are difficulties in writing on the problem of evil, and Whitehead would be the first to admit the imperfection of the treatment of it which he presents in *Process and Reality* though this book, his wife tells us, was the one which he most wanted to write. He later said that he should have written in the first page and "repeated at intervals" how inadequate it was for the expression of the philosophical ideas it contains.[41]

But though Whitehead's words on the problem of evil that we have most recently quoted sound somewhat formal, he has small friendliness for the "sophism that all is for the best in the best of possible worlds."[42] In another volume he speaks of this theory as "an audacious fudge produced in order to save the face of a Creator constructed by contemporary, and antecedent, theologians."[43] We sense his very real social concern when he speaks about the value of revolt against the "facile solution," which is often accepted "by fortunate people, that the sufferer is the evil person."[44]

Here humanitarian reform was prominent in Whitehead's mind. In his world-view, however, he recognized the limitedness of all forms of actuality. What we call totality is always under restrictions which are in the background. He did not blame the finiteness of our earthly achievements upon an overall evil. "This finiteness," he wrote, "is not the result of evil, or of imperfection. It results from the fact that there are possibilities of harmony which either produce evil in joint realization, or are incapable of such conjunction."[45]

It is our problem to bring to achievement effective "possibilities of harmony" and good insofar as we can. We must, that is, be creative—

looking to the future. For Whitehead, feelings of distress concerning evil should not hamper us in our constructiveness, and in this he is close to Wordsworth. He is also close to the spirit of love which is a central thread in various works of literature (for example, in Dante), and in *The Prelude* where love is thought of as the beginning and ending of all things. Wordsworth's summation concerning the source of all things appears in these lines:

> for here
> Do we begin and end, all grandeur comes,
> All truth and beauty, from pervading love . . . (149—)

Love as a central theme in this portion of *The Prelude* is brought into juxtaposition with truth, as we see. Wordsworth gives us next his famous passage "Behold the fields," recalling the springtime pastures of Westmoreland and Lancastershire, though specific places are not indicated. In these lines, not fully quoted here—with their reference to "rising flowers"—we have a sense of budding and burgeoning growth, in a word, of process. If one has ever been present in spring lamb-dropping time in Montana, the tenderness of Wordsworth's writing here will be full of memorable associations. The poet, however, moves on at once to personal human love. Such love is evidently very important in his eyes, but from this point he nevertheless proceeds to a higher love. Whitehead, thinking of the divine, similarly moves from a consideration of the merely personal in such situations, for, as he says, there is a danger if "personal love is simply a clinging to a condition of selfish happiness."[46] In discussing this he is concerned about transcendence. For Wordsworth, likewise, the "higher love" comes to man accompanied with a sense of "awe"—that is, it has its connection with the "divine" and with a broad religion. This is a case which, in Whitehead's terms, represents the universal Eros in action.

We would expect to find Wordsworth making references to "the soul" as he speaks of the higher love and of awe, and he does so. Whitehead's remarks about the soul can be brought to consideration in this context—for example, his idea that, in its action "by synthesis," the soul "creates a new fact which is the Appearance woven out of the old and new"; this action of the soul as it gives rise to fact "in its turn passes into the future."[47] It is the Eros Whitehead is mainly speaking of when he makes these remarks; in terms that we would like to use for the purpose of providing an adaptation of Wordsworth's ideas, this Eros produces an action beyond that of any merely self-oriented love. And it can scarcely be thought of in operation (looking as it does into the future) except as an action which is employing the imagination. The imagination also appears specifically in Wordsworth's thought in *The Prelude* with regard to the subject of love. This operative love, as he declares,

> cannot be
> Without imagination, which, in truth,
> Is but another name for absolute strength . . . (166—)

The quotation from *The Prelude* here appears in a form which is somewhat curtailed so that the reader can see the stress that Wordsworth gives to the imaginative "strength" which is within us and which has exceedingly great operational force. It is in itself an "amplitude of mind," as Wordsworth says. Whitehead also, in discussing "a mental side" shortly before the passage we have quoted concerning the creation of a new fact or circumstance, brings out an important distinction having reference to the feature of mentality which in the creation of "a new fact" includes, as we saw, a created "Appearance" that passes onward into further experience.[48] This is "a mental side" of the action which "the Soul" produces. But the spirit of man has more than "a mental side" in Whitehead, as is true also in Wordsworth.

In saying that more than mind is required of the being who is truly human we are thinking again of the need for transcendence. We have quoted from Wordsworth a few lines ending on the word "strength"; this strength he connects with mind, along with "reason in her most exalted mood." The mental "stream" of the higher reason, and its origin, Wordsworth says he has been trying to trace

> From darkness, and the very place of birth
> In its blind cavern . . . (173—)

The "blind cavern" of early experience brings Plato to our consciousness (because of Plato's thought about the cave and our consciousness of transcendence), and along with it we may think of Whitehead's continued preoccupation with the spiritual in contrast to the material. From the blind "cavern," Wordsworth tells us, he emerged mentally to "light" as well as to "open day," which is a kind of light of earthly experience. In addition the poet relates this action to the subject of "Nature"; observing this similarity between Wordsworth and Whitehead, we need to remind ourselves of the fact that the subject of nature is a perennial one not only in the poet but also in Whitehead—for example, it is treated in his volumes *The Principles of Natural Knowledge*, *The Concept of Nature*, and *Nature and Life*. His essay "The Relatedness of Nature" in *The Principles of Relativity* and his chapter on "Relativity" in *Science and the Modern World*[49] might be cited as further examples.

The theme of nature we have largely touched upon earlier, except that we may now stress the importance of a question that Whitehead presents: "What is nature made of?" Answers of Greek philosophy on this question include that given by Plato, in which, as Whitehead says, "the forms of thought are more fluid than in Aristotle"; and because of their fluidity Whitehead ventures to believe they are "the more valuable."[50] They express "a distinction between the general becoming of nature and the measurable time of nature." Such a Platonic view has an affiliation with the views of Whitehead and is closer to Wordsworth than is the more fixed and static conception of Aristotle on this subject.

Whitehead's rejection of the idea of a static nature is emphasized very strongly in *Modes of Thought* when he proceeds from reflection on the development of vegetable nature to that of higher forms, including the mental aspects of humanity. In his terminal chapter in this connection, he expresses his opposition to a "sharp division between mentality and nature"; having presented three points with reference to this, he comes to a fourth point, "the task of defining natural facts, so as to understand how mental occurrences are operative in conditioning the subsequent course of nature."[51]

Our conception of "natural facts," that is, must include the "mental" factor which has a tremendous effect on the happenings of the world. Clearly, an increasingly great understanding of psychology is important here, as well as of other social subjects. One instance of

Whitehead's concern about such mental aspects in nature appears in *Adventures of Ideas*, where he devotes an entire section of over a hundred pages to the topic of the social under the general heading "Sociological." The mental factor in nature is to be seen again in a statement he makes in *Symbolism* about "thought" in its relation to nature: "When it abstracts, thought is merely conforming to nature—or rather, it is exhibiting itself as an element in nature."[52]

Thought is then, in a sense, nature, but it is not the totality which is the natural world. In Wordsworth's presentation there is—to recapitulate—the mental as "amplitude of mind" or "reason in her most exalted mood" along with nature; in Whitehead we see a widely operative "thought" which, as we have indicated in our quotation from his volume *Symbolism*, is "an element in nature." For an understanding of Wordsworth's presentation we find ourselves following a "stream"—which corresponds to the highest phases of the mental, being in itself a kind of "moving soul" proceeding beyond initial darkness toward light. For Whitehead the "forms of thought" applied to the constitution of nature have a similar flowing or "fluid" quality. In Book Thirteen Wordsworth, then, had "traced" or followed the "stream," which is at once mind in the higher sense and nature, but he also tells how he

> afterwards
> Lost sight of it bewilder'd and engulph'd ... (177—)

This last-mentioned stage when Wordsworth felt "bewilder'd and engulph'd" refers of course to his dark period, which we have discussed. In our references to the "stream" of the moving "soul" coupled with nature, we must not lose sight of nature as most spontaneous readers of Wordsworth feel its presence. That Whitehead is somewhat similar to this spontaneous reader may be seen in one of his statements about what is needed for the "best thinking" of human beings. In his remarks on this subject he seems almost to be reflecting Wordsworth directly when he states that "what is wanted is contact with the elemental processes of nature during those years of youth when the mind is being formed."[53] It was renewed contacts of this very sort that helped in a measure to bring Wordsworth out of that dark period which followed his French Revolutionary experience.

Wordsworth's escape from his time of distress may be illuminatingly related, once more, to Whitehead's chapter "Nature Alive," which, in its consideration of "life," deals at once with it as "the central meeting point of all the strains of systematic thought, humanistic, naturalistic, philosophic."[54] Whitehead is referring here to the weakness of a "conclusion respecting nature, considered in abstraction from the notion of life." In an earlier book he speaks similarly when he regretfully points out that "the course of nature" has been "interpreted as the history of matter."[55] In a passage from *Modes of Thought*, which we quoted a moment ago, he spoke of that which is human, using the word "humanistic," and we have seen that a human being's profound capacity for thought as well as the psychology involved in his function as a human being is central in Whitehead's thinking, as it is in that of the poet. For both men, thought is a part of nature, and it is little wonder that, after Wordsworth's dark period of bewilderment and loss had passed, he took joy in trying to follow his "stream" (the "soul") as he found himself confronted by it

> as it rose once more
> With strength, reflecting in its solemn breast
> The works of man . . . (179—)

When the poet speaks here of the "works of man" he has in mind that which is human (a concept for which Whitehead, in a passage we have quoted, uses the term "humanistic"). Wordsworth thinks also of what he calls "the face of human life"; the humanistic activity, that is, has a "face"—is not a mere dead abstraction. Human developments possess a life within them. This inward life Whitehead also recognizes, and he has a position for it in his philosophy. Indeed, the inward life as treated by Whitehead receives most tremendous emphasis. But this is by no means all. For both Wordsworth and Whitehead man has participated in creating the whole immense world of ideas. Having considered in part the "stream" in its relation to man's "works," we are then brought in *The Prelude* to

> The feeling of life endless, the great thought
> By which we live, Infinity and God.   (183—)

From the clearly human emphasis in these lines—if we take them with what we have previously referred to, using such key words as "reason" in its highest, its most "exalted" expression—the poet moves on to a new point. He includes in such *reason* the intuitive as well as nature. Wordsworth thus develops his theme until he has reached the problem of immortality. What he terms the "feeling of life endless" (immortality) brings us to the fact that he had felt intimations concerning this earlier, and in the period from 1803 to 1805 while contemplating the problem he had written a separate poem about these feelings. Do we find any parallel to this in Whitehead? We may say that, in his philosophy, the eternal or the immortal can be related to things that are enduring in life. But he goes further than this when he declares that "things which are temporal arise by their participation in things which are eternal."[56]

This is a remark that Whitehead makes after emphasizing again that to some degree his thought is Platonic. The importance to him of the eternal or the timeless is brought out elsewhere in his suggestion that, although merely "a selection of eternal objects" may be felt or experienced by a person at a given time, those which are not being experienced may still be of influence; "those eternal objects which are not felt are not therefore negligible."[57] Far from being negligible, they are part of the eternal which connects us all. Indeed, in speaking of occasions of experience (spots of time could be an example) he says, to quote from one of his other volumes, "Every occasion is a synthesis of all eternal objects,"[58] under certain restrictions. There is a connection, also, between all occasions of experience, one with the other. Here we have an example (among many examples) of his approach to the eternal, or to infinity.

We have considered in the present chapter the fact that Wordsworth, in Book Thirteen of *The Prelude*, refers rapidly to a series of conceptions such as the tendency toward the highly sense-directed life, the idea of a universe of death, the topic of the divine, fear as resolved by love, as well as the subjects of pain and joy. When he mentions these matters in Book Thirteen of the 1805 *Prelude*, one cannot help but sense their importance in his mind. The topics—as we saw also with reference to the subjects mentioned in the previous chapter—are highly interrelated. Many of the ideas that we found in

Wordsworth, as we can say again, are dealt with, albeit with more subtlety, by Whitehead. We shall see that this is true of certain other important ideas that will be presented in the next chapter. There we shall include a further comment on "life endless" or immortality, as well as on a number of other topics constituting the substance of the conclusion of this last book of *The Prelude* which we have been discussing.

Notes

[1]*Adventures of Ideas*, p. 236. It is the primary ground.

[2]*Ibid.*, p. 244.

[3]*Ibid.*, p. 245.

[4]*Ibid.*, p. 247.

[5]*Ibid.*, p. 251. See also George H. Mead on this sort of philosophy in *The Philosophy of the Present* (La Salle, Ill.: Open Court, 1932, 1959), p. 23.

[6]*Ibid.*, pp. 251-252.

[7]*Ibid.*, p. 240.

[8]*Ibid.*, p. 360.

[9]*Ibid.*, p. 361.

[10]*Modes of Thought*, p. 184.

[11]*Ibid.*, p. 153.

[12]*Ibid.*, p. 185.

[13]*Science and the Modern World*, p. 109. He refers also to a view of "mechanism of God," which he criticized.

[14]*Ibid.*, p. 112.

[15] *Ibid.*, p. 146.

[16] *Ibid.*, p. 147.

[17] *Modes of Thought*, p. 138. We have tried to present Whitehead's view here and in the following paragraph with as few technicalities as possible.

[18] *Ibid.*, p. 199.

[19] *Ibid.*, pp. 199-200.

[20] *Ibid.*, p. 200.

[21] *Ibid.*, pp. 199-200.

[22] *Ibid.*, p. 200.

[23] *Ibid.*, p. 201.

[24] *Adventures of Ideas*, p. 205.

[25] *Ibid.*, p. 211.

[26] *Ibid.*, p. 213.

[27] *Science and the Modern World*, p. 148. See also p. 150.

[28] *Adventures of Ideas*, p. 215; see also p. 210 for Whitehead's opposition to a methodology of science which he feels is unduly restrictive.

[29] *Ibid.*, p. 311.

[30] *Ibid.*, p. 319.

[31] *Ibid.*, p. 342.

[32] *Ibid.*, p. 343.

[33] *Ibid.*, p. 350.

[34] *Ibid.*, p. 356.

[35] *Ibid.*, p. 357.

[36] *Ibid.*, p. 377.

[37] *Ibid.*, p. 333.

[38] *Ibid.*, p. 369. Not only "pain," but "fear" also finds a place in Whitehead; for the latter, see *Symbolism*, p. 45. See also footnote 56 below.

[39] *Process and Reality*, p. 516.

[40] *Ibid.*, p. 517. This passage from *Process and Reality* needs to be supplemented by remarks that Whitehead makes in pp. 524-526.

[41] *Dialogues of Alfred North Whitehead*, p. 363.

[42] *Religion in the Making* (New York: Macmillan, 1926), p. 48.

[43] *Process and Reality*, p. 74. He realizes that Leibniz is worthy of great admiration, apart from this attitude with regard to evil. There is an allusion to Leibniz in our paragraph.

[44] *Religion in the Making*, p. 49.

[45] *Adventures of Ideas*, p. 356. This is a sentence which deserves very special emphasis.

[46] *Ibid.*, p. 373.

[47] *Ibid.*, p. 355.

[48] *Ibid.*

[49] We see that "abstraction" directs "attention to something which is in nature" and which thereby isolates it "for the purpose of contemplation." Note this in *Science and the Modern World*, p. 173.

[50] *The Concept of Nature*, p. 17.

[51] *Modes of Thought*, p. 214.

[52]*Symbolism*, (New York: Capricorn Books, published by permission of Macmillan, 1957), p. 26. Originally published in 1927.

[53]*Dialogues of Alfred North Whitehead*, p. 71.

[54]*Modes of Thought*, p. 202.

[55]*The Concept of Nature*, p. 16.

[56]*Process and Reality*, p. 63.

[57]*Ibid.*, p. 66.

[58]*Science and the Modern World*, p. 252.

Chapter Sixteen

Concluding Ideas in the 1805 "Prelude" As Related to Whitehead

We have seen that Wordsworth in his reflection upon what he called "life endless" brought this topic together with a "great thought" back of our entire existence. He included in the great thought, which he held to be fundamental, the concept of "Infinity," as well as that of the divine. In the *Prelude* passage quoted near the close of the last chapter, the conceptions of "life endless" and "Infinity" are related. In referring to "life endless" (connected with timelessness) we asked whether there is a parallel to the poet's thought and that of White-head. A part of the answer is that, just as Wordsworth has his "Ode on the Intimations of Immortality," and other pertinent material separately conceived, so Whitehead has an essay, "Immortality," and various statements bearing upon the topic which appear from time to time in a number of volumes he has written. Things that are important to Wordsworth in this matter are important to Whitehead also.

For Whitehead the very act of valuing something is related to the apparently timeless, to immortality, and to the idea of the divine.

But valuing, in our human experience, must necessarily operate through finitude. That is, value in the abstract, after its transformation into "Evaluation,"[1] performs the act, or function, of a modification within the expanse (or within the events) of time. Value itself for Whitehead is timeless, eternal, just as love—through the action of God—is eternal. The evidence for the fact of Whitehead's belief in the latter point must wait upon the discussion to be presented near the middle of the present chapter in which reference is made to *Process and Reality* and God's "tenderness" and his "infinite patience." Within ourselves, however, value undergoes a "transformation," as treated in the essay "Immortality"; for example, we modify things in our minds, such as our thought about the education we might have received in a different city or under varying other circumstances. The value appears in the excellence as well as in the disadvantages (negative values) which the imagined education might possess. We have a definite affective or emotional response when we regard such things (education could continue to be our example) as having value. The same is true of customs which we hold to be important. Customs involve value theory.

A further analysis of value, which is related to Wordsworth's concept of "life endless" and to his feeling about the divine, cannot at present appear. But Whitehead for his own part finds in Plato stimulating suggestions about value and about the feelings human beings have in regard to it. He decries, however, Plato's remoteness from life *as lived* and the attacks Plato makes upon actualities as mere shadows. Value must not be too abstract. Here we may think of John Dewey's emphasis upon actualities. In the page from which we have quoted in the "Immortality" essay Whitehead also rejects emphatically Plato's "feeble" conception of "imitation," which may be found troublesome for one thing because, if actuality is a mere representation or an imitating of the ideal, there is a kind of presumption that the "imitation," if it were all that it should be, would produce identity.

Where then, in such a slavish conception of imitation, would there be room for the unique individual person who does certain things in his own highly special fashion? There is an area in human life in which things that we do can be done by no other person. Whitehead is a strong believer in such independency. He applies it to some of the most precious features of education. Speaking to a group of listeners he remarked, "In reality you educate yourselves. No one else can do it for you."[2] In *The Prelude* Wordsworth, too, recognizes something inviolable within the self that must find its expression, as we have seen, and we shall see this again in a later passage of the poem. In such matters as these we have no helpers. We must stand independently. He would by no means deny that we are all immensely helped by others, nor would Whitehead deny this. We are, then, faced here with a kind of paradox; we shall have to return to it near the middle of the chapter.

Along with Whitehead's independency, which we notice, we see that he is definitely drawn to the ideal, and he opposes strongly the trend in our own time toward "the pragmatic dismissal of 'immortality.' " We can think of the idea of immortality as being involved with the long history of the creative as it manifests itself in human experience. Even in ordinary life the creative—which projects indefinitely toward the future—is constantly active. And at this point we may think again of Dewey and what he calls the "genetic-functional" approach to first principles. It is the activity-doctrine of Dewey that speaks to us here in all its emphasis upon what we today call the relevant needs of mankind. With regard to this approach to the relevant, Whitehead stresses the fact that "William James and John Dewey will stand out as having infused philosophy with new life, and with a new relevance to the modern world."[3]

At the very moment that Whitehead had been making this acknowledgment, however, Dewey had been criticizing the philosophy of organism. In making his attack, Dewey had suggested that Whitehead ought to choose "between the 'genetic-functional' interpretation of first principles and the 'mathematical-formal' interpretation." The words concerning the controversy are Whitehead's. He declined, however, to make such a choice. "Our present problem," he explained, "is the fusion of two interpretations." What is implied is that the Deweyan principle which Dewey would like to impose (as well as the alternative concerning the "mathematical-formal") is not so inclusive as the principle behind the philosophy of organism.

Whitehead here was thinking of the importance of interaction. In his philosophy the thought we may have about the *value* of a given action modifies the character of what we may choose to create. This is true throughout our lives. In certain ways, even the child touches the edge of the philosophical: such knowledge "enters while we still remember the rocking cradle."[4] The experience of the abstract concept of number, for example, arrives thus early. The knowledge, like much philosophic insight, is vague. Dewey's own word "genetic-functional"[5] is an example also of vagueness; the "compound word 'genetic-functional' means an ultimate metaphysical principle from which there is no escape." Here Whitehead explains that he is "in complete agreement with Dewey."

The willingness of Dewey to proceed on the basis of action where knowledge may be cloudy is the important underlying factor here. It must be steadily kept in mind, as we have said, that we can at times perceive some things in a "flash" which will bring about intuitive understanding. Whitehead says that he cannot "discern any reason, apart from dogmatic assumption, why any factor in the universe should not be manifest in some flash of human consciousness."[6]

It is to "value-theory"[7] rather specifically that Whitehead turns near the conclusion of his argument. He speaks of the "enjoyment of the values of human art, or of natural beauty, our horror at the obvious vulgarities and defacements which force themselves upon us," and he feels that we all tend to have such value responses. They seem very clear, but they nevertheless reach toward a profundity; they "disclose the very meaning of things." These ideas in Whitehead have their connection with certain concepts that appear four years later in the "Immortality" essay.

The idea of immortality is then connected with his view that "value issues into modification of creative action."[8] Putting the matter in a different way, Whitehead says that "value is saved from the futility of abstraction by its impact upon the process of Creation." The importance of "effectiveness in action" receives further emphasis in the page we have cited, as does the concept of the "persuasive force" of value. These points might seem to stress a kind of instrumentalism such as Dewey favors, but Whitehead's thought goes beyond instrumentalism.

Value as related to immortality presents difficulties which will inevitably cry for further clarification, but Whitehead's belief in the "immortality," or eternal quality, of certain active ideas should be kept steadily in mind. The belief in the immortality of certain concepts or ideals may itself be valued. This has a positive connection with Plato, and ultimately with a partial overcoming of determinism and coercion. We can never completely overcome determinism or force in a finite world. But as Whitehead states in *Process and Reality*, we are brought "back to some restatement of Platonic realism, modified so as to avoid the pitfalls"[9] concerning which many philosophers have been victims—among them Descartes, Locke, and those in their later tradition. These thinkers, if followed consistently, "in the end lead to Hume's extreme of sensationalism."[10] In subsequent philosophy, and even in popular thought down to the present, there have been many followers of this tradition, emphasizing sensation. To understand Whitehead it is important to remember that in "the illumination of consciousness" there is a factor of "a nonsensuous perception"[11] which he believes can be demonstrated.

We have spoken of the *action* of ideas and have alluded to Dewey. The course of this action of ideas makes clear that Whitehead is no stranger to the mundane world. Philosophy, as he views it, should be strongly interested in action. Belief in the "immortality" of ideas is connected with what Whitehead calls "conceptual valuation," which becomes in its action "a persuasive force in the development of the Universe."[12] Persuasion for Whitehead is the reverse side of compulsion in the world. It concerns persons and social movements, and it has wider applications. It is related to what he calls the "World of Value." This area, along with "Value" itself, has an immortal or timeless factor, though the "World of Value," like "Value" also, has, as we have said, to be brought into dynamic relation with a finite world. He is close to Wordsworth here.

Again and again Whitehead stresses in his volumes the importance of activity and things which are instrumental. He speaks, for example, of the fusion of the "World of Value" with the "World of Activity"; in this process of fusion we can see "that either world can only be described in terms of factors which are common to both of them."[13] Here each "World" has an aspect which is related to that of the other. He gives special stress to the fact that the correlative aspects of "factors are the famous 'Ideas,' which it is the glory of Greek thought to have explicitly discovered, and the tragedy of Greek thought to have misconceived in respect to their status in the Universe." Their real status, contrary to the Greek interpretation, is not one of "independent existence."

The thing to be remembered is that "every entity is only to be understood in terms of the way in which it" interacts with and "is interwoven with the rest of the Universe." The word "understood" here might well have been underlined. The "entity" is to be comprehended only in terms of a seamless coat of which the "entity" is a part. Personality is such an entity. As Whitehead views the matter of personality, then, he is struck by what he calls its "survival"[14]; this survival aspect he connects with the theory of value and also with his doctrine of immortality.

We have referred to Whitehead's opposition to the "pragmatic dismissal of immortality." His attitude toward the pragmatic philosophy is complex; for example, it might seem that some of his remarks *against* the independent existence of anything would appear to have a pragmatic tinge. One might suppose that natural law is under question along with the denial of "independent existence." We find, however, that he opposes the "modern fashion to deny any evidence for the stability of natural law"; it is true that "natural law" has come under serious questioning, but the complete denial of it is an undermining of our very necessary general stability. Here personality needs to be considered. "The outstanding example of such stability" generally, according to Whitehead, "is Personal Identity."[15] And this fact of personal stability or identity, if we are willing to accept his mode of supporting it, points in the direction of a belief in immortality. The problem itself presents an important example of the linking of a universe of activity and one of value.

In various works Whitehead has much to say about the integration of personality (for example, near the close of *Modes of Thought* where he speaks of the soul's lasting self-identity), and we have spoken, at the end of the second last paragraph, of the survival of personality, which he deals with in his essay on "Immortality." In this connection Whitehead mentions that this survival possesses its stability as a result of the *action* of value. Indeed, we find a statement, shortly after he makes this point, that he regards self-identity (the personal self) as "the extreme example of the sustained realization of a type of value."[16] Our existence has value in our continuing experience. At a later point in this essay he does not hesitate to contrast "temporal personality" on the one hand (as seen in the "World of Change") with "immortal personality"[17] on the other hand, which he connects very especially with value. We may relate this to the fact that, in another work, he refers to the question of the degree to which "a support" may be given for the soul's "existence beyond the body,"[18] and two sentences later he says, as we will emphasize, "In some important sense the existence of the soul may be freed from its complete dependence upon bodily organization."

We have mentioned Whitehead's belief in the relationships of all the occasions of experience one with another. Now we would stress the fact that the almost universal movement of the world itself contains for Whitehead a kind of intimation of eternity; in his view, also, "the World of Action" has a kind of "immortality"[19] which is derived from its "transformation" into what he would call the very nature of the divine. It is human action he is considering here. Such immortality as the world of action possesses "is beyond our imagination to conceive." That is, we cannot begin to conceive it fully.

The reason for this impossibility in our conceptions, doubtless, is that to conceive the immortality of "the World of Action" would take us into the infinite. In our *attempt* to conceive such a thing, however, a great force of the imagination is active. In effect Whitehead himself is stressing this when he says, "What does haunt our imagination is that the immediate facts of present action pass into permanent significance for the Universe."[20] In the context there is an importance in a human being's striving—in his motions *toward* what Whitehead refers to as "Achievement," such as it may be. The effort at Achievement—indeed, the very notion of achievement—is an outgrowth of the total background Whitehead has in mind. It is also true even of what he has to say about the concept of "Failure"; at times this is a wrong concept to hold, and it needs careful pondering. But even actual failure itself has a *value* which cannot be denied.

Whitehead makes clear that he does not hold his views on these particular matters dogmatically. He is very far from the dogmatic in all of his thinking. But like Wordsworth he has, as we have said, intimations of immortality. He and Wordsworth both admit the difficulties here in regard to the whole problem. His personal explanation has in part been presented dogmatically (that is in a direct statement), for the purpose of the exposition. But he is not, for example, basing his views on the conception of anything involving essence. He feels, however, that there is an endless vista ahead as to those things which endure, along with mankind's enlightenment, which has been slowly growing and enlarging. This tremendous vista has its place in our thought with regard to "life endless" (in Wordsworth's term) along with the divine.

The *Prelude* passage concerning life endless (which we quoted toward the end of Chapter Fifteen) was followed immediately by mention of "the great thought" involving "Infinity"; a further "great thought" is also in the poet's mind, but this we will speak of later. For Wordsworth "Infinity" is indeed, as he holds, a subject for far-reaching reflection. Preliminary to considering this subject, let us for a moment give imagination the exercise of conceiving a line following a ray of light extending to us from the central point of a distant and enormously large sun. Then, if we imagine that we have moved some ten or twenty feet to the left, let us think again of another ray streaming to us from the center of this gigantic sun. This second ray, like the first, represents a line, and the two lines, formed by the swiftly descending rays, may be thought of as two nearly equal lines of an almost unbelievably large triangle with approximately a twenty-foot base near our feet. The apex of this triangle would be a far-distant acute angle.

We can imagine any number of triangles like this triangle (in proportions), but different in size; hence it is one example of a class of triangles. The class is that of triangles which have two equal sides. Since, if we wished, we could vary indefinitely the length of the third side, or base, we would have in these triangles multiple examples of infinite classes, or at least of classes which approach infinity as a limit. The enormous triangle itself, as we think of the minuscule man standing close to its base, may help us to see how small a human being or the individual person is when compared to the great triangle itself.

The many possible variations in a set of triangles such as we have described may serve to suggest the abstract concept of possible variations itself, and to bring to our minds once more an example of what Whitehead calls an eternal object. Such an "object" is multiform. And it may be seen that it has relations to a multitude of other objects—for example, it has a relation to the two right-angled triangles which would be formed if the enormous triangle were divided by dropping a perpendicular line from its apex to a point near our feet where we are imagined as standing on the earth. Thinking, then, of the smallness of man and of this so-called eternal object (the enor-

mous triangle with its variations), we can probably see why Whitehead suggests that we are somewhat at a loss as we imagine the reach
of these concepts. He suggests that for the full *valuation* of the entire
quantity of eternal objects we need God; that is to say, we have need
of God at least for "the unconditioned conceptual valuation of the
entire multiplicity of eternal objects."[21] Value is eternal.

But now, since we have decided to give somewhat extensive rein to
the imagination in thinking about the enormous triangle, we could
imagine again a human being who might travel along the lines following a ray of light toward the zenith and the distant sun (since we can
imagine anything), and in the reference to the man we can, with an
effort, see perhaps what Whitehead means by his term "concretizing."
It is a relative term. The man we are imagining as following a ray of
light toward the distant sun is entering in experience into our picture
of the great triangle, and we thus, through the example of the man,
are concretizing the whole adventure or conception. We would
require, according to Whitehead's philosophy, "a principle of concre-
tion," and in the triangle and the man taken together we can see an
example of such a far-reaching principle. It can be ideational. The
triangle, whether thought of as small or large, is a single pregnant
instance of an "eternal object" in an occasion of experience. Whitehead speaks of various "occasions" of experience—for example
"occasions of bodily existence, or the soul's existence."[22] (He usually
speaks of exceedingly brief occasions, within a fraction of a second,
but we are not thinking of this extreme kind of brevity here.)

The "occasion" we are referring to is within the mind, but like the
occasion of experience in one's memory of Hamburg (or of Cologne
after the bombing), it is nonetheless real for all that. And when we
consider that we have also to value these things as bad, or as good, we
may be able to see why Whitehead says, "There must be value beyond
ourselves."[23] Moreover, we can perhaps see why he connects this
short statement to remarks which he makes about God or Deity. In a
page immediately following that containing these comments he refers
to ideals of various kinds including even "ideals defaced." Here the
personal appears. The experience itself of any one of these ideals is
"the experience of the Deity of the universe." It is an example of what
we were speaking about when we mentioned that the eternal, or the
immortal, can be related to things that are enduring in life or indeed
instrumental.

We have quoted Whitehead earlier to the effect that he does not hold dogmatically a position concerning immortality; as he conceives the problem, he would not wish his position to be understood as being based upon a generality taken from any person's lips or from an institution which includes professions held to be authoritative and under no obligation to submit to the questioning of any mere man. We need to ponder Whitehead's statements in the spirit of a poet, and Wordsworth would be a good example of such a ponderer. All of the statements Whitehead has made with reference to the immortality topic are connected with the seeming infinity of the universe, and this, though it provides a challenge, also represents definite limitations for us. Thus Whitehead, as we have said, disagrees with Plato insofar as Plato seeks ideas which are ultimate and therefore to be described as leading to the substance of things essential.

Wordsworth also holds certain views that are not in accordance with the philosophy of Plato; like Whitehead he prefers not to make any extravagant imaginative leaps into infinite regions. Nevertheless, following upon his reference in *The Prelude* to "infinity," the first of the great conceptions central to our very existence, he makes place for the second conception—God, though the idea of God is for him entwined with the first, infinity. Whitehead, similarly—though he has been deeply concerned with the subject of immortality (or infinity) and feels strongly about it—does not, on the basis of the problem of infinity, *seek* God, though he believes God is there for us in part to perceive. Again we may say that he is not dogmatic. He is making an inquiry. In a quest of this sort he says we cannot find, "we cannot rely on any adequate explicit analysis."[24]

We have commented upon the subject of the infinite subsequently to our observations on "life endless" because this is the order which Wordsworth used in his mention of the two matters. Following, as we do, the order he uses in referring to what he regards as the great idea which enables us actually to live or have a sense of existence, we come to his final reference in the context—that is, as we have seen, to "God." In going back to an earlier part of Whitehead's essay "Immortality," we may observe that his theory of value is connected with "the unification of personality."[25] This latter expression covers, in some measure, Wordsworth's aim in writing his poem *The Prelude*. For Whitehead the term *unification of personality* is directly related to the divine. It is even central to our very conception of the deity.

For Whitehead, then, the unification of personality is at the heart of "the concept of God." Indeed, he states it without reservation. Whitehead wishes to find God (though he cannot directly seek him), and Wordsworth in *The Prelude* has the same indirect goal. This is what the final book in the poem is leading toward. As to religion, Whitehead has learned much from the traditions of Greece and of Judaism, along with those of Christianity and even the Far East, "the Hindu Buddhistic tradition."[26] But Whitehead's thought departs considerably from that seen in what he calls the "diffused" deity of India; he thinks of God as "the intangible fact at the base of finite existence."

We spoke of the unification of personality at the head of the previous paragraph. Wordsworth, in his conceptions regarding the higher reason (as well as the intuitive, nature, and infinity), was directing his thought, as we saw, toward personality—that is, individual identity, and finally toward God. Do these things, along with the theme of the imagination—which is by no means peripheral— harmonize in any further ways with the ideas of Whitehead? We do not see a complete harmony of the two men when we observe Whitehead's statement about the "coordination of many personal individualities as factors in the nature of God." Philosophic thought had not advanced (or proceeded) in this highly personalistic way at the time of Wordsworth's writing. For Whitehead, in contrast to Wordsworth, mankind can accomplish, in thought concerning "the World of Value," such a "coordination of many personal individualities," and it can lead the human being toward a conception of God.

The many distinctly "personal individualities" are important to Whitehead, especially in the long process of development toward an increased harmony of persons one with another. The importance of man as a reality within God is not, however, the whole story. He tells us at once that "the coordination of many individualities" in the essence of the deity needs supplementation. Such coordination is "only half the truth." The important thing is the stress we must place upon God himself. "The emphasis upon the divine factor in human nature is the essence of religious thought." There is a God within. But as he thinks of God he feels that change, rather than a static condition, must be constantly stressed.

And here there arises a problem concerning the incompatibilities within the idea of deity recognized by many religious thinkers of the world, including "impossibility such that God himself cannot surmount it"[27]; but, though theologians have wrestled with this aspect of the divine, Whitehead grants, they have not dealt with it in terms applicable to the world of human beings. The theologian has recognized that *intrinsic* incompatibility is a problem in relation to the nature of God, but "this notion of incompatibility has never been applied to ideals in the Divine realization." And part of the "Divine realization" occurs with reference to the lives of persons. Again Whitehead thinks of the "Eros," which is "the active entertainment of all ideals, with the urge to their finite realization, each in its due season." Here he calls upon the principle of "process" which, he concludes, is "inherent in God's nature"; that is, it is by process that "his infinity is acquiring realization."

As human beings we must not be rendered helpless when we sense the presence of "incompatibilities"; we "entertain" them and do something with them, as we can, and our acts of thought or overt behavior are directed toward "physical realization." Such situations, which involve conflict, arise "in each finite occasion." Moreover, they have a relation to the civilization that we, along with others, produce. When we are functioning fruitfully, "fresh experimentation" has to occur. But there is always the danger that, through our own default or that of others, "the society in question lacks imaginative force." We have seen this occurring in various decades in our own century.

It is in such a situation that satire becomes prominent. The significance of literary satire has been insufficiently understood. In certain periods satire is very important (indeed, useful), but it does not, according to Whitehead, occur prominently during a period in which a society is healthy. He thinks here of the time when Sinclair Lewis was writing and there were other important satirists at work elsewhere, for example in England. Lewis receives no mention, but we can see Whitehead's principle at work as we reflect on the satire of "clock-work" oranges that in a later period became prominent. In a world of "incompatibilities" such as are present in a time which gives rise to satire, the appropriate treatment of these incompatibilities appears in this form of literature. Satire arises when evils are rampant. We need to become acquainted with such evils and to struggle with them in order to overcome them. They are connected with gross social evils which we can conceive as being saddening to God as well as to man.

But, though Whitehead is struck by incompatibilities and the problem that they present in an age of satire, he is still more impressed by the unification that occurs and the togetherness of all things that may be produced after the long ordeal has been in process of proceeding. So also in Wordsworth, if we will recall the stream that he has metaphorically followed in *The Prelude* and its progression (he uses the word "progress," but without honorific suggestion), we find a motion in the direction of a bringing together of all things. This theme of togetherness involves the action of combined forces. In his statement of what he has been moving toward he presents these lines:

> Imagination having been our theme,
> So also hath that intellectual love,
> For they are each in each, and cannot stand
> Dividually.—Here must thou be, O Man!
> Strength to thyself . . . (185—)

The view that things have to work together, one with another, is exemplified here in the union of the imagination, of intellectual factors, and of the love which, as in Whitehead, binds together all things. We can recall Whitehead's statement about "togetherness" and compare it to Wordsworth's statement. But it is to be remembered also that, while there is the principle of togetherness in Whitehead, there is in addition the factor of an extreme individual self-unification, the need to have strength within oneself—as Wordsworth also indicates in the last line of the passage we have most lately quoted. Again we must confront the question of "fixity and distinction"[28] (Whitehead's expression) as it applies to the notion of a firmly integrated self. Is a most extreme form of "fixity and distinction" absolutely necessary to a sense of the individuality of the self? At times people seem to think so. But certain examples of the foundations of the world which in the past have been most extremely maintained have been crumbling, and some thinkers feel scarcely any sense of fixedness or distinction at all, even in personality. As an example of a writer on this subject Carl Rogers could be cited here.

Many of the suppositions of this kind of fixity, Whitehead says, "have explicitly vanished," though "in fact they dominate learned literature." Obviously we need to discover how to regain them or to get along without them. Whitehead is somewhat ironical here as he thinks of the defects, in width of scope, displayed in "learned literature." Actually, we find this long-entertained notion of fixity and distinction, in its extreme form, unconsciously present not only in many scholars but in creative writers such as Waugh, Graham Greene, and others, though Whitehead does not mention specific writers of this kind. But with reference to fixity he does add the remark—still ironically—that mankind, in reference to fixity, has been so unfortunate as to "preserve the errors of the past, as well as its wisdom." We tend to fossilize many of the absolutistic errors of the past even in our terminology, inveterately taking for granted their absoluteness. This is a point that Whitehead goes on to develop in the context from which we have quoted.

Because of the danger of fossilizing errors, even "dictionaries," in Whitehead's view, "are public dangers"; we have to look beyond the dictionaries to the living experience of men—experience on which the imperfect dictionaries have attempted to crystallize their narrowly conceived conceptions. Notions of the fixity of things represent a hazard, but the important point, nevertheless, is that every single individual, in his self-distinction, is "a special mode of coordination of the ideal world" whereby he can play his part, despite its limitations in "effectiveness." There does exist a "maintenance" of self, of "character," but if this maintenance of self were too fixed and absolute we could never embrace "the infinitude of possibility." Herein lies the danger of an absolute in fixity within the self. After all, it is true that "a perspective of ideal existence enters into the finite actuality." For Whitehead, indeed, all values for *us* arise out of circumstances of finitude, and herein we have to consider again the instrumental.

Would one wish to have the element of unity so magnified or inflated in the personality that the openness of ideal possibilities would cease to exist? Notions with regard to the personal existence of the self are difficult, but they have a connection, Whitehead believes, with the divine. It is in the context of such thinking that we can understand more profoundly Whitehead's philosophy in its likeness to that of Royce. Whitehead faces the difficulties of the concepts of loyalty to the self, to philosophy, and even to God somewhat as

Royce does, as we will observe in the sequel. And the practical, or instrumental, is important in both men. But we must now return to Wordsworth.

The poet's emphasis upon "strength to thyself" at the close of the *Prelude* passage last given is no minor indication of the place of independency in his conception of his own being and in his philosophy. One cannot yield one's right to free thought and to the action of one's own reason. In our century, pragmatism has opened the way to a new notion even of the means of inquiry. Wordsworth's approach to things is somewhat in the spirit of these ways of proceeding, but our point may be best understood if one takes recourse to Whitehead's approach in *Process and Reality* to what he calls "pragmatic" valuation in relation to "transcendent creativity in various temporal instances."[29]

In referring to this "pragmatic" factor, Whitehead is speaking of God "as the outcome of creativity, as the foundation of order, and as the goal towards novelty." In Whitehead the word "pragmatic" always needs careful consideration. He goes on in a moment to mention that "every actual entity, including God, is something individual for its own sake"; insofar as this latter point concerning individuality is true every actual entity "transcends the rest of actuality." This statement applies to the human being in his more ultimate reality, but it has its connection with many other things in the universe. The person has, almost unqualifiedly, his own individuality in his right to action (as well as in his obligations to action), but viewed in another way he may be thought of as a mere actual occasion related to other actual occasions. Man is not so gigantic as he thinks he is; though he has an almost unqualified right to action, he may behave unwisely, and he may be quite wrong in some of the acts he is guilty of. This is an aspect of man that is implied in the discussion. Whitehead does not forget the importance of the personal.

When Whitehead proceeds with the development of his thought he uses the idea of an actual entity (and this includes man) in such a way as to represent "a conditioned actual entity of the temporal world"; the idea of an actual entity does not include God or go beyond this type we have considered, "unless God is expressly included in the discussion."[30] To make his position clearer he adds that "the term 'actual occasion' will always exclude God from its scope." Here he is contrasting the expression "actual occasion" against that of an "actual entity" with the reservation he has indicated.

It has been thought at times that Whitehead's God, although the God as perceived has grandeur in the immense reach which he possesses, can scarcely be thought of as being available to man in his needs or as providing for man any degree of dignity. But the opposite is the case. The fact that, for Whitehead, God is not to be referred to as an "actual occasion" does not mean that he is not actual; rather, it means that he is more than an occasion—that is, more than an occasion of experience. We may be able to perceive Whitehead's view in part if we think of God as again and again providing an actual occasion of experience for *us*, through the extent of his care and his tenderness, and of course in many other ways beyond care and tenderness.

We ourselves, for example, at times practice "revolts of destructive evil"[31] (and we suffer them in relations with others); we are not now speaking of the good these revolts may at times accomplish according to the philosopher, but of the fact that all along there is an operative growth of God's nature, partly through us. Man surely acquires a dignity in such a view. It is an operative growth that Whitehead centers upon in thinking of God. "The image—and it is but an image—the image," he reiterates emphatically, "under which this operative growth of God's nature is best conceived, is that of a tender care that nothing is lost." It is the sequence, or the consequence, of God's eternal living, operative force that is important, as Whitehead conceives it. God "saves the world" and he does this in that "it passes into the immediacy of his own life. It is the judgment of a tenderness which loses nothing that can be saved."

Beyond this, in thinking of the "consequent nature" of God, Whitehead feels that an additional "image" is required, which is that of God's "infinite patience." And again, after another sentence, he re-emphasizes the point of patience: we can "conceive the patience of God, tenderly saving the turmoil of the intermediate world by the completion of his own nature." Within a single page in speaking of God Whitehead throws stress three times on the root term related to tenderness, as we have indicated here. And he even applies to God, in the page following, the expression "tender patience" once more. We need not think of Whitehead's conception of God as being remote

from man except by our own failure to strive toward intuitive understanding, or by our neglect of the statements he has made.

Returning to the importance of Wordsworth's idea of "strength"
within the "self" we may stress not only a pragmatic factor, if carefully viewed, but its wider connections, which are even related to a
kind of grandeur. It has uses which are extensive. Imagination and
what Wordsworth has called intellectual love cannot be thought of as
dividual; they cannot "stand" as divided, within the human soul, and
the human being, too, must be capable of holding himself erect in his
own self-integrated person. To use the poet's own words:

> No Helper hast thou here;
> Here keepest thou thy individual state:
> No other can divide with thee this work;
> No secondary hand can intervene
> To fashion this ability . . . (189—)

For the poet "this ability" is within the individual as a "prime and
vital principle" in "the recesses" of the person's "nature," remote from
that which is "outward"; thinking of selfhood, he says directly that
without the inwardnesses it "is not thine at all." Thought about the
cruciality of a sense of one's own personal identity (of loving the self
properly, as a modern psychologist might say) was important to
Wordsworth; the sense of spirit within the self has a place, the poet
says, which is inviolable to "any reach of outward fellowship," and,
indeed, otherwise does not exist or, to re-emphasize, "is not thine at
all." The idea, in Wordsworth's presentation of it, represents a kind of
individual personalism, as we have used the term heretofore, but the
word could possibly be troublesome because it has been employed at
times in the sense of an extreme private subjectivism. In speaking of
Wordsworth and Whitehead, what we intend by the term *personalism* is very far from such subjectivism; the self-sense, in its wholesome
and social form, gives rise, for Wordsworth, to a result leading to
inward happiness which he expresses in the lines announcing

> joy to him,
> Oh joy to him who here hath sown, hath laid
> Here the foundations of his future years!   (197—)

This very private joy resulting from a firm sense of the personal self—apart even from "all that friendship, all that love can do" in bringing happiness—might appear to be expressed rather extremely. He does not deny the help we receive from others. The conception that Wordsworth wishes to present—we stress again—includes the fruits of friendship and love, but he points out that these cannot be effectively attained if personal identity fails to shape itself firmly. This is implied, because he never underestimates the importance of love and friendship. Rather, he speaks of these matters immediately. We will recall Whitehead's emphasis upon tenderness as we think of the poet's warm sense of friendship, shown in a passage that follows. For Wordsworth the concept of tenderness appears as he develops the idea of private and personal experience. What he presents is a kind of counterpoise to the dangers in the evil of pride—or, as we would express it today, the illusion of omnipotence. This counterpoise appears when he doubly emphasizes (by word, and by allusion to the early life of childhood) the proper place of humility in any life which attains, day by day, a deeper valuation of wisdom.

Concern about the personal (and one's own personal identity) has a relation to the theory of value and ultimately to the problem of evil, to which we have given consideration. Now, in view of Whitehead's references to tenderness, which certainly have personal significance, we may consider whether tenderness has for Whitehead a relation to value. Valuation is involved with contraries. Oppositions in our processes of thought occasionally disturb us: they are, seemingly, obstructions to us, but oppositions are internally necessary even to thinking. They are important in understanding the nature of conceptions, and for Whitehead tenderness is thought of by way of opposition to the despotic. Valuation, according to Whitehead, is, however, timeless. It has something of the eternal in it. All value is *related* to finitude, and in its connection with activity what is necessary to value is "origination"[32] of pattern. But "infinitude," which we may associate with pattern, "is mere vacancy apart from its embodiment of finite values," and, related to this, "finite entities are meaningless apart from their relationship beyond themselves. The notion of 'understanding' requires some grasp of how the finitude of the entity in question requires infinity, and also some notion of how infinity requires finitude." We have been quoting from the important essay

"Mathematics and the Good," which needs, in the philosopher's own view, to be associated with his latest and most profound work.

We can appreciate Whitehead's feelings about internal conflict and his effort at explanation if we bring in a reference, somewhat later-ally, to a very large topic, immortality, although Whitehead seems to make of it what he calls a "side-issue"[33]—or something small. How can immortality be small? The reference to be considered includes the observation that "the topic of 'The Immortality of Man' is seen to be a side issue in the wider topic, which is 'The Immortality of Realized Value' "; the importance of valuation, thus, is to be regarded as transcendent in our minds. But, for all the transcendency, the self is not minimized; indeed, the personality is maximized because of the very fact of value. Whitehead, we may say again, for all his abstrac-tion, does not forget the personal.

The topic of value has a relationship to still another subject, love, as applied to persons, which is important to Wordsworth—as it is, also, to Whitehead. In reading the poet's lines one may think also of Whitehead's remarks revealing the deepest concern for persons; indeed the poet's feeling reaches not only to persons but to creatures at a lower level than that of humanity. In *The Prelude* Wordsworth's remarks on personality, or the self—coupled with his recognition of the need for the virtue of humility—are followed by a beautiful expression of personalism in a final tribute he pays to his sister, in which we see again the love he felt for her as well as that which he received from her in turn. And it will recall Whitehead to our minds when we see that it is tenderness to which Wordsworth wishes to give continuing emphasis following the lines

> Child of my Parents! Sister of my Soul!
> Elsewhere have streams of gratitude been breath'd
> To thee . . . (211—)

Wordsworth proceeds at once to speak in the passage of the "tenderness" he had reciprocally experienced in his relations with Dorothy. The concern for the personal is equally important in Whitehead, for example, in his conception of "the World of Value in the guise of the coordination of many personal individualities" which are "factors in the nature of God."[34] No person is too small to be included. But there is a further point to be recalled, and this concerns the human factor as it is brought out in his statement "The emphasis upon the divine factor in human nature is the essence of religious thought." Included in his distinctly human view is the importance of compassion and love. Arising from the world of valuation are such human experiences as sympathy and tragedy, as well as many others coming from the "World of Value," including happiness. This latter we may consider as parallel to Wordsworth's "joy," which we have already mentioned.

The main strand of tenderness which we have in mind here appears elsewhere in Whitehead's work—for example, in the concluding part of *Process and Reality*. The statement near the terminal point of the work comes as a climax after he has dealt with three historic strands in religious history; he calls it a "suggestion" and tells us, "It dwells upon the tender elements of the world, which slowly and in quietness operate by love; and it finds purpose in the present immediacy of a kingdom not of this world."[35]

This may be very close to a definitive presentation of the philosopher's religious outlook. But it needs nevertheless to be supplemented by a remark he made later about the value of learning what we can from religions of various types. This we have quoted in part near the close of Chapter Thirteen, but the point must be re-emphasized here. It is important, he says, for people to remember that in considering "religious opinions" they can "borrow" ideas "from each other" and can proceed to new points of view by "imperceptible transitions." Most important, "they can learn to understand each other"[36] and to have affection one for another. This needed understanding (along with affection or "love") is deeply pervasive in Whitehead's philosophy, and it also has what he tends to call a sociological character.

It would take us too far afield to try to cover evidences of the warmth of the person Whitehead and his direct feeling for others as individuals. In his philosophy, however, he sees the danger of an attenuation of "human personality"[37] and he goes on to speak of the importance of "personal unity" and the place of selves in a world. Here he considers history. In earlier times various thinkers endeavored to conceive of the difficult concept of the self—for example, in "the Epicurean doctrine of a Concilium of subtle atoms"; related to this Epicurean view, and important further to the sense of self, is "the Humanitarian doctrine of the Rights of man," as well as "the general Common Sense of civilized mankind"—all being part of our communal life. Whitehead stresses the fact that these sociological aspects related to love, along with other examples, represent doctrines which "dominate the whole span of Western thought." He feels there is a matter of great philosophical importance in all this and that it makes necessary a renewed deep probing into the nature of self. Hence it is that he remarks, "Any philosophy must provide some doctrine of personal identity."

It is not too much to say, then, that the combination of a needed understanding and love connected with Whitehead's philosophy has an ultimate character which is sociological. This latter term is applied by the philosopher very broadly, for example when he includes such chapter headings as "The Human Soul," "The Humanitarian Ideal," "From Force to Persuasion," and "Foresight" under the general heading "Sociological" in the first part of his *Adventures of Ideas*. The "sociological" is needed as a corrective which is necessary for the purpose of broadening a too-limited view of his search into the personal. That search covers the cosmological and the divine element, which includes the sociological, for, as he says, "The great social ideal for religion is that it should be the common basis for the unity of civilization."[38]

The social, as connected with love or with human concern, may not seem very directly connected with what Whitehead calls "Freedom and Equality," which he regards as "an inevitable presupposition for modern political thought"[39]; in this latter, the political view, as he says, "God has been a great resource: a lot of things, which won't work on Earth, can be conceived as true in his sight." In another way of looking at the matter, there is a truth which to many people may not seem true but, nevertheless, in the history of mankind, proves fruitful in the "growth of the idea of the essential rights of human beings, arising from their sheer humanity"; this has a connection with the great Depression and the serious problem which has been sometimes referred to insensitively as the excess of the availability of human beings who seek daily labor. Perhaps it is necessary at times to use abstract expressions somewhat like this. We do have an excess of human beings in certain portions of the total world, and something must be done—is being done—about this. Whitehead saw this problem. Perhaps we do have an excess of human beings who seek daily labor, and it may be necessary that more people should enjoy a good deal of leisure, and that the free hours made available may have, through education, a real value for individuals.

Whitehead himself sometimes uses very abstract language when he speaks of labor and its problems. But he communicates his idea directly when, in speaking of the Depression, he says: "In any industrial district in the world today, it is a grim joke to speak of freedom. All that remains is the phantasm of freedom, devoid of opportunity."[40] Thus, despite occasional abstractness of expression in Whitehead, we observe in such things as he here presents his recognition of a definite and tragic evil. The personal is involved here. As he puts matters, "for more than a hundred years" the problem of those who were out of work "has always been there."[41] Such an evil will almost inevitably "settle on the whole industrial world as a permanent factor in life, unless the great corporations can adapt their mode of functioning." His words are prophetic. This adaptation he regarded as an absolute necessity. The "permanent factor" has now settled on our whole culture, but he was able to anticipate what a magnified personal problem the world has to face today. It was his view that Depressions, if left to themselves, would get worse, not automatically become better.

All this has a bearing on personal concern for the rights of ourselves and others viewed as spiritual equals. An adaptation of the whole civilization and its mode of functioning is of course now in process. What we are faced with is partly a psychological problem, not merely an economic one. Philosophy, as Whitehead saw, is also involved. This he states clearly. And his view is very pertinent to Wordsworth's larger sense of evil and its relation to people in a tragic world. All of this, as we have said, involves the personal. And personalism is related to tolerance.

But we must resume our consideration of personalism in its more direct sense. In addition to the personal element in Wordsworth's last tribute to his sister in *The Prelude*, this same element in its relation to love and friendship appears in a final tribute to Coleridge. Considering, as he says, the "theme" that he has been treating, it would be impossible for him to remain silent concerning what he owes to his

friend, who seemed given to this earth "to love and understand"; the
spirit of Coleridge found its "way" to effect a purpose

> and thus the life
> Of all things and the mighty unity
> In all which we behold, and feel, and are,
> Admitted more habitually a mild
> Interposition, and closelier gathering thoughts
> Of man and his concerns . . . (253—)

The concerns of human beings regardless of class or other elements
of status were important in Wordsworth's eyes, and he thinks of them
in relation to what friendship and Coleridge had meant to him. From
Coleridge he says he had gained a greater sense of the necessity of
connecting the smaller parts of thought one with another; that is,
from Coleridge had come "closelier gathering thoughts" as applied to
"man and his concerns" at whatever level. Whitehead, like Wordsworth, recognizes the worth of the man Coleridge. But the philosopher thinks of him mainly in connection with his influence upon the
development of Wordsworth's thought.[42] The points with regard to
Coleridge's influence indicated in *The Prelude* have a relationship to
Whitehead's statements.

Returning now to Wordsworth's reference to "closelier gathering
thoughts" and to "man and his concerns," we can see in some of the
characters Coleridge portrayed—and whom Wordsworth appreciated—a recognition of the importance of people at the lower human
levels, as they are often hastily conceived to be. As an illustration of
this type of portrayal we have the superstitious ancient mariner and
his uneducated fellow associates. Coleridge was interested also in the
lower creatures at all levels (for example, in the albatross), but it is the
"human creature" that Wordsworth speaks of rather abstractly as he
now thinks of the work of his friend. Indeed, the two men together
shared closely in the work which they did. Wordsworth, through his
relations with Coleridge in that earlier period, had been able to attain
a profound "joy," even a "rapture," which he associates with a
veritable

> Hallelujah sent
> From all that breathes and is . . . (262—)

But this "Hallelujah" cry was not a mere youthful enthusiasm for people; rather, it had been "balanced," he says, through his experience with Coleridge and others. By such means it came about that "God and man divided, as they ought," the "system of the world," each participating in and contributing to the universe "which God animates." In *The Prelude* Wordsworth does not wish to presume too much as to his own powers, but he takes as a supposition the fact that the analysis which he has tried to present may confirm the possibility that he has been earnestly striving on the right track in order to try to become a poet and to make a contribution to man. For this purpose, he realizes, "knowledge" is necessary, and this of course means labor; he does not go on the assumption that all things come to one through wishing for them. In recording the story of his attempted growth, he admits that

> much has been omitted, as need was;
> Of Books how much! and even of the other wealth
> That is collected among woods and fields . . . (279—)

The long attempt at an examination and analysis of what books meant to Wordsworth or Whitehead—historically speaking—is not part of our purpose here. Wordsworth in *The Prelude* at once proceeds to another topic—beyond that of books—the "other wealth" which came to him from "woods and fields"; this wealth reaches one slowly, he says, and cannot be acquired carelessly, but is, rather, carefully collected with conscious attention. Thus he refers to what he has in mind as being a deliberate, though a "secondary grace"; but though it is a thing which is "outward," he makes clear that there is more to nature than this outwardness.

Even the outwardness, the "secondary grace"—including such external things, perhaps, as an unusually able botanist might observe—would be momentously important in his eyes, as they are to Whitehead. It is true that some five years earlier than the writing of this part of *The Prelude* Wordsworth spoke (in "A Poet's Epitaph") of a peeping scientist who, when visiting his mother's grave, would stoop to "botanize" with regard to some technicality he was able to observe there. But this is not to say that he opposed botanizing. In *Process and Reality* (p. 212) Whitehead alludes to the passage in Wordsworth's "A Poet's Epitaph," without mentioning the title, but it seems that he did not realize how close he and the poet are in their attitudes toward observation. Apart from the topic of outward observation, Wordsworth sees something which is related to morality in the world of nature when it is carefully studied. Even in the field of botany this notion with regard to morality could perhaps receive a degree of substantiation, but doubtless the world of animal life would for most people provide a better exemplification of it. The poet uses for a description of this mirroring value the figure of a "softening mirror"—that is, it is not an exact mirror which he has in mind.

Whitehead similarly recognizes the pertinency of something analogous between morality as seen in human beings and that to be observed in the world of lower nature. Various references to this could be found, including in them his view of the deeper relationship of all parts of the universe, even the atoms, one to another. But we would especially stress here his considered judgment that morality itself "can be discerned in the higher animals"[43]; this statement may seem somewhat more bizarre than anything as to the "softening mirror" which Wordsworth may have had in mind. The poet's view does not seem a particularly intemperate one. Wordsworth's image of the "softening mirror" modifies his idea that things in animal life are analogous to those found in human existence. Has this analogy between the life of human beings and that in lower nature any relation to philosophy? The poet's "softening mirror" image modifies the vision of what might be too baldly or too mechanically observed. In any event, in his remarks he is thinking mainly of what we may learn by looking at things that are seemingly "outward" or external; he is referring to what Whitehead in various contexts calls practical observation.

Following the references in Wordsworth to that which is "outward" or external, the poet mentions that the subject of the imagination, "the main essential power"—which he feels he has "track'd"—might have been next followed by the treatment of the topic of the fanciful. The latter force in man needs, he says, to be both "purified" and "steadied." If this purification and steadying is accomplished in a person, it would be possible to return to "the Rivers and the Groves" with a new insight, beyond that acquired through mere external vision, returning to them, indeed, so that one might

> behold
> Another face, might hear them from all sides
> Calling upon the more instructed mind
> To link their images with subtle skill . . . (295—)

What is the "subtle skill" that the poet here refers to? It is the power of fantasy (Wordsworth's "Fancy") which, though it is subject to the danger of extravagance, is capable of being put to constructive uses. It brings a kind of "togetherness" (Whitehead's word, though he uses it in various other connections, aside from those having to do with fantasy), just as the imagination functions in a unified way with even more special force. Sometimes this "subtle skill" (the fanciful) accomplishes its work by humor, or "elaborate research," as Wordsworth says; here man may use "forms and definite appearances" which apply not only to the rivers and the groves but to "human life"—appearances having a way of working upon us by means of an "involuntary sympathy" excited by the "being" or the fanciful (or fancy-creating) self that is internal to us—a special selfhood

> Where meditation cannot come, which thought
> Could never heighten. (305—)

The passage in *The Prelude* from which this is drawn deals with conscious and unconscious human behavior, or with what Wordsworth refers to explicitly as "our internal being"; these conscious and unconscious emotions (including "delight") work upon the "fancy," and help man to develop psychologically a particular structure within the self. Here we may consider again (as a comparison to Wordsworth's thought) Whitehead's theory about the complexity of man's feelings and the fact that ideas and emotions intermingle and become beliefs. But it is the psychological structure involved in the process that Whitehead fixes most attention upon in various books, and it is this kind of structure to which Wordsworth also refers.

For Whitehead, and for Wordsworth, the experiencing of feelings as well as notions must be regarded as central, and this is true also of feelings and notions of large generality: they are central to civilization. The point is illustrated, as Whitehead says, by the fact that, "as we first recall ourselves to civilized experience," we characteristically settle upon such broad feelings as whether a given thing is "important" or "difficult"; thus we are using the particular and the vague.[44] We use "a large, vague characterization indicative of some form of excitement arising from the particular fact in the world without." The word "excitement" (as a form of centered emotion) is vital in Whitehead's philosophy. In his view, the "sense" or fact "of importance (or interest) is embedded in the very being of animal existence."[45]

It is not a low thing that Whitehead is thinking of here when he uses the word "animal," but something which is a part of our total life. It makes us what we mainly are: persons having psychological structures of broad feelings and emotions of such generality that we hardly notice them. Our very beings are constituted by multiple perspectives which we have.

For our special nature, perspective is exceedingly important. Some things, in our feelings, are negligible in their relation to us, and "'to be negligible' means 'to be negligible' " so far as our coordinations of feeling are concerned. "Thus," Whitehead says, "perspective is the outcome of feeling"[46] which we happen to possess. It is living emotion that he is concerned with here. In *Adventures of Ideas*, also, he deals with such living emotion; he quotes George Foot Moore about broad feelings shared by many people through a "community of the feelings by which ideas are 'emotionalized' and become beliefs and motives."[47] In this connection Whitehead refers also to J.H. Denison's *Emotions as the Basis of Civilization* as "a work of importance." He does not use such words of appreciative recognition lightly. Wordsworth refers comparably to an emotion, using the conception of an "involuntary sympathy," which is deeply within us. Attentiveness is essential in all of the interests such as this.

But even more important, we may add that, according to Wordsworth, there are aspects of the world still "nearer to ourselves" (closer to our inward being) which, because they may be discovered only in our self-inspection, we may "overlook," but most especially—and this is to be noted carefully—we overlook the world which is near to the self as it appears in other people. We know that we are given to introspection, but we overlook the fact that various examples of introspection (and other inward actions) are going on importantly in others. We can observe this fact, that is, if we look for it with care. The

way other people see and feel things is important. This, as Wordsworth tries to explain it, is a "marvellous world" (which he examined
first in his "own heart"), but one which he saw also in the world
outside himself and

> In life among the passions of mankind
> And qualities commix'd and modified
> By the infinite varieties and shades
> Of individual character.   (310—)

As we think of the life which Wordsworth refers to with its "pas-
sions" and "qualities" strangely "commix'd and modified,"—along
with "the infinite varieties and shades" of human beings which must
be kept in mind—we have some sense also of the intermingling of
psychological forces that Whitehead also dwells upon. There is a
parallel here. These things which Wordsworth, too, chooses to examine are exemplified, if anyone would observe them closely, in the life
of a crowded school. Wordsworth holds that he was fortunate in not
being placed in the hands of a tutor for private education; rather, he
was

> forced
> In hardy independence, to stand up
> Amid conflicting passions and the shock
> Of various tempers, to endure and note
> What was not understood though known to be ... (316—)

Here we have an attempted summing up of the objective gathering
of facts about the self and human life (what Whitehead calls "assemblage") appearing in Wordsworth's line concerning things in his
experience that were sensed, or, in the poet's expression just quoted,
"not understood though known to be." Thus one gathers the narrow
assemblage of facts, whether for the purpose of botany or with the
intent of understanding the world and the human self as a prepara-
tion for the writing of poetry. Analogously, Whitehead's term
"assemblage" can be used also in regard to philosophy: he applies the
term to the work of William James, who, though he thought to some
extent about system, "above all . . . assembled. His intellectual life

was one protest against the dismissal of experience in the interest of system."[48] William James was distinctly personalistic.

Wordsworth, similarly, does not wish to be *ruled* by system; what he seeks is evidently a balance between system and the close attention to experience. This principle of balance is the ideal to which Whitehead is himself devoted. Whether he or Wordsworth attains it adequately is a difficult question to answer. That they strive toward such a balance is evident. Wordsworth sought to move

> Among the mysteries of love and hate,
> Honour and shame, looking to right and left,
> Uncheck'd by innocence too delicate
> And moral notions too intolerant
> Sympathies too contracted.   (321—)

There is always a danger in adopting a strongly moralizing vantage point, as Wordsworth here realizes. Whitehead is aware of this too, and in various places in his writing he emphasizes the weakness of moralism. What he fears is stagnation in the name of morals; this is "the deadly foe of morality." He suggests that "the champions of morality" are too often "the fierce opponents of new ideals."[49] He objects to intolerant moral notions just as Wordsworth does. The mere conformation to static codes misses the point with regard to an enlarging morality needed as "the aim at that union of harmony, intensity, and vividness which involves perfection of importance for that occasion."[50] Codes "are useful, and indeed essential, for civilization. But we only weaken their influence by exaggerating their status."

The tolerance which is prominent, then, in Wordsworth and Whitehead has another connection in that it recognizes the importance of the personal self and shows concern for variegations of individual character. The thought about variegations which we have in mind suggests something more than variations—perhaps allowing for the admittance of occasional marked eccentricities; these neither Wordsworth nor Whitehead would view with unfriendliness. And here we touch the edge of personalism once more. Personalism may be seen also in *The Prelude* in what Wordsworth refers to as "one word more of personal circumstance"; the point appears in the expla-

nation he gives of the three years which he spent without "a permanent abode," and he makes clear once more the devoted love which he
felt for his sister Dorothy. She was undoubtedly one of his very great
loves, and he rightly refers to her as

> that Sister of my heart
> Who ought by rights the dearest to have been
> Conspicuous through this biographic verse,
> Star seldom utterly conceal'd from view . . . (339—)

The poet's additional "word of personal circumstance" (apart from
the "undomestic Wanderer's life" which he led) has further to do with
excursions he made as a result of "personal friendships" or "chance"
happenings. One outgrowth of these wanderings (which, as he says,
he made "excursively" as his "slender means" made them possible)
resulted in a gift which was bequeathed to him by Raisley Calvert. So
strongly does he feel about the generosity of his friend, who at the
time was dying, that it is his hope in *The Prelude* to make the name of
Calvert endure, and with this in mind he declares—

> it shall live, if words
> Of mine can give it life . . . (350—)

Through personalism the spirit of a concern for all men and for
democracy is incipient. Calvert had hoped to promote something
pointing toward the good, and in the utmost generosity he made it
possible for Wordsworth to "pause for choice"—that is, to have
sufficient time to make plans to the best of his ability for a worthwhile
career. And his was the career of a highly personal, democratic writer,
especially in its important stages. The poet, thus, became an exceedingly free person, even to the point of no longer having to think of his
own "maintenance," and he was able to turn to his career in a way
which would not have been possible otherwise. Had it not been for
this "bequest" (in 1795), *The Prelude* and certain other works might
never have been written. Having commented on Calvert with affection and appreciation, Wordsworth turns again with gratitude to the
subject of friendship and in a most personal way addresses Coleridge
once more in the words

> Call back to mind
> The mood in which this Poem was begun,
> O Friend! (370—)

Personalism appears again here in the description given by Wordsworth of the way in which he had begun writing *The Prelude*— in "distraction and intense desire"; the intensity of the poet's feeling concerning this poetical work is significant, indeed even the fact that he addresses his own past life as if it were a living being. He had spoken to it (his life), in effect saying, "Where art thou"? And he found that it gave a response most eagerly—in a "voice" which would have implied a reproach if he had not heeded it. What had his past life, which was still a living thing, been like? What was it now, being—as it were—a living thing within his own mind? He had been in the past, as he says, a "world" unto himself, and he still thinks of personality in this way. What he implies is that everyone is a world. It will be recalled that Wordsworth had said earlier that a person is "a memory to himself"; we have mentioned this more than once. So likewise "a world" of the past is a memory, and a person is a world.

Writing *The Prelude*, Wordsworth says very personally, he had tried to be heedful of the "sorrows of the earth"; he had written with the intention of "centering all in love," but in a spirit which is completely "gratulant," as he explains, "if rightly understood." Here, in using the word "gratulant," he is speaking in the manner of a past era. By the use of this expression he wishes to convey his feeling of gratefulness for the life that has been his. He would give thanks, accepting the grace that has come to him, but not regarding it as a mere code to which one is required to conform; rather, he says, he would choose to speak in a spirit of rejoicing.

Wordsworth's personal modesty is further revealed in his thought that everything that lies ahead—so far as his promise and power are concerned—will be uncertain, but he looks back, and he urges Coleridge likewise to look back, to the days when, among grassy hills, and with "happy heart" as he says, there came into being Coleridge's story of the "bright-eyed Mariner" and that of the character Christabel, in addition to personal performances of Wordsworth's own concerning two things to which he makes allusion, a

> moonlight ride
> Near the loud Waterfall; or her who sate
> In misery near the miserable Thorn . . . (401—)

We are still considering the importance of the personal as we reflect upon the first of Wordsworth's poems to which he makes allusion here in *The Prelude*. The "moonlight ride" and the reference to an almost deafening "Waterfall" must be first given attention. The distracting sound of the waterfall has an effect on one of Wordsworth's characters, a mother—and has a non-effect on her son. In the image of "the loud Waterfall" we have an allusion bringing to mind the character of the son in Wordsworth's "The Idiot Boy." This character has the habit of obliviousness, though through no fault of his own. The boy, oblivious to the thundering sound and "headlong force" of the water, as well as to the sad searching of his loving mother, sits thoughtlessly beneath the luminously shining moon. Perhaps it was no accident that Wordsworth chose to refer to the pathos and irony of this human poem of his own about a character who had tragically been deprived of almost all mental faculties. Here surely, the poet may have thought, is the ultimate disaster that can befall a person, especially as that disaster is combined with the human pathos in the life of a mother concerned about a lost son who is bereft of sense.

It is the personal element that engages our attention, especially as we try to view the situation through Wordsworth's eyes. Some readers may say that the poet's intention is of no importance, but we do get added insight into his work if we reflect upon what he is trying to do. The *Prelude* passage that has been last quoted also includes an allusion to another of Wordsworth's works about human tragedy—a poem which tells of a thorn tree which has grown no higher than "a two year's child"; it concerns a dead child whose life is symbolized in the small thorn tree. Nevertheless, with all the sadness implicit in the allusions which Wordsworth includes, he adds a note of happiness as he thinks of the personal companionship that he and his friend enjoyed at the time of their experience which he is calling back to memory. It is this joy which he hopes will also come to Coleridge. It is given intimate expression in the lines:

When thou dost to that summer turn thy thoughts,
And hast before thee all that then we were,
To thee, in memory of that happiness
It will be known, by thee at least, my Friend,
Felt, that the history of a Poet's mind
Is labour not unworthy of regard . . . (404—)

The note of individual friendship is enlarged upon by an additional personal explanation concerning the composition of *The Prelude*. The "later portions" of this "Gift" (*The Prelude*), which Wordsworth had planned to present to Coleridge, were written, he says during periods "of much sorrow, of a private grief"; here he is referring to the "enduring" pain caused by the death of his brother John, who died by drowning in a faraway sea. Personalism thus appears once more in the poem. The "frame of mind" Wordsworth considers in reference to this is presented in *The Prelude* as that of a somewhat philosophical-meditative individual existence which turns his thought with even deeper feeling to the loss. Wordsworth does not make this explicit. Understandably he prefers to use allusions in this situation. But it is notable that he combines closely a reference to "meditative History" (his own) and an event involving profound feeling. The "frame of mind" which he has created in writing *The Prelude* also "enabled" him, he says, to be reconciled more completely to the suffering that had come to him. Philosophy, though imperfect, helps in such a situation: even the activity in attempting to clarify thought may be a help. And thinking of Coleridge he feels that a further

comfort now, a hope,
One of the dearest which this life can give,
Is mine; that thou art near, and wilt be soon
Restored to us in renovated health . . . (421—)

Personalism, then, as we have been thinking of it, undoubtedly plays a part in Wordsworth's thought, as it does in Whitehead's. It might perhaps seem that we have exaggerated its presence in the latter's philosophy. We wish in using the term to have it apply in part to the profounder aspects of personality. In discussing what White-head calls the "Requisites for Social Progress" such a personalism as we have in mind has a significant place. According to his "metaphysical doctrine" he says what man needs is "to increase the depth of individuality."[51] This increase in depth of the personal has its aesthetic side for Whitehead. But the aesthetic value is related to fairness; it is a corrective to injustice, which sometimes appears in thinking. "We must foster the creative initiative towards the maintenance of objective values." Whitehead also thinks here of art and of the creative in the broadest sense. He would include in it even the operation of factories with their machinery and with the "community of operatives" which is involved. It must be remembered that all this comes under a general chapter heading, "Requisites for Social Progress," but we cannot do more now than touch the surface of the degree of personalism in Whitehead's thought.

As we have examined Wordsworth and personalism the element of tragedy has repeatedly appeared to be close at hand. This brings us again to the problem of evil, although we have already had to deal with it in earlier pages. It is impossible ever to bring to completion one's treatment of the problem of evil. Inevitably, we cannot look beyond this dark problem to a resolution of all the confusions that flesh is heir to so that a cheerful culmination may be provided. We cannot look very far beyond a painful vision of today which in its full reaches covers a vast, dark night of the soul. What we can do is to see in Wordsworth and Whitehead glimpses that give to us a measure of light.

Whitehead never minimizes the problem of evil, in part because he had suffered—as had Wordsworth—a tragic loss which was forever in his mind when he was writing his later books[52]: the death of his very young son Eric, who was shot down in conflict in one of the rickety early war planes of 1918. This was at a point when the war had almost been brought to an end. Personalism, then, has its notable relations to suffering and loss. Whitehead's feelings near the close of World War I can only be imagined. But we can sense his feeling about war in the twentieth century as that feeling is expressed in the 1946 essay "An Appeal to Sanity." In it he refers to the irony of "local wars." Is this an anticipation of what we have learned about Vietnam and the Near East? It is not too much to say that this is so. In the essay he deals with the importance (and danger) of "contagious emotion." He asks also whether there is a justification for "isolation"; what, in other words is the duty, as he says, of a "powerful nation when evil is turbulent in any part of the world?"

It would be quite wrong to affirm that we cannot stay for an answer to a question of this kind. We *must* stay. Certainly also it is difficult for us to deny the importance of personalism after we have experienced the news of the terrible events of war and rumors of war in the modern world, with its Cambodias, Beiruts, and Angolas. But the situation is so desperate that we may also feel the need for Whitehead's conviction, apart from all distresses, that compensatingly in the world there is an element of the divine. There is also a requirement—related to God, so he holds—for creative action.

Despite Whitehead's feeling of the need for action rather than vacillation in a world of insane decimations, his thought has affiliations with an outlook that may be associated with a religion somewhat like the experiential religious outlook of the Quakers. He has some of their idealism and some of their earthly practicality. What we tend to remember in such an outlook, however, concerns a kingdom not altogether of this world, along with the strong desire to try to make the earth, whatever it may be essentially, a place of communion and beauty and fairness. Here we may think again of Martin Buber. In *The Prelude* of more than one hundred and seventy years ago Wordsworth moves forward toward a contemplation of his age which may remind us in some respects of our own. It was an age which he feels may be "too weak to tread the ways of truth"—one which, as he viewed it, was falling back repeatedly to the worship of countless false deities. Though men stoop (as human beings have done in our own time) "to servitude," to baseness, and though whole nations sink "to ignominy and shame," there still may be solace

> in the knowledge which we have,
> Bless'd with true happiness if we may be
> United helpers forward of a day
> Of firmer trust . . . (436—)

This was a *Prelude* passage which Wordsworth hoped to apply, in its aspiration, to Coleridge and to himself. With the help of some source higher than that of man, a poet could—so he hoped—make a difference in the world's events, might be able in part to teach the world that "the mind of man" itself may become far more wonderful than "the earth" on which human beings dwell. The mind of man is potentially capable of greater things than it has thus far ever beheld in its best dreams because it has within it, as compared to the external world when taken by itself, far more of the character which is divine. This is Wordsworth's view.

The final word in *The Prelude* is, in actuality, the term "divine." For Whitehead, as for Wordsworth, it is possible to attain a kind of mysticism of the divine in the sense of what the philosopher calls "direct insight into depths as yet unspoken."[53] But "the purpose of philosophy," Whitehead declares, "is to rationalize mysticism: not by explaining it away, but by the introduction of novel verbal characterizations, rationally coordinated."[54] If we avail ourselves rationally of a thing which he regards as ultimately mystical we will be making more readily available the essence of what he elsewhere calls the dream.

It has been mentioned that his thought has affiliations that may be associated with an experiential religious outlook somewhat like that of the Quakers. It is their individual tolerance that he is especially struck by.[55] He also felt drawn in a friendly way toward the views of certain Congregationalists[56] who came to visit him in order to share ideas. The individual and personal contribution in these religions seems to have been for him the most important point; it is through the personal in religion that "individuals can make imperceptible transitions."[57] The transitions he has in mind have to do with the general growth of religion in the course of centuries.

We can all help each other in this long process. He was interested in the Quaker religion and a variety of other religions, then, but his interest in the Quakers did not extend to the endorsement of pacifism in World War I. In this he was different from his friend Bertrand Russell, who later acknowledged that Whitehead, during the war years when he had differences with Russell, was basically an example of tolerance.[58] The basis of tolerance, according to Whitehead, is that "all points of view" are needed; others can contribute through many ages to the understanding of the wide universe. These others, of course, make mistakes which require critical attention. "The duty of tolerance is our finite homage to the abundance of inexhaustible novelty which is awaiting the future, and to the complexity of accomplished fact which exceeds our stretch of insight."[59]

Tolerance, for the philosopher, also requires individual thinking and decision. Whitehead's reference to the Hebrew heritage (which acts as a complement of the Greek gift to mankind) shows his realization that within the best Jewish tradition there is the recognition of a philosophy which includes the love of one's fellow human being as one should love sister or brother. In the Hebrews and the Greeks then—through their refusal to be content with what has become merely acceptable in contrast to exceptional behavior—there lies a "hope which never deserted their glimpses of perfection."[60] This aspect of Whitehead's tolerant philosophy needs to be joined with the historical record concerning the man of Nazareth, even though that record is, as he says, "fragmentary"[61] and incapable of exact verification.

Whitehead would not personally attempt the scholar's *effort* to reconstruct such a history, though the effort at reconstruction is needed in every age. What is immediately important can be found in the evocative value that remains in the life story of this man in its several aspects, including among other elements "the bare manger: the lowly man, homeless and self-forgetful, with his message of peace, love, and sympathy: the suffering, the agony, the tender words as life ebbed, the final despair: and the whole with the authority of supreme victory." It is for Whitehead a mystical victory, although the human factor receives stress.

But we must never forget the Hebrew and the Greek heritage. Can we doubt, Whitehead wonders, that the strength of religion "lies in its revelation in act, of that which Plato divined in theory?" The flash of the divine in human experience is in this instance what Whitehead treasures. Even art, like an act, can be religious. Art in itself, he says elsewhere, can give "an elation of feeling which is supernatural."[62] He does not falter at the word *supernatural* here. One of the best examples in art lies in the handling of the sculpture and the tracery in a cathedral—sculpture and tracery which draw "the eye upward to the vaulting above" and in addition draw it sidewise to the "symbolism of the altar."[63] It is the Cathedral at Chartres to which he refers. Anyone who has stood in that cathedral, or who has examined a variety of pictures of it, is likely to remember the sculpture and the tracery, and how they draw "attention by their beauty and detail." The vaulting itself seems like a live and violent example of action. Yet "supreme individuality" is not lost in the vast whole.

Earlier in the volume *Adventures of Ideas*, Whitehead pays tribute to this individuality in the Cathedral.[64] He speaks of individuality later as he refers to reality and indeed to "the harmonizing of harmonies, and of particular individual actualities as the sole authentic reality."[65] The importance to Whitehead of individual entities is evident here. His conception of the individual is very wide. The theory of the importance of the individual (if humanity and justice are kept paramount) leads to love, and, as he says, "love, above all things, is personal." The personalism of Whitehead's philosophy is ever-present as an undercurrent even when it may not be manifested on the surface.

In Whitehead's view, nothing comes without a dream of the ideal. Here we can think of our American use of such a conception as the dream. The American conception of it is too narrow, for the Whiteheadian dream is many-sided. But the dream in itself is never a completely unrealizable thing. It includes an ideal wherein a society has its purpose of actively accomplishing all the ends associated with a spiritual and contributory peace. Indeed, "a society is to be termed civilized" if, along with bringing about other things—including its art, its devotion to truth, and its dedication to a daring of adventure—its "members participate" in producing a state of affairs including "Peace."[66] For Whitehead this "Peace" is no "negative conception"; it is active, it is a thing that "crowns the 'life and motion' of the soul." The peace that he seeks thus involves emphatically a dynamism of action.

What he has called "the dream" he associates particularly with the spirit of youth,[67] but this spirit can manifest itself at any age. Tragedy may come with the dream, as it will, but it does not negate the active forces which are at work within the dream. It would be difficult to exaggerate the importance of what Whitehead in his philosophy develops as the relation between the ideal and "Peace." And it would be difficult to overstate the importance of what he terms the dream.

Our purpose now should be to conclude by trying to interrelate within ourselves whatever seems of value in the most perceptive thoughts and feelings of the poet Wordsworth and the philosopher Whitehead. Such an effort should especially draw one to the many respects in which their works may be related to the poetry and the thinking of their time and ours. This will appear particularly in relation to the ideal as it is connected with the pursuits of human beings who would promote the arts and the general good without losing an emphasis on the importance of the life of every human being, regardless of ethnic or any other affiliations which that individual may have. The "general good" is sometimes too narrowly conceived. The dream, which is the ideal, should never be forgotten.

Notes

[1]"Immortality," *Essays in Science and Philosophy*, p. 63. "Evaluation" is not abstract; it is a real action in the world and often leads to a practical effort to change things. See also *Process and Reality*, p. 525.

[2]"Education and Self-Education," *Essays in Science and Philosophy*, p. 128.

[3]"Analysis of Meaning," *Essays in Science and Philosophy*, p. 94. The genetic approach concerns the way things are brought about, developed, or changed; thus it has to do with how things function or work. This is Dewey's "genetic-functional" approach.

[4]*Ibid.*, p. 94. It enters into our experience.

[5]*Ibid.*, p. 95.

[6]*Ibid.*, p. 95.

[7]*Ibid.*, p. 98. Whitehead's theory contrasts with Dewey's view that knowledge is essentially an instrument which functions to change a situation in the practical world.

[8]"Immortality," p. 63.

[9]*Process and Reality*, p. 79.

[10]*Ibid.*, p. 196.

[11]*Adventures of Ideas*, p. 236.

[12]"Immortality," p. 63.

[13]*Ibid.*, p. 64.

[14]*Ibid.*, p. 65. Assessment of the *value* of life is connected with belief or unbelief in personal survival. It is of "personal identity" that he speaks.

[15]*Ibid.* It would be hard to *value* or to assess the excellence of a given philosophy (say Dewey's) if the self had no stability.

[16]*Ibid.*, p. 66.

[17]*Ibid.*, p. 69.

[18]*Adventures of Ideas*, p. 267.

[19]*Essays in Science and Philosophy*, p. 72.

[20]*Ibid.*, p. 72.

[21]*Process and Reality*, p. 46.

[22]*Modes of Thought*, p. 223.

[23]*Ibid.*, p. 140.

[24]*Essays in Science and Philosophy*, p. 73.

[25]*Ibid.*, p. 69.

[26]*Ibid.*, Assessment of *value* or relative excellence appears in his attitudes toward these religions.

[27]*Adventures of Ideas*, p. 357.

[28]*Essays in Science and Philosophy*, p. 67. See also Carl R. Rogers, *Carl Rogers on Personal Power* (New York: Delacorte Press, 1977), p. 74, on "person-centered education"; the person "shares in the responsible choices and decisions" and a "climate" is provided for the "aims."

[29]*Process and Reality*, p. 135.

[30]*Ibid.*, p. 135. See also p. 33 for the fact that actual entities "are also termed 'actual occasions.' " The exception to this, as has been made clear above, is God. Although Whitehead can be very abstract, he does not forget the importance of the immediate and personal.

[31]*Ibid.*, p. 525.

[32]*Essays in Science and Philosophy*, p. 81. The next quotation is from pp. 81-82.

[33]*Ibid.*, p. 65.

[34]*Ibid.*, p. 69. We are often in *self-conflict* when a problem of value arises, and this is particularly true of highly personal matters.

[35]*Process and Reality*, p. 520. The three strands are the "Caesars, the Hebrew prophets, and Aristotle." The statement coming after the indication of the three strands is a "suggestion" concerning Galilean beginnings.

[36]*Adventures of Ideas*, p. 220.

[37]*Ibid.*, p. 239. The next quotation is from pp. 239-240.

[38]*Ibid.*, p. 221.

[39]*Ibid.*, p. 15.

[40]"The Study of the Past," *Essays in Science and Philosophy*, p. 117.

[41]*Ibid.*, p. 118. See also in Rogers, *On Personal Power*, p. 109, the danger of "a propagandistic, dogmatic leadership."

[42]*Science and the Modern World*, p. 120.

[43]*Modes of Thought*, p. 39.

[44]*Ibid.*, p. 6.

[45]*Ibid.*, p. 12. The parentheses are in Whitehead's book and provide valuable emphasis.

[46]*Ibid.*, p. 13.

[47] *Adventures of Ideas*, p. 299.

[48] *Modes of Thought*, p. 4.

[49] *Adventures of Ideas*, p. 346.

[50] *Modes of Thought*, p. 19. Note Whitehead's use of the word *perfection*.

[51] *Science and the Modern World*, p. 287. Sociality also remains. Compare Martin Buber, *A Believing Humanism*, p. 128. Buber, in referring to Christian, Jewish, and other faiths, indicates the danger if one "measures the value of the others by its own, identifies the particularity of its own religion with the essence of all religion . . ." See also our Chapter XIII, footnote 77.

[52] These later volumes begin with *The Concept of Nature* (1919) and include his major philosophical works.

[53] *Modes of Thought*, p. 237.

[54] *Ibid.*, p. 237.

[55] *Ibid.*, p. 63.

[56] *Dialogues of Alfred North Whitehead*, p. 183.

[57] *Adventures of Ideas*, p. 220. Note, on p. 219 of the volume, the contribution that Pericles can make to modern religion.

[58] *The Autobiography of Bertrand Russell, 1872-1914* (Boston: The Atlantic Monthly Press, Little, Brown and Co., 1967), p. 188. Russell says of Whitehead, "He was more tolerant than I was, and it was much more my fault than his that these differences caused a diminution . . . of our friendship." We can recall here that Russell's wife was a Quaker.

[59] *Adventures of Ideas*, p. 65.

[60] *Ibid.*, p. 13. Compare, also, the influence of many religions in Martin Buber's work, especially in *Daniel*, trans. by Maurice Friedman (New York: Holt, Rinehart and Winston, 1964); note especially p. 5.

[61] *Ibid.*, p. 214.

[62] *Ibid.*, p. 348.

[63] *Ibid.*, p. 364.

[64] *Ibid.*, p. 339.

[65] *Ibid.*, p. 376.

[66] *Ibid.*, p. 367.

[67] *Ibid.*, p. 381. Here Whitehead says we find "always the dream of youth and the harvest of tragedy."

Index

At times this short index combines items for the purpose of relating them, and it often excludes names frequently referred to in the book.

269